COURSE 2

McDougal Littell Middle School

Math

Larson   Boswell   Kanold   Stiff

Notetaking Guide

The Notetaking Guide contains a lesson-by-lesson framework that allows students to take notes on and review the main concepts of each lesson in the textbook. Each Notetaking Guide lesson features worked-out examples and Your Turn Now exercises similar to those found in the textbook. Each example has a number of write-in boxes for students to complete, either in class as the example is discussed or at home as part of a review of the lesson. Each chapter concludes with a review of the main vocabulary of the chapter. Upon completion, each chapter of the Notetaking Guide can be used by students to help review for the test on that particular chapter.

McDougal Littell
A HOUGHTON MIFFLIN COMPANY
Evanston, Illinois • Boston • Dallas

Contributing Author

The authors wish to thank the following individual for her contributions to the Notetaking Guide.

Penny Ann Dowdy

ISBN-13: 978-0-618-25618-1   ISBN-10: 0-618-25618-0

18 19 20 -1409- 12 11 10 09

Contents

Notetaking Guide

Contents

Contents

Contents

Describing Patterns

Goal: Describe patterns using whole number operations.

EXAMPLE 1 **Recognizing and Extending a Pattern**

City Bus Kristen needs to take the city bus to work. She starts work at 5:00 P.M. The bus stops at the bus stop every 30 minutes. If the bus stops at the bus stop at 3:45 P.M., at what times are the next three stops? What time should Kristen take the bus to be to work on time if her bus ride to work is 15 minutes?

To answer the question, start with 3:45 P.M. and repeatedly add [ ] minutes to the time.

Time of first stop: 3:45 P.M.

Time of second stop:

Time of third stop:

Time of fourth stop:

Because 3:45 P.M. and [ ] are too early for Kristen to take the bus and [ ] is too late, she should take the bus at [ ] to be to work on time.

EXAMPLE 2 **Extending a Numerical Pattern**

Describe the following pattern: 55, 49, 43, 37, ... Then write the next three numbers.

55, 49, 43, 37, [ ], [ ], [ ], . . .

The three dots at the end of a list of numbers mean that the numbers and the pattern continue without end.

Describe the following pattern: 4, 8, 16, 32, ... Then write the next three numbers.

Need help with whole number operations? See pp. 688–690 of your textbook.

You

to get the next number in the pattern.

4,   8,   16,   32,   ,   ,   , . . .

Your turn now **Describe the pattern. Then write the next three numbers.**

1. 729, 243, 81, . . .

2. 40, 33, 26, . . .

3. 3, 11, 19, . . .

EXAMPLE 4 **Extending a Visual Pattern**

Quilt A patchwork quilt has squares that follow a pattern. What are the next three squares that the quilter would make?

Solution

Look for a repeated pattern in the quilt squares. Each square has two triangles facing the same direction. Then each square rotates 90° in a counterclockwise direction from the previous square.

Answer:

4.

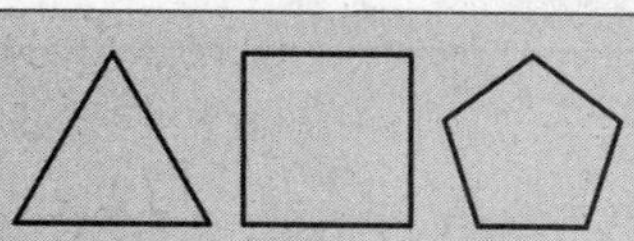

5.

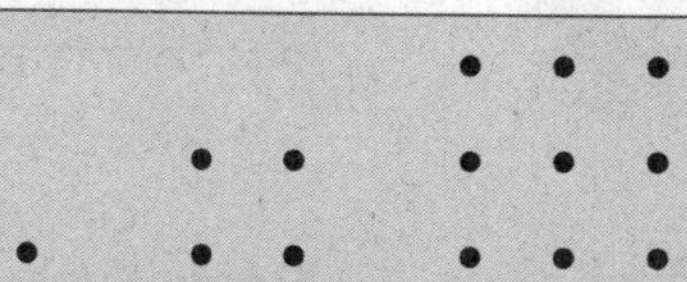

Variables and Expressions

Goal: Evaluate variable expressions.

Vocabulary

Variable:

Variable expression:

Evaluate:

EXAMPLE 1 **Evaluating Variable Expressions**

a. Evaluate $x + 7$ when $x = 4$.　　　**b.** Evaluate $y - 5$ when $y = 13$.

Solution

a. $x + 7 = $ [ ]　　Substitute [ ] for x.

$= $ [ ]　　Add.

b. $y - 5 = $ [ ]　　Substitute [ ] for y.

$= $ [ ]　　Subtract.

Your turn now Evaluate the expression when $d = 3$ and $t = 11$.

1. $6 + d$	**2.** $t - 7$	**3.** $d + 10$

Multiplication and Division Expressions

The expression 2×5 can also be written as ☐ $\cdot$ ☐. There are several different ways you can write multiplication and division expressions.

Multiplication: ☐ is another way of writing $5 \cdot n$.

☐ is another way of writing $a \cdot b$.

☐ is another way of writing $3 \cdot 7$.

Division: ☐ is another way of writing $x \div 4$

EXAMPLE 2 Evaluating Variable Expressions

a. Evaluate $6g$ when $g = 5$.

b. Evaluate $\dfrac{s}{3}$ when $s = 15$.

Solution

a. $6g = $ ☐   Substitute ☐ for g.

$= $ ☐   Multiply.

b. $\dfrac{s}{3} = \dfrac{☐}{☐}$ Substitute ☐ for s.

$= $ ☐   Divide.

---

your turn now Evaluate the expression when $r = 2$ and $z = 9$.

4. $4r$	**5.** $5z$	**6.** $\dfrac{z}{3}$

Waiter To find the amount of money earned by a waiter at a restaurant, you can evaluate the expression $w + t$, where w is the wages earned and t is the amount of tips left by customers. Find the amount of money earned by a waiter who made $25 in wages and $30 in tips.

Solution

$w + t = $ ▢ $ + $ ▢   Substitute ▢ for w and ▢ for t.

$= $ ▢   Add.

Answer: The waiter earned $ ▢ .

Powers and Exponents

Goal: Write repeated multiplication using exponents.

Vocabulary

Power:

Base:

Exponent:

Powers and Exponents

Numbers 4^6 = $4 \cdot 4 \cdot 4 \cdot 4 \cdot 4 \cdot 4$

The power is read

        is a factor   times.

Algebra If n is a nonzero whole number, then:

$$a^n = a \cdot a \cdot a \cdot \cdots \cdot a$$

        is a factor   times.

The power is read

EXAMPLE 1 Writing Powers

There were $3 \cdot 3 \cdot 3 \cdot 3 \cdot 3$ fans in attendance at Mica's first football game. What is another way to write the number of fans at Mica's football game?

$$3 \cdot 3 \cdot 3 \cdot 3 \cdot 3 = \boxed{}$$

        is a factor   times.

Answer: There were   fans at Mica's football game.

Evaluate the power.

a. 5^3 b. 9^2 c. 2^1

Solution

a. $5^3 = $ ☐   Write ☐ as a factor ☐ times.

  $= $ ☐   Multiply.

b. $9^2 = $ ☐   Write ☐ as a factor ☐ times.

  $= $ ☐   Multiply.

c. $2^1 = $ ☐   Write ☐ as a factor ☐ time.

You can read 5^3 as "5 to the third power" or as "5 cubed." You can read 9^2 as "9 to the second power" or as "9 squared."

Your turn now **Write the product as a power.**

1. $3 \cdot 3 \cdot 3$	2. $4 \cdot 4 \cdot 4 \cdot 4 \cdot 4$	3. $10 \cdot 10 \cdot 10 \cdot 10$

Evaluate the power.

4. 1^6	5. 3^6	6. 7^4

EXAMPLE 3 **Evaluating Powers with Variables**

a. Evaluate y^3 when $y = 4$.   **b.** Evaluate g^2 when $g = 10$.

Solution

a. $y^3 = \boxed{}$ Substitute $\boxed{}$ for y.

$= \boxed{}$ Write $\boxed{}$ as a factor $\boxed{}$ times.

$= \boxed{}$ Multiply.

b. $g^2 = \boxed{}$ Substitute $\boxed{}$ for g.

$= \boxed{}$ Write $\boxed{}$ as a factor $\boxed{}$ times.

$= \boxed{}$ Multiply.

Your turn now **Complete the following exercises.**

7. Evaluate b^3 when $b = 6$.	**8.** Evaluate p^5 when $p = 2$.

9. To get a result of 1,000,000, you raise 10 to what power?

Order of Operations

Goal: Evaluate expressions involving two or more operations.

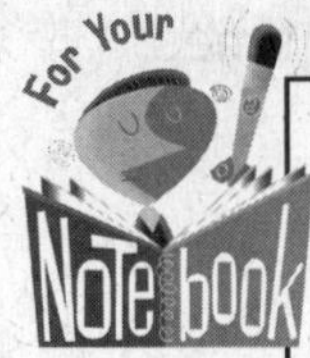

Vocabulary

Order of operations:

Order of Operations

1. Evaluate expressions   .

2. Evaluate   .

3.   from left to right.

4.   from left to right.

EXAMPLE 1   **Following Order of Operations**

Babysitting You earn spending money by babysitting. You charge $5 per hour plus a flat fee of $2 per child. Find the amount you earned babysitting 1 child for 4 hours.

$2 + 5 \times 4 =$ First multiply   and   .

       $=$ Then add   and   .

Answer: You earned $.

EXAMPLE 2   **Evaluating a Variable Expression**

Evaluate $a + \dfrac{b^2}{3}$ when $a = 7$ and $b = 6$.

$a + \dfrac{b^2}{3} =$ Substitute   for a and   for b.

$= 7 + \dfrac{36}{3}$ Evaluate the power.

$=$ $=$ Divide   and   . Then add   and

 Evaluate the expression.

1. $8 + 3 \times 4$	**2.** $32 - 3^3 \div 9$	**3.** $8 \times 4 + 5^2$

4. Evaluate the expression $t - 3v^3$ when $t = 100$ and $v = 2$.

EXAMPLE 3 **Using the Left-to-Right Rule**

a. $15 - 8 + 9 - 3 = \boxed{}$ Subtract $\boxed{}$ from $\boxed{}$.

$= \boxed{}$ Add $\boxed{}$ and $\boxed{}$.

$= \boxed{}$ Subtract $\boxed{}$ from $\boxed{}$.

b. $100 \div 10 \div 2 = \boxed{}$ Divide $\boxed{}$ by $\boxed{}$.

$= \boxed{}$ Divide $\boxed{}$ by $\boxed{}$.

EXAMPLE 4 **Using Grouping Symbols**

Thinking of the letters PEMDAS might help you remember the order of operations:
Parentheses
Exponents
Multiplication
Division
Addition
Subtraction

a. $6(10 - 5) = \boxed{}$ Subtract $\boxed{}$ from $\boxed{}$.

$= \boxed{}$ Multiply $\boxed{}$ and $\boxed{}$.

b. $\dfrac{6 \cdot 6}{8 + 4} = \dfrac{\boxed{}}{\boxed{}}$ Multiply $\boxed{}$ and $\boxed{}$. Add $\boxed{}$ and $\boxed{}$.

$= \boxed{}$ Divide $\boxed{}$ by $\boxed{}$.

c. $(4 + 7)^2 - 20 = \boxed{}$ Add $\boxed{}$ and $\boxed{}$.

$= \boxed{}$ Evaluate the power.

$= \boxed{}$ Subtract $\boxed{}$ from $\boxed{}$.

5. $25 - 10 + 3 - 5$	**6.** $(9 - 4)(5 - 2)^3$	**7.** $\dfrac{9 + 5}{63 \div 9}$

EXAMPLE 5 **Using Order of Operations**

Basketball The point values for certain baskets in basketball are shown in the table. You make 12 field goals, 5 free throws, and 3 three-point field goals. Your friend makes 15 field goals, 3 free throws, and 4 three-point field goals. How many more points did your friend score than you?

Type of Basket	Points
Three-point field goal	3
Field goal	2
Free throw	1

Solution

You need to evaluate the expression
$(15 \cdot 2 + 3 \cdot 1 + 4 \cdot 3) - (12 \cdot 2 + 5 \cdot 1 + 3 \cdot 3)$.

$(15 \cdot 2 + 3 \cdot 1 + 4 \cdot 3) - (12 \cdot 2 + 5 \cdot 1 + 3 \cdot 3)$

$= \underline{}$ $\boxed{}$ first.

$= \underline{}$ Add $\boxed{}$, $\boxed{}$, and $\boxed{}$

           Add $\boxed{}$, $\boxed{}$, and $\boxed{}$.

$= \boxed{}$ Subtract $\boxed{}$ from $\boxed{}$

Answer: Your friend scored $\boxed{}$ more points than you.

Equations and Mental Math

Goal: Use mental math to solve an equation.

For Your Notebook

Vocabulary

Equation:

Solution:

Solving an equation:

EXAMPLE 1 **Checking Possible Solutions**

Tell whether the value of the variable is a solution to $f + 7 = 13$.

a. $f = 8$ **b.** $f = 6$

Solution

Symbol	Meaning
=	is equal to
$\stackrel{?}{=}$	is equal to?
≠	is not equal to

a. $f + 7 = 13$ Write original equation.

Substitute ⬚ for f.

The equation ⬚ true, ⬚.

b. $f + 7 = 13$ Write original equation.

Substitute ⬚ for f.

The equation ⬚ true, ⬚.

Your turn now   **Tell whether the value of the variable is a solution of the equation.**

1. $4t = 20;\ t = 6$	**2.** $17 - p = 12;\ p = 5$	**3.** $12 \div d = 4;\ d = 3$

 Using Mental Math to Solve Equations

Equation →	Question →	Solution →	Check
a. $5 + v = 9$	[ ] plus [ ] equals [ ] ?	[ ]	[ ]
b. $s - 7 = 4$	[ ] minus [ ] equals [ ] ?	[ ]	[ ]
c. $5h = 35$	[ ] times [ ] equals [ ] ?	[ ]	[ ]
d. $j \div 6 = 8$	[ ] divided by [ ] equals [ ] ?	[ ]	[ ]

Your turn now Solve the equation using mental math.

4. $2n = 18$	**5.** $22 = k - 8$	**6.** $4 + r = 17$	**7.** $56 \div w = 8$

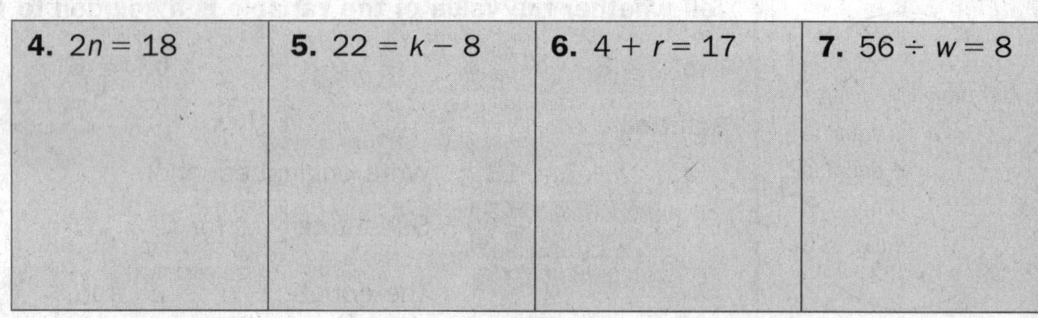

Distance, Speed, and Time

Words Distance traveled is equal to the [ ] (rate of travel) times the [ ] .

Algebra $d =$ [ ]

Numbers distance = 2 feet per second $\cdot$ 30 seconds = [ ]

 Using Mental Math to Solve an Equation

Race Walker A race walker travels at a speed of 5 miles per hour. She tallies her training schedule and finds that she walked 100 miles this month. How much time did she spend walking this month?

Solution

(formula box)   Write formula for distance.

(box) = (box)   Substitute the values you know.

(box) = (box)   Use mental math to solve the equation.

Answer: She walked (box) hours this month.

Your turn now   **Solve the following problem.**

8. A high speed passenger commuter ferry is advertised as being able to make a 16 mile crossing between land and an island in only 48 minutes. How many minutes does it take the ferry to travel 1 mile?

Perimeter and Area

Goal: Use formulas to find perimeter and area.

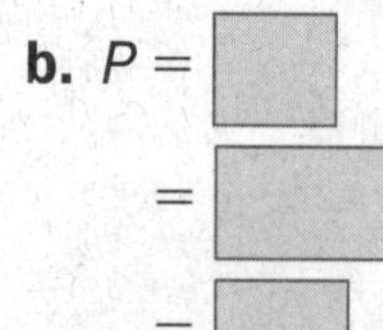

Vocabulary

Perimeter:

Area:

Perimeter and Area

	Rectangle	Square
	width w / length ℓ	side length s
Perimeter P	$P =$	$P =$
Area A	$A =$	$A =$

EXAMPLE 1 Finding Perimeter

Find the perimeter of the rectangle or square with the given dimensions.

  a. $\ell = 6$ feet, $w = 3$ feet   **b.** $s = 5$ centimeters

Solution

a. $P =$

$=$

$= \quad =$

b. $P =$

$=$

$=$

Answer: The perimeter is   feet.

Answer: The perimeter is   centimeters.

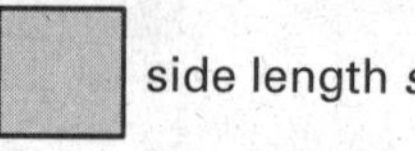

Your turn now **Find the perimeter of the rectangle or square.**

1. 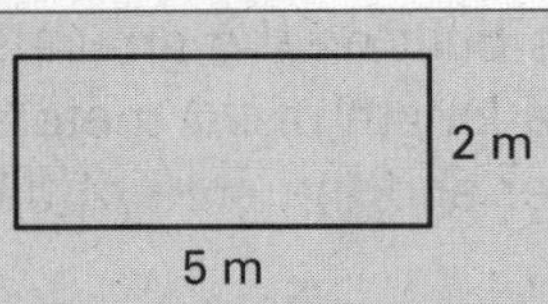
2 m
5 m

2. 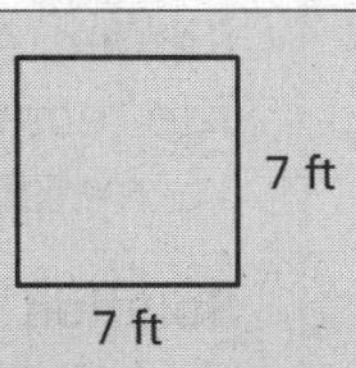
7 ft
7 ft

EXAMPLE 2 Finding Area

Find the area of the rectangle or square with the given dimensions.

a. $\ell = 10$ feet, $w = 4$ feet

b. $s = 12$ centimeters

Solution

a. $A =$ ______
$=$ ______
$=$ ______

Answer: The area is ______ square feet.

b. $A =$ ______
$=$ ______
$=$ ______

Answer: The area is ______ square centimeters.

Your turn now **Find the area of the rectangle or square.**

3. 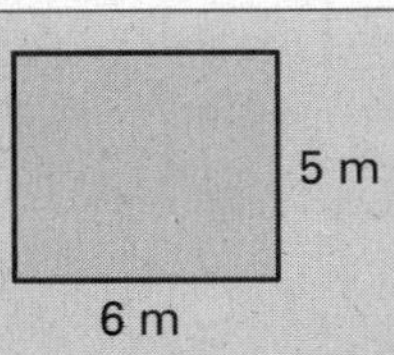
5 m
6 m

4. 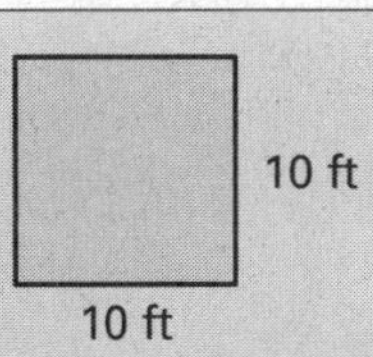
10 ft
10 ft

5. Find the perimeter and the area of a rectangle that has a length of 12 inches and a width of 9 inches.

Garden A hidden garden was built on the grounds of a castle. The rectangular garden had a length of 20 meters and a width of 15 meters. Find the perimeter and the area of the garden.

Solution

$P =$ 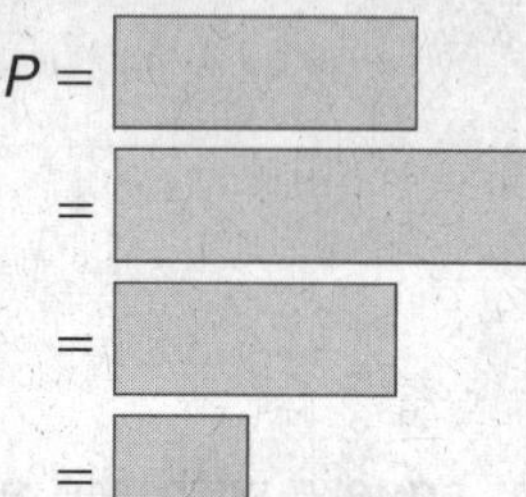

$=$

$=$

$=$

$A =$ 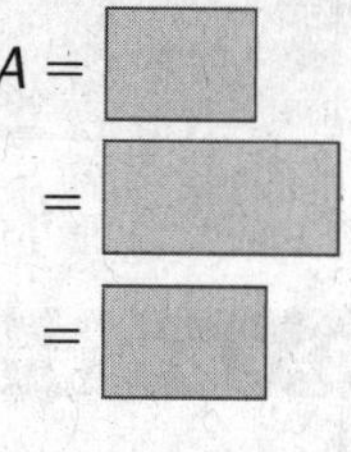

$=$

$=$

Answer: The perimeter is   , and the area is   .

A Problem Solving Plan

Goal: Use a 4-step plan to solve many kinds of problems.

EXAMPLE 1 Understanding and Planning

Commercials A programmer at a television station has exactly 160 seconds of time to fill with commercials. The programmer must choose 3 commercials from the table, and one of the commercials must be the station's commercial. What commercials can the programmer use?

Commercial	Time (seconds)
Station Commercial	45
A	30
B	55
C	80
D	60

To solve this problem, you need to make sure you understand the problem. Then make a plan for solving the problem.

Read and Understand
What do you Know?

The programmer must fill ____________ of commercial time.

The programmer must choose ____ commercials.

____________ must be included.

What do you want to find out?

Make a Plan
How can you relate what you know to what you want to find out?

Your turn now   **Use the information in Example 1.**

1. How many seconds long is the station commercial?

2. How many seconds does this leave for the remaining two commercials?

EXAMPLE 2   **Solving and Looking Back**

To solve the television commercial problem from the previous page, you nee
to carry out the plan from Example 1 and then check the answer.

Solve the Problem

Because of the station commercial requirement, there are ⬚ − ⬚ =

⬚ seconds for playing the other two commercials. Make a list of all the
combinations of the other two commercials and the time it takes to play ther

Commercials	Total Time (seconds)
A: 30 sec, B: 55 sec	
A: 30 sec, C: 80 sec	
A: 30 sec, D: 60 sec	
B: 55 sec, C: 80 sec	
B: 55 sec, D: 60 sec	
C: 80 sec, D: 60 sec	

Answer: The programmer must play the station commercial and commercia

⬚ and ⬚.

Look Back

The answer lists exactly 3 commercials, one of which is the station
commercial, totaling to ⬚ seconds + ⬚ seconds = ⬚ seconds.

Notice the pattern of commercial pairings in the table:

A B C D

A B C D

A B C D

Using a pattern like this guarantees that you don't forget any commercial pairings.

3. Suppose the station commercial was 50 seconds long. Now what commercials would the programmer need to play?

Problem Solving Plan

1. [____________] Read the problem carefully. Identify the question and any important information.

2. [________] Decide on a problem solving strategy.

3. [__________] Use the problem solving strategy to answer the question.

4. [______] Check that your answer is reasonable.

Words to Review

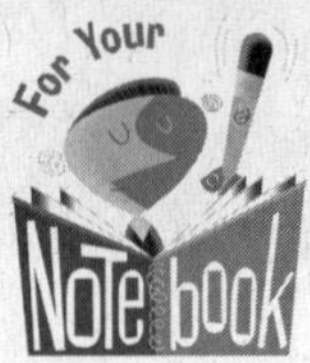

Give an example of the vocabulary word.

Variable

Variable expression

Evaluate

Power

Base

Exponent

Order of operations

Equation

Solution

Solving an equation

Perimeter

Area

Review your notes and Chapter 1 by using the Chapter Review on pages 44–45 of your textbook.

Comparing, Ordering, and Rounding Decimals

Goal: Compare, order, and round decimals.

Vocabulary

Decimal:

Decimals and Place Value

hundred thousands · ten thousands · thousands · hundreds · tens · ones · tenths · hundredths · thousandths · ten-thousandths · hundred-thousandths

fifteen and two tenths

fifteen and eight hundredths

EXAMPLE 1 Comparing Decimals

Baby Weights At Jason's 6-month checkup, he weighed 15.2 pounds. At Ali's 6-month checkup, she weighed 15.08 pounds. Compare the weights of the babies to determine who weighed more.

The ☐ and ☐ digits are the same.

15.**2**0 ←— Write a ☐ as a placeholder.

15.**0**8

The ☐ digits are different. ☐, so ☐.

Answer: Because 15.2 ☐ 15.08, ☐ weighed more.

Your turn now Copy and complete the statement using <, >, or =.

1. 15.3 __?__ 15.09	**2.** 6.3 __?__ 6.30	**3.** 9.238 __?__ 9.36

EXAMPLE 2 Ordering Decimals

Order 6.14, 6.3, 6.07, 6, and 6.27 from least to greatest.

On a number line, mark tenths between [ ]. Mark hundredths by dividing each tenth into [ ] equal parts. Then graph each number.

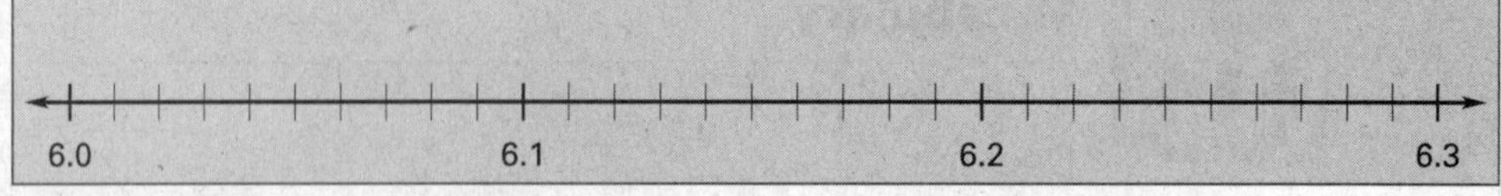

From least to greatest, the numbers are [ ].

Rounding Decimals

To round a decimal to a given place value, look at the digit in the place to the [ ].

- If the digit is less than [ ], round down.
- If the digit is [ ] or greater, round up.

EXAMPLE 3 Rounding a Decimal

Round 8.548 to the nearest tenth.

8.548

You want to round to the nearest [ ].

Because the hundredths' digit is less than [ ], round [ ] and drop the remaining digits.

Answer: The decimal 8.548 rounded to the nearest tenth is [ ].

Your turn now Order the numbers from least to greatest.

4. 7.59, 8.2, 8.15, 7.95, 7.85	**5.** 1.36, 1.4, 1.59, 1.92, 1.5

6. Round 61.0962 to the nearest hundredth.

Adding and Subtracting Decimals

Goal: Add and subtract decimals.

Vocabulary

Front-end estimation:

EXAMPLE 1 **Adding and Subtracting Decimals**

a. 2.149 + 1.32

$$
\begin{array}{r}
2.149 \\
+\ 1.320 \\
\hline
\end{array}
$$

⟵ Write ☐ as a placeholder.

b. 5 − 3.18

$$
\begin{array}{r}
5.00 \\
-\ 3.18 \\
\hline
\end{array}
$$

⟵ Write ☐ as placeholders.

Your turn now Find the sum or difference.

1. 42.9 + 26.5	**2.** 4.62 + 3.4	**3.** 2.859 + 3.48
4. 2.5 − 0.9	**5.** 8.43 − 6.21	**6.** 1 − 0.16

 Evaluating a Variable Expression

Evaluate $4.9 + t - v$ when $t = 3.42$ and $v = 3.8$.

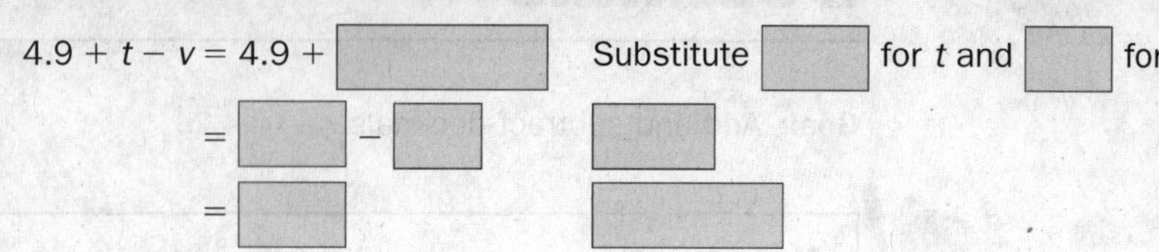

WATCH OUT!
Don't forget to add and subtract from left to right.

$$4.9 + t - v = 4.9 + \boxed{} \qquad \text{Substitute } \boxed{} \text{ for } t \text{ and } \boxed{} \text{ for}$$

$$= \boxed{} - \boxed{} \qquad \boxed{}$$

$$= \boxed{} \qquad \boxed{}$$

Your turn now Evaluate the expression when $d = 5.82$ and $f = 4.9$.

7. $d + f$	**8.** $d - f$	**9.** $11 - f - d$

 Estimating a Sum

Lunch Joel and Manny are eating lunch at a deli. Joel's lunch cost $6.75, and Manny's lunch cost $5.40. They want to order two chocolate shakes, which will cost an additional $3.89. They have $15.00 to pay the bill. Can they buy the milkshakes?

Solution

1. Add the front-end digits: the dollars.

$6.75
$5.40
+ $3.89
$\boxed{}$

2. Estimate the sum of the remaining digits: the cents.

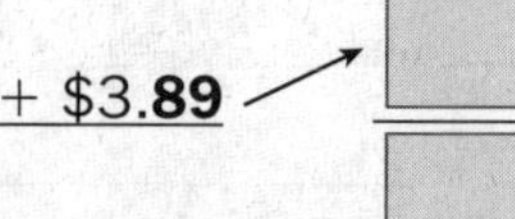

$6.**75**
$5.**40** →
+ $3.**89**

3. Add the results.

$\boxed{}$
+ $\boxed{}$
$\boxed{}$

Answer: The estimated sum is $\boxed{}$ than $15, so they $\boxed{}$ bu the milkshakes.

Multiplying Decimals

Goal: Multiply decimals.

Vocabulary

Leading digit:

Multiplying Decimals

Words   Multiply decimals as you would ___________. Then place the ___________ in the product. The number of decimal places in the product is equal to ___________ ___________.

Numbers $0.7 \times 0.3 =$ ___

EXAMPLE 1   **Multiplying Decimals**

$$
\begin{array}{r}
2.56 \\
\times\ 0.43 \\
\hline
768 \\
1024 \\
\hline
1.1008
\end{array}
$$

___ decimal places

$+$ ___ decimal places

___ decimal places

a. 0.55 ☐ decimal places

× 12 + ☐ decimal places

☐

☐

☐ ☐ decimal places

Answer: 0.55 × 12 = ☐

✓ **Check** Because $\frac{1}{2}$ of 12 is ☐ , the product is reasonable.

b. 1.168 ☐ decimal places

× 0.07 + ☐ decimal places

☐ ☐ decimal places

Answer: 1.168 × 0.07 = ☐

✓ **Check** Because 1 × 0.07 = ☐ , the product is reasonable.

Your turn now Find the product. Then check that your answer is reasonab▶

1. 2.5 × 3.9	**2.** 0.43 × 0.16	**3.** 5.103 × 2.9

 Multiplying Decimals to Find Area

Table Top Alonzo is building a table to hold his model train. The table top is going to be 4.75 feet long and 3.5 feet wide. What is the area of the table top?

Solution

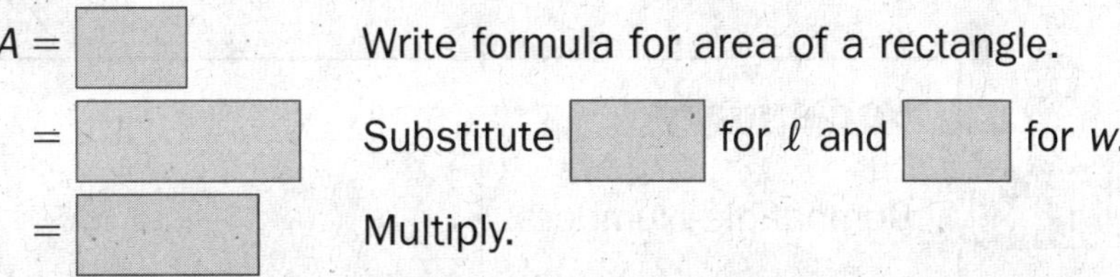

$A = \boxed{}$ Write formula for area of a rectangle.

$ = \boxed{}$ Substitute $\boxed{}$ for ℓ and $\boxed{}$ for w.

$ = \boxed{}$ Multiply.

Answer: The area of the table top is $\boxed{}$.

Your turn now **Find the area of the rectangle.**

4.

5 cm

1.68 cm

5.

6.5 in.

15.2 in.

Dividing Decimals

Goal: Divide decimals.

Vocabulary

Compatible Numbers:

EXAMPLE 1 **Dividing a Decimal by a Whole Number**

Gift Joy and her three cousins spent $21.40 on a gift for their grandfather.
Each cousin contributed the same amount of money. How much did each
cousin spend?

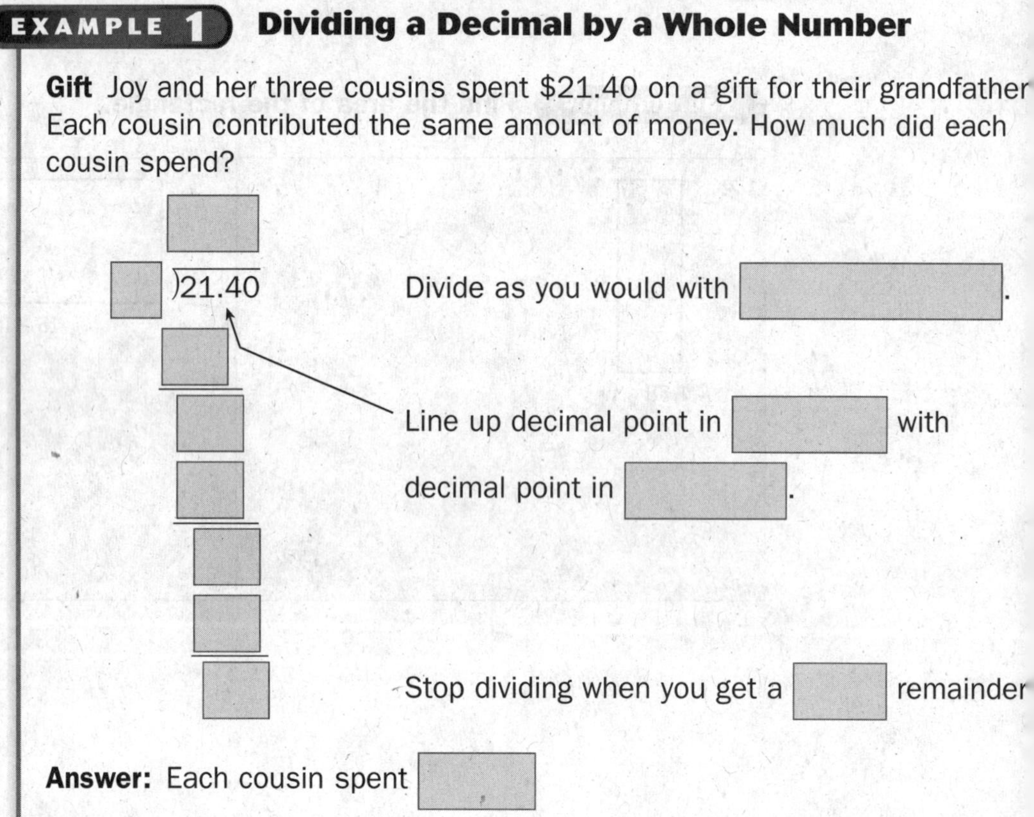

Divide as you would with [ ].

Line up decimal point in [ ] with decimal point in [ ].

Stop dividing when you get a [ ] remainder.

Answer: Each cousin spent [ ].

Your turn now Find the quotient. Then check your answer.

1. 253.4 ÷ 7	**2.** 14.76 ÷ 3	**3.** 91.8 ÷ 9

┌───┐

Dividing by a Decimal

Words   When you divide by a decimal, multiply both the divisor and

the dividend by a [   ] that will make the divisor a

[   ].

Numbers $12.5\overline{)8.75}$ ⟶ $[\quad]\overline{)87.5}$ with quotient 0.7

└───┘

EXAMPLE 2   **Dividing Decimals**

Divide: **a.** $6.826 \div 0.002$ **b.** $12 \div 2.4$ **c.** $0.028 \div 0.5$

Solution

a. $0.002\overline{)6.826}$ To multiply divisor and dividend by [   ],

move both decimal points [ ] place(s) to the right.

$$
\begin{array}{r}
3413 \\
2\overline{)6826} \\
\underline{6} \\
8 \\
\underline{8} \\
2 \\
\underline{2} \\
6 \\
\underline{6} \\
0
\end{array}
$$

b. $2.4\overline{)12.0}$ To multiply divisor and dividend by [ ], move both decimal

points [ ] place(s) to the right. Write [ ] as a placeholder.

$$
\begin{array}{r}
5 \\
24\overline{)120} \\
\underline{120} \\
0
\end{array}
$$

c. $0.5\overline{)0.028}$ To multiply divisor and dividend by 10, move both

decimal points [ ] place(s) to the right.

$$
\begin{array}{r}
0.056 \\
5\overline{)0.28} \\
\underline{25} \\
30 \\
\underline{30} \\
0
\end{array}
$$

Line up [   ].

WATCH OUT!
Don't forget to write
zeros as placeholders
in the quotient.

4. $19.6 \div 0.5$	**5.** $48.45 \div 5.7$	**6.** $0.495 \div 8.25$
7. $16.0125 \div 9.15$	**8.** $75 \div 3.2$	**9.** $9.6 \div 4$

EXAMPLE 3   Rounding a Quotient

Socks A pack of six pairs of socks costs $9.75. Find the price of one pair
socks. Round to the nearest cent.

In Example 3, you are rounding to the nearest cent, or hundredth. Divide only until the quotient reaches the thousandths' place. Then round.

Solution

1. Divide $9.75 by 6.

```
     1.625
  6)9.750
     6
     37
     36
      15
      12
       30
       30
        0
```

Write and bring down ▢ as a placeholder.

Stop dividing when the quotient reaches the ▢ place.

2. Round the quotient to the nearest cent. $1.625 ⟶ ▢

Answer: The price of each pair of socks is ▢.

Scientific Notation

Goal: Read and write numbers using scientific notation.

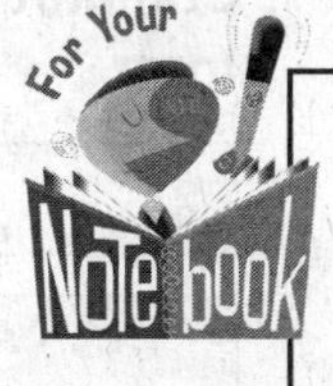

Vocabulary

Scientific notation: [_____________]

Using Scientific Notation

A number is written in scientific notation if it has the form $c \times 10^n$ where c is [_____] 1 and less than 10 and n is [_____].

Standard form	Product form	Scientific notation
2,860,000	2.86 × [____]	[____] × $10^{\square}$

EXAMPLE 1 **Writing Numbers in Scientific Notation**

Budget The budget to support the national parks in the United States was $64,500,000 in 1998. To write 64,500,000 in scientific notation, use powers of 10.

Powers of ten:
$10^1 = 10$
$10^2 = 100$
$10^3 = 1000$
$10^4 = 10,000$
$10^5 = 100,000$
$10^6 = 1,000,000$

Standard form	Product form	Scientific notation
64,500,000	[____] × [________]	[____] × $10^{\square}$

Answer: The budget for national parks in the United States was $[________] in 1998.

 Writing Numbers in Standard Form

Write the number in standard form.

a. 3×10^5 **b.** 6.702×10^9

Solution

You read 3×10^5 as "three times ten to the fifth power."

	Scientific notation	Product form			Standard form
a.	3×10^5	$3 \times$			
b.	6.702×10^9		$\times$		

Your turn now   **Write the number in scientific notation.**

1. 27,500,000	**2.** 10,200,000,000	**3.** 3,600,000

Write the number in standard form.

4. 6.37×10^4	**5.** 2.09×10^7	**6.** 1×10^1

Population The population of Alaska was about 6.35×10^5 in 2001. The population of Nebraska was about 1.71×10^6 in 2001. Which state had the greater population?

Solution

To compare numbers written in scientific notation, first compare the ☐. If the exponents are ☐, then compare the ☐.

Alaska: 6.35×10^5 Exponent is ☐.

Nebraska: 1.71×10^6 Exponent is ☐.

Because 5 ☐ 6, 6.35×10^5 ☐ 1.71×10^6.

Answer: ☐ had the greater population.

✓ **Check** Write the numbers in ☐ and compare.

$6.35 \times 10^5 = $ ☐

$1.71 \times 10^6 = $ ☐

So, 6.35×10^5 ☐ 1.71×10^6.

Your turn now   **Copy and complete the statement using <, >, or =.**

7. 3.4×10^{30} __?__ 2.05×10^{32}	**8.** 2.59×10^{15} __?__ 2.06×10^{15}

Measuring in Metric Units

Goal: Measure and estimate using metric units.

Vocabulary

Metric system:

Metric units of length:

Mass:

Metric units of mass:

Capacity:

Metric units of capacity:

Benchmarks

1 millimeter is about the thickness of a dime.

1 centimeter is about the width of a large paper clip.

1 meter is about the height of the back of a chair.

1 kilometer is about the combined length of 9 football fields.

1 milligram is about the mass of a grain of sugar.

1 gram is about the mass of a small paper clip.

1 kilogram is about the mass of a textbook.

1 millimeter is about the capacity of an eyedropper.

1 liter is about the capacity of a large water bottle.

1 kiloliter is about the capacity of 8 large trash cans.

EXAMPLE 1   Using Metric Units of Length

Estimate the length of a key by imagining paper clips laid next to it. Then measure the key with a metric ruler to check your estimate.

Solution

1. About ☐ large paper clips fit next to the key, so it is about ☐ long.

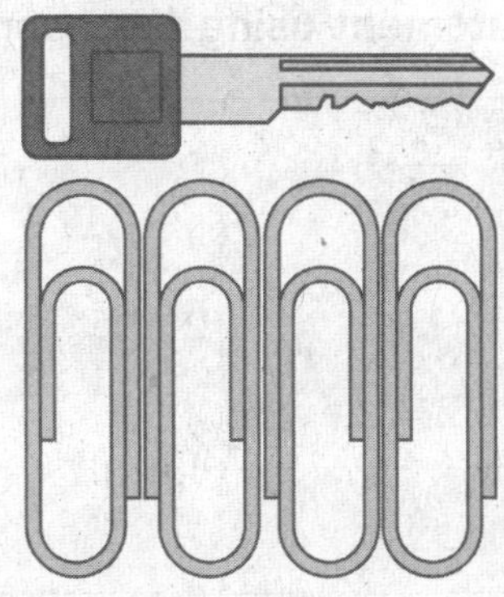

2. Measure using a ruler.

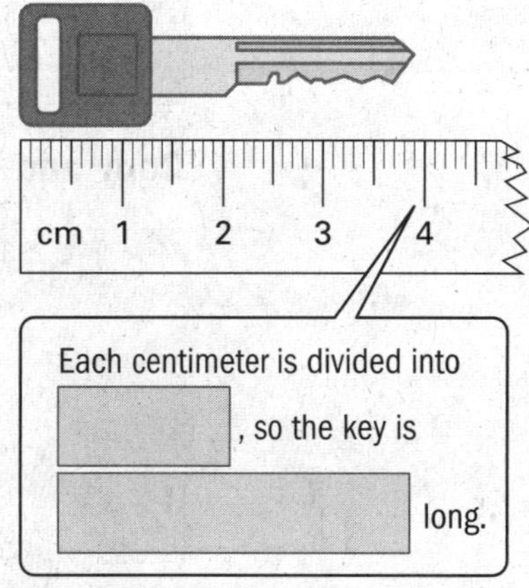

EXAMPLE 2   Measuring Mass

Find the mass of the plastic model of bananas.

Each gram is divided into ☐ , so the mass of the model is ☐ .

EXAMPLE 3   Using Metric Units of Mass

Copy and complete the statement using the appropriate metric unit: The mass of a computer monitor is 5 _?_ .

The mass of a computer monitor is ☐ than 5 grains of sugar (5 ☐), and is also ☐ than the mass of 5 paper clips (5 ☐).

Because a good estimate for the mass of a computer monitor is 5 ☐ , the appropriate metric unit is ☐ .

Answer: The mass of a computer monitor is 5 ☐ .

1. Estimate the length of a video cassette in centimeters. Then use a metric ruler to check your estimate.

Copy and complete the statement using the appropriate metric unit.

2. The mass of a cat is 4 _?_ .	**3.** The mass of a rubber band is 175 _?_ .

EXAMPLE 4   **Measuring a Liquid Amount**

Find the amount of liquid in the measuring cup.

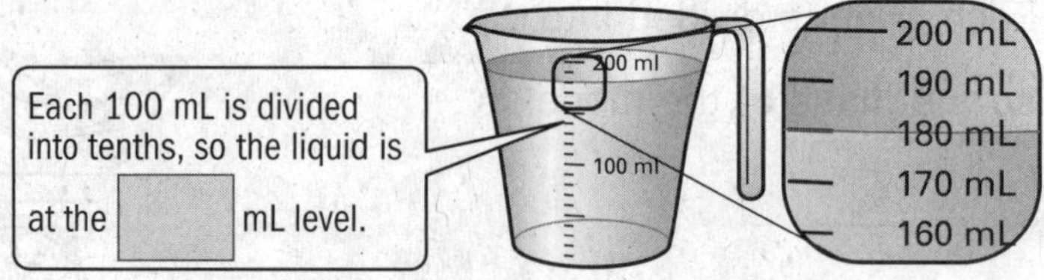

Answer: The measuring cup contains ☐ milliliters of liquid.

EXAMPLE 5   **Using Metric Units of Capacity**

What is the most reasonable capacity of a bucket?

 A. 6 L   **B.** 65 mL   **C.** 75 L   **D.** 2 kL

Solution

Both ☐ (☐ large water bottles) and ☐ (☐ large trash can

would overfill a bucket. Using ☐ (☐ eyedroppers) would be too

little. That leaves ☐ (☐ large water bottles), which seems reasonabl

Answer: The most reasonable capacity of a bucket is ☐ .

1. Spoon	**2.** Hot tub	**3.** Drinking glass
A. 1.3 kL	**A.** 1.3 kL	**A.** 1.3 kL
B. 250 mL	**B.** 250 mL	**B.** 250 mL
C. 2 mL	**C.** 2 mL	**C.** 2 mL

Converting Metric Units

Goal: Convert between metric units.

The metric system is a [   ]. Metric prefixes are associate with decimal place values.

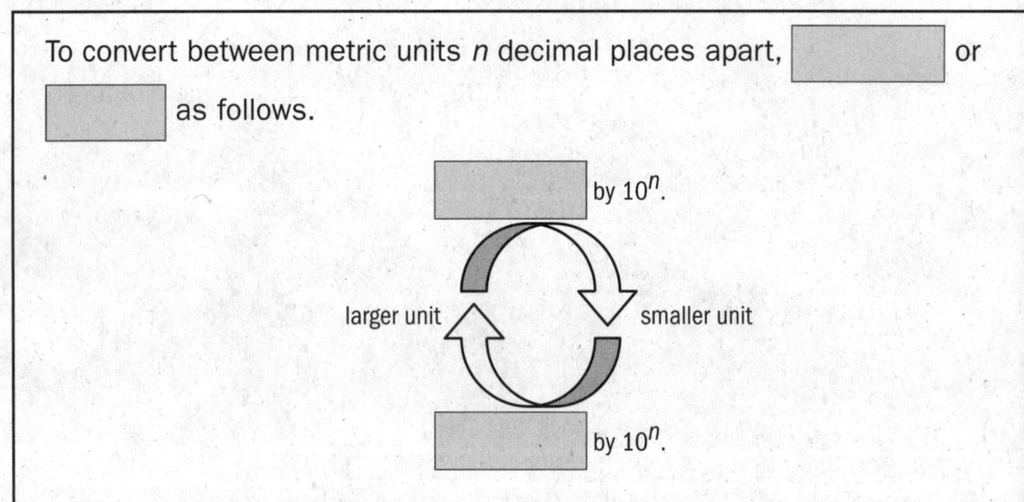

To convert between metric units n decimal places apart, [   ] or [   ] as follows.

EXAMPLE 1   Converting Metric Units of Length

The height of a chain-link fence is 137 centimeters. How many meters tall is the fence?

Solution

You are converting from a smaller unit (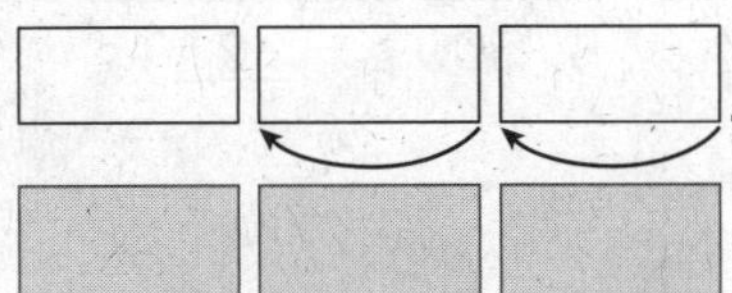) to a larger unit

([ ]), so [ ] by a power of 10.

From [ ] to [ ], the decimal point is moved

[ ], so divide by [ ], or [ ].

$137 \div$ [ ] $=$ [ ]

137 centimeters $=$ [ ] meters

Answer: The fence is [ ] tall.

EXAMPLE 2   Converting Units of Mass and Capacity

Copy and complete the statement.

a. 4620 g = __?__ kg   **b.** 27 L = __?__ mL

Solution

a. To convert from grams to kilograms, [ ].

$4620 \div$ [ ] $=$ [ ], so 4620 g = [ ] kg.

b. To convert from liters to milliliters, [ ].

$27 \times$ [ ] $=$ [ ], so 27 L = [ ] mL.

1. 5600 m = _?_ km	**2.** 68 m = _?_ mm	**3.** 275 cm = _?_ m
4. 382 mm = _?_ cm	**5.** 500 g = _?_ kg	**6.** 1.75 kL = _?_ L

EXAMPLE 3   **Comparing Metric Measures**

Copy and complete the statement using <, >, or =.

a. 650 cm _?_ 6 m   **b.** 1.6 kg _?_ 1525 g

Solution

a. 650 cm _?_ 6 m   Strategy: Convert meters to ☐

650 cm _?_ ☐ cm   6 × ☐ = ☐ , so 6 m = ☐ cm.

650 cm ☐ ☐ cm   Compare.

Answer: 650 cm ☐ 6 m

b. 1.6 kg _?_ 1525 g   Strategy: Convert kilograms to ☐ .

☐ g _?_ 1525 g   1.6 × ☐ = ☐ ,

                                      so 1.6 kg = ☐ g.

☐ g ☐ 1525 g   Compare.

Answer: 1.6 kg ☐ 1525 g

To compare two measurements that have different units, convert one of the measures so that both have the same units.

1. 6.8 kL __?__ 6725 L	**2.** 2.1 g __?__ 2100 mg	**3.** 7.3 mm __?__ 73 cm

EXAMPLE 4 Using Metric Units of Length

Garden Beds Hank is planting a garden in his yard that is 8.5 meters long. Suppose the garden is divided into smaller beds that each measure 212.5 centimeters in length. How many small garden beds would there be?

Solution

1. Convert 8.5 meters to ____________ by multiplying by ______.

8.5 × ______ = ______, so 8.5 m = ____________.

2. To find the number of gardens, divide the ________________________

by ____________________.

______ cm ÷ ______ cm = ______

Answer: The garden would be divided into ______ smaller beds.

Words to Review

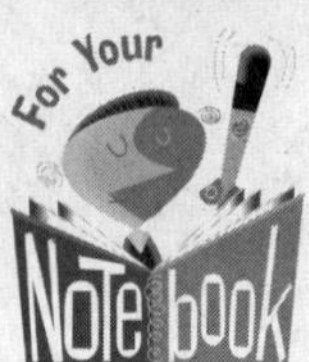

Give an example of the vocabulary word.

Decimal

Front-end estimation

Leading digits

Compatible numbers

Scientific notation

Metric system

Meter

Millimeter

Centimeter

Kilometer

Mass

Gram

Milligram

Kilogram

Capacity

Liter

Milliliter

Kiloliter

Review your notes and Chapter 2 by using the Chapter Review on pages 92–93 of your textbook.

Mean, Median, and Mode

Goal: Describe data using mean, median, and mode.

Vocabulary

Mean:

Median:

Mode:

Range:

EXAMPLE 1 **Finding a Mean**

Heights The students in Ms. Whitney's class practice measuring by finding each other's heights. The results are shown below. Find the mean height.

$$1.6 \text{ m} \quad 1.8 \text{ m} \quad 1.5 \text{ m} \quad 1.3 \text{ m} \quad 1.9 \text{ m}$$
$$1.4 \text{ m} \quad 1.6 \text{ m} \quad 1.5 \text{ m} \quad 1.8 \text{ m} \quad 1.6 \text{ m}$$

Mean =

=

=

Answer: The mean height of the students is ___________.

EXAMPLE 2 **Finding Median, Mode, and Range**

Find the median, mode(s), and range of the numbers below.

54   58   51   48   63   59   57   52   54   58

Write the numbers in order from ____________.

____

Median: Because there is an even number of data values, the median is the ____________.

$$\text{Median} = \frac{\boxed{}}{\boxed{}} = \frac{\boxed{}}{\boxed{}} = \boxed{}$$

Modes: The numbers that occur most often are ____ and ____.

Range: Find the difference between the greatest and the least values.

Range = ____________ = ____

Your turn now **Find the mean, median, mode(s), and range.**

1. 6, 2, 7, 11, 2, 10, 5, 3, 8

2. 27, 63, 49, 34, 70, 58, 55, 68

 Choosing the Best Average

School Play The numbers of tickets sold for the upcoming school play are listed below.

86　30　28　9　26　32　34　42　35　28

Which average best represents the number of tickets sold?

Solution

Compare the mean, median, and mode.

Mean: ␣␣␣␣␣␣␣␣␣ = ␣␣

Median: 9　26　28　28　**30**　**32**　34　35　42　86

␣␣␣ = ␣

The median is ␣.

Mode: The number of tickets most often sold is ␣.

Answer: The ␣␣␣ best represents the number of tickets sold.

Bar Graphs and Line Graphs

Goal: Make and interpret bar graphs and line graphs.

Vocabulary

Bar graph:

Line graph:

EXAMPLE 1 **Making a Bar Graph**

Use a bar graph to represent the data in the table.

School Population				
School	**Smith**	**Hall**	**Greenman**	**Carlson**
Students	651	703	528	639

1. Choose a scale.

The largest data value is ▢ . So, start the scale at ▢ and extend

to a value greater than ▢ , such as ▢ . Use increments of ▢

2. Draw and label the graph.

Use the scale to determine the length of the bar

Include horizonta gridlines.

All of the bars should have the same width.

 Make a bar graph of the data.

1.

Football Players	
Grade Level	**Number of Players**
9th	3
10th	8
11th	23
12th	28

TV Stations The table shows the number of stations available to Satellite TV and Cable TV in a community during four years.

To make a double bar graph of the data, start by drawing bars for the Satellite TV stations. Then draw bars for the Cable TV stations.

Year	Satellite	Cable
1998	50	37
1999	84	52
2000	100	75
2001	125	130

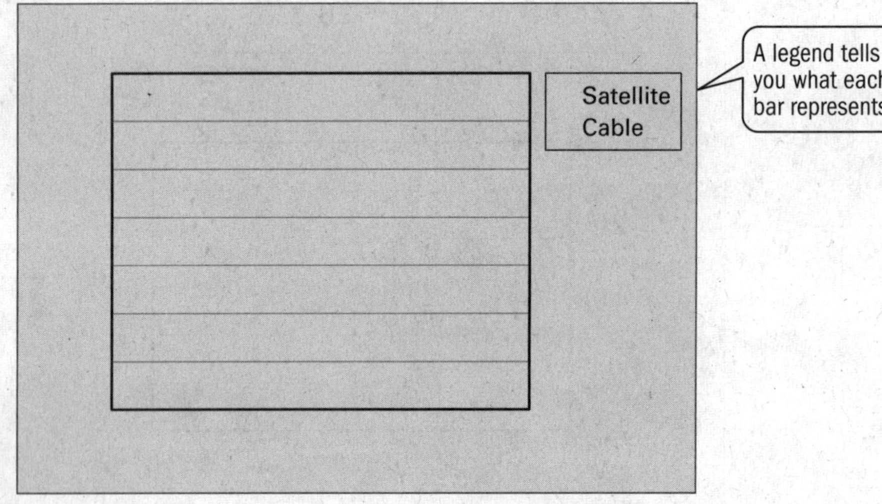

A legend tells you what each bar represents.

Ice Skating School The line graph shows the enrollment at the Kids on Ice Skating School from 1995 through 2000. What conclusion can you make about the line graph?

In the line graph, the break in the vertical axis allows you to focus on the values between 125 and 185.

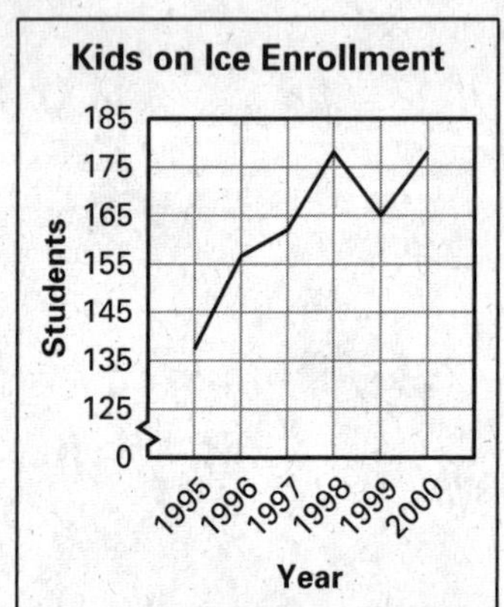

Answer: The line graph shows that the enrollment ☐ between ☐ and ☐, but there was a ☐ from ☐ to ☐ From ☐ to ☐, the enrollment ☐.

Bike Riders Use the table to make a line graph of the number of students riding their bikes to a certain school from 1995 through 2000.

1. Choose the horizontal and vertical axes. Years from 1995 through 2000 will be shown on the [   ] axis. The greatest number of bike riders is 36. So, start the [   ] axis at 0 and end with 40, using increments of 5.

Year	Bike Riders
1995	12
1996	15
1997	21
1998	33
1999	36
2000	31

2. Draw and label the graph.

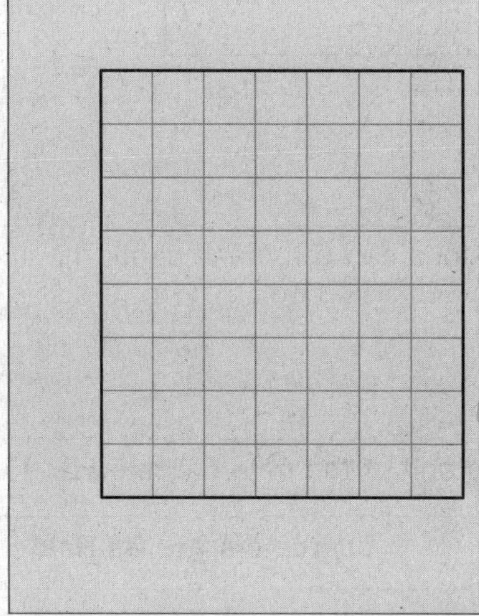

Plot a point for each year. Then connect the points with line segments.

Include evenly spaced horizontal and vertical gridlines.

2. Make a double bar graph of the data collected by a car dealership in one month.

Types of Vehicles People Bought					
Vehicle	**Sedan**	**SUV**	**Station Wagon**	**Truck**	**Van**
Male	12	18	2	15	3
Female	10	15	6	11	5

3. What conclusions can you make about the line graph in Example 4?

4. Make a line graph of the data collected by a customer service call center.

Customers Are On Hold					
Time	8 A.M.	10 A.M.	Noon	2 P.M.	4 P.M.
Average Hold Time (in minutes)	1	3	7	5	2

Stem-and-Leaf Plots

Goal: Display data using stem-and-leaf plots.

Vocabulary

Stem-and-leaf plot:

EXAMPLE 1 **Making a Stem-and-Leaf Plot**

The table shows the number of phone calls received by a telethon each hour for ten hours. Display the numbers of phone calls on a stem-and-leaf plot.

Hour	Number of Calls Received	Hour	Number of Calls Received
1	15	6	27
2	21	7	53
3	36	8	52
4	31	9	39
5	38	10	20

Solution

1. The numbers range from ☐ to ☐, so let the ☐ be the tens' digits from ☐ to ☐. Let the ☐ be the ones' digits.

2. Write the ☐ first. Draw a ☐ next to the stems. Then record each number of phone calls by writing its ☐ on the same line as the corresponding ☐.

3. Make an ordered stem-and-leaf plot.

Unordered Plot

Ordered Plot

Key: ⬜ | ⬜ = ⬜

Key: ⬜ | ⬜ = ⬜

EXAMPLE 2 **Interpreting a Stem-and-Leaf Plot**

100-Meter Hurdles Sophia runs the 100-meter hurdles for her track team. Her race times (in seconds) are listed below. Use a stem-and-leaf plot to order the data. Then make a conclusion about the data.

18.5   21.3   19.0   19.6   17.8   22.4   21.6   19.3   18.9   22.8   21.3

Solution

Begin by making an unordered stem-and-leaf plot. Because the race times range from ⬜ to ⬜, the stems are the digits in the ⬜ places. The leaves are the digits in the ⬜ place.

Then make an ordered stem-and-leaf plot.

Unordered Plot

Ordered Plot

Key: ⬜ | ⬜ = ⬜

Key: ⬜ | ⬜ = ⬜

Answer: Sophia runs ⬜ races under 20 seconds than ⬜ 20 seconds.

1. The number of customers visiting Tyrone's book shop each day are listed below. Make an ordered stem-and-leaf plot of the numbers.

18 12 20 32 15 45 53 18 23 24 39 27 19 26 17 20

2. Use the stem-and-leaf plot from Exercise 1 to determine the number of customers greater than 32.

3. Use the stem-and-leaf plot from Exercise 1 to make a conclusion about the daily number of customers in Tyrone's store.

Box-and-Whisker Plots

Goal: Display data using box-and-whisker plots.

Vocabulary

Box-and-whisker plot:

Lower quartile:

Upper quartile:

Lower extreme:

Upper extreme:

 Making a Box-and-Whisker Plot

Ages The ages of the skaters at the Aurora Skating Rink are listed below. How can the data be displayed so that it is divided into quarters?

6, 8, 9, 12, 13, 14, 14, 15, 15, 16,
16, 18, 18, 19, 25, 27, 28, 32, 42, 56

If a data set has an odd number of values, the median value is not included in either the lower half or the upper half.

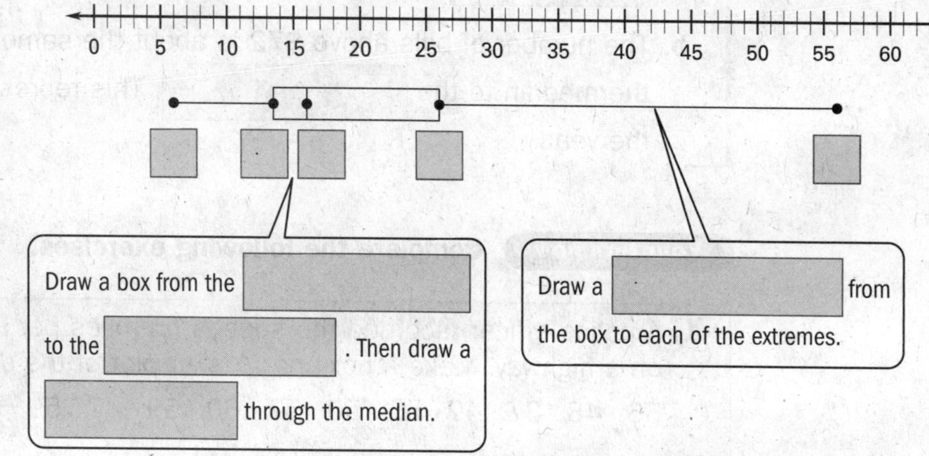

Plot the lower extreme, lower quartile, median, upper quartile, and upper extreme using a number line.

Draw a box from the ______ to the ______ . Then draw a ______ through the median.

Draw a ______ from the box to each of the extremes.

Electric Bills The amounts of the electricity bills in the Nguyen's home in a year are displayed in the box-and-whisker plot below.

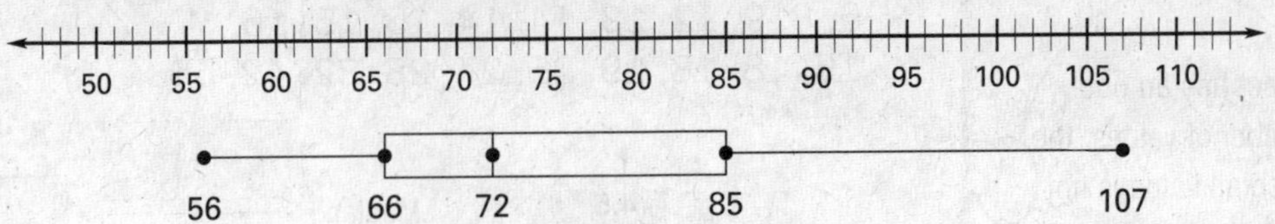

a. If the Nguyen's electricity bills were under $66 in the months that they did not run the air conditioner, then about what fraction of the year did they not run the air conditioner?

b. If the electricity bills over $72 represent the months where the average outdoor temperature was at least 85°F, then about what fraction of the year was the average temperature at least 85°F?

Solution

a. The number of bills under $66 is about the same on the number line as ____________________________________, which represents about ____________ of the year.

b. The number of bills above $72 is about the same as the number from the median to the ________________. This represents about ______ of the year.

Your turn now **Complete the following exercises.**

1. A police officer recorded the speeds (in miles per hour) of cars traveling on a highway. Make a box-and-whisker plot of the data listed below.

    56 48 37 49 55 50 57 60 59 47 59 57 55 58 54 48

2. Use the box-and-whisker plot from Exercise 1 to make a conclusion about the data.

3. In Example 2, is the number of electricity bills between $66 and $72 necessarily less than the number of bills between $72 and $85?

 Comparing Box-and-Whisker Plots

DVDs The box-and-whisker plots below represent the prices of DVDs at two different stores. What conclusions can you draw about the data?

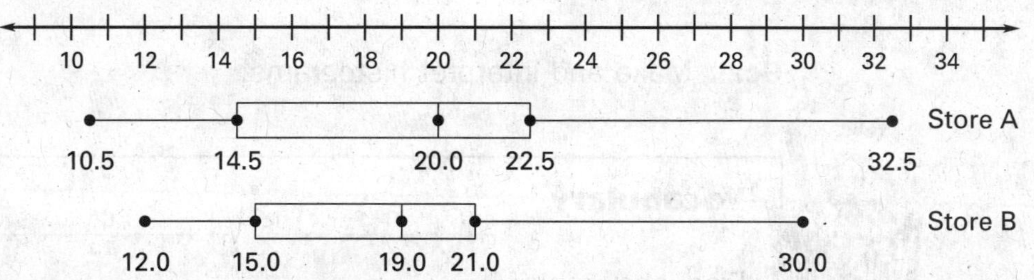

Solution

In general, Store A has a ▢ range of prices. ▢ has the most expensive DVD, but also has the least expensive DVD. The median price of Store B's DVDs is ▢ than the median price of Store A's DVDs.

Histograms

Goal: Make and interpret histograms.

Vocabulary

Frequency table: data in intervals

Frequency: # of values

Histogram: graph from freq. table

EXAMPLE 1 Making a Frequency Table

Auction The sellers on an Internet auction site tracked how many people viewed the auction each day. The data are listed below. Make a frequency table of the data.

15, 28, 36, 16, 18, 27, 40, 39, 25, 19, 36, 19, 42, 39, 27, 30, 49, 6, 27, 38, 0, 42, 37, 26, 17, 16, 25, 31, 29, 8, 10, 28, 34, 16, 9, 40, 32

Solution

1. Choose intervals of __=__ that cover all the data values, which range from ___ to ___. In the table, each interval covers __49__ whole numbers. The first interval is __0__ and the last interval is ______.

2. Make a __________ next to the interval containing a given number of viewers of the auction.

3. Write the frequency for each interval by __________ of tally marks for the interval.

Viewers	Tally	Frequency
0–9	IIII	4
10–19	THL IIII	9
20–29	THL IIII	9
30–39	THL THL	10
40–49	THL	5

Phone Calls A business kept track of how many phone solicitors called them. The table shows the number of phone calls received each day. Make a histogram of the data.

Phone Calls	Tally	Frequency
0–4		8
5–9		0
10–14		12
15–19		18
20–24		9

Solution

1. Draw and label the [ ] and [ ] axes.

   List each interval from the frequency table on the [ ].

   The greatest frequency is [ ]. So, start the vertical axis at [ ] and end it at [ ], using increments of 2.

2. Draw a bar for [ ]. The bars should have [ ] width.

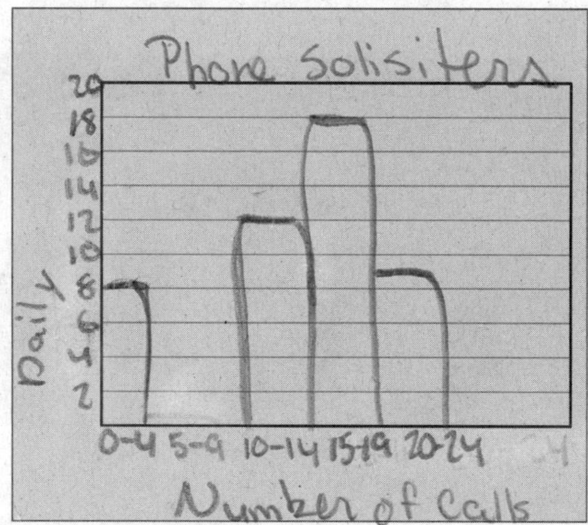

Include [ ] grid lines.

Bars that are next to each other should [ ] gap between them.

1. The runs scored by the school baseball team in each game are listed below. Make a frequency table of the data.

2, 8, 0, 3, 5, 10, 2, 1, 3, 1, 0, 14, 2, 3, 5, 0, 6, 2, 12, 4, 8, 2

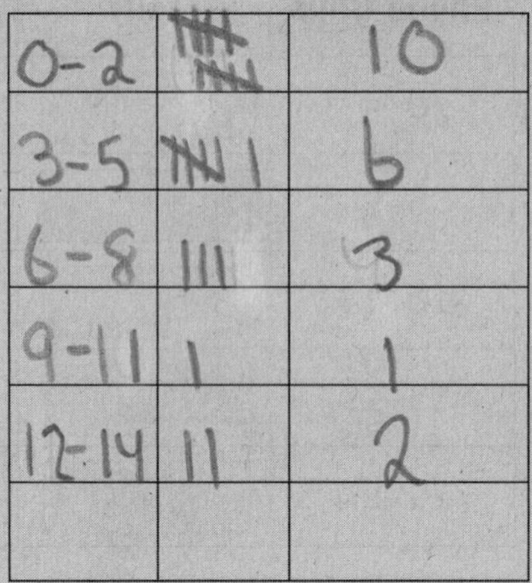

2. Make a histogram of the data in Exercise 1.

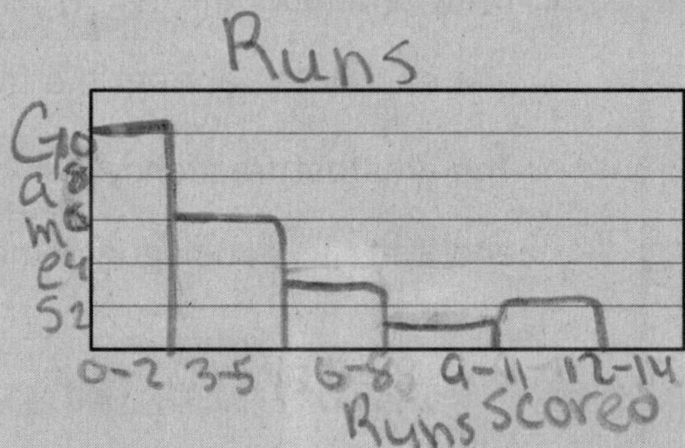

 Interpreting a Histogram

Traffic Patterns City officials are looking at traffic patterns at their major intersection. They have tracked the average number of cars backed up at the stoplight between 5 A.M. and 6:59 P.M. Make a conclusion about the data.

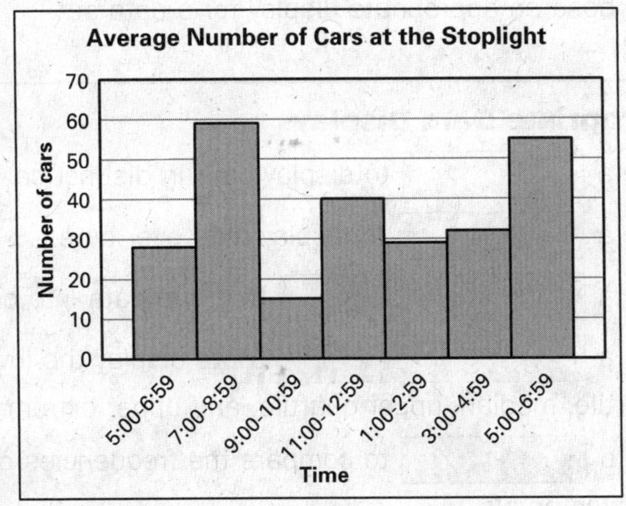

Answer: The number of cars [   ] most as people would be traveling to and from work and lunch.

Appropriate Data Displays

Goal: Choose an appropriate display for a data set.

Appropriate Data Displays

- Use a [   ] to display data in distinct categories.
- Use a [   ] to display data over time.
- Use a [   ] to group data into ordered lists.
- Use a [   ] to display the lower extreme, lower quartile, median, upper quartile, and upper extreme of a data set.
- Use a [   ] to compare the frequencies of data that fall in equal intervals.

EXAMPLE 1 **Choosing an Appropriate Data Display**

A movie theater manager wants to display the attendances to the movies shown in the theaters. What data display(s) should she use to see how the data are distributed, without displaying the individual data?

Answer: Either a [   ] or a [   ] will show how the data are distributed without showing individual data.

EXAMPLE 2 **Identifying Misleading Data Displays**

Is the graph potentially misleading? Explain.

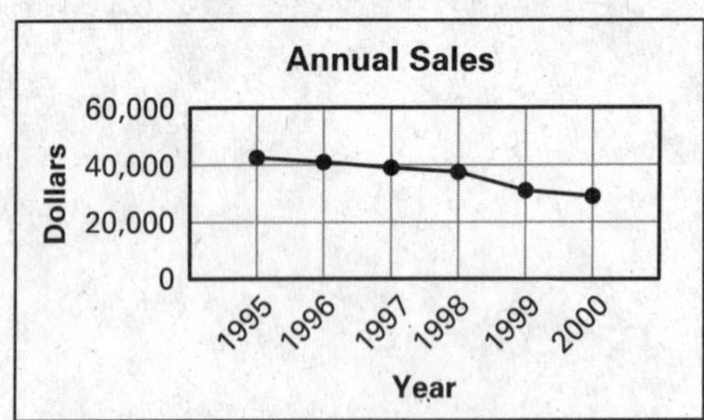

Solution

The graph could be misleading because the vertical scale uses [   ]. The graph indicates a [   ] change in sales. If the vertical scale had [   ] increments, the change in sales would look more significant.

1. A bookstore sells eight different types of books. Which data display(s) should be used to compare the number of each type of book in stock?

2. Redraw the line graph in Example 2 with smaller increments on the vertical scale. Compare the two graphs. What do you notice?

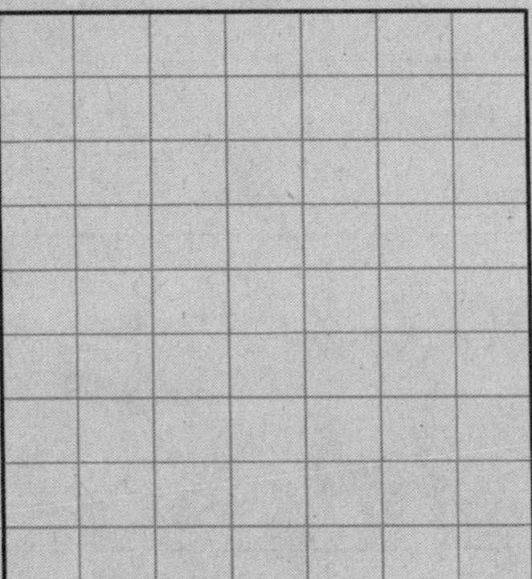

Words to Review

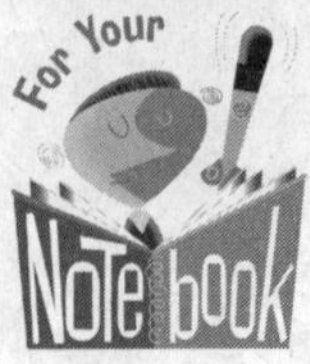

Give an example of the vocabulary word.

Mean

Median

Mode

Range

Bar graph

Line graph

Stem-and-leaf plot

Box-and-whisker plot

Lower quartile

Upper quartile

Lower extreme

Upper extreme

Frequency table

Frequency

Histogram

Review your notes and Chapter 3 by using the Chapter Review on pages 142–143 of your textbook.

Prime Factorization

Goal: Write a number as a product of prime numbers.

Vocabulary

Prime number:

Composite number:

Prime factorization:

Factor tree:

EXAMPLE 1 **Writing Factors of a Number**

Gardening Mrs. Gilbert bought 48 plants to put in her garden. She wants to break the plants up into groups that are the same size. Find the possible group sizes by writing all the factors of 48.

$48 = 1 \times$ ▢

$= 2 \times$ ▢

$= 3 \times$ ▢

$= 4 \times$ ▢   48 isn't divisible by ▢ . Skip to ▢ .

$= 6 \times$ ▢   48 isn't divisible by ▢ . Skip to ▢ .

$= 8 \times$ ▢   Stop when the factors ▢ .

Answer: The factors of 48 are ▢ .

Identifying Prime and Composite Numbers

Tell whether the number is *prime* or *composite*.

a. 52

b. 17

Solution

a. The factors of 52 are

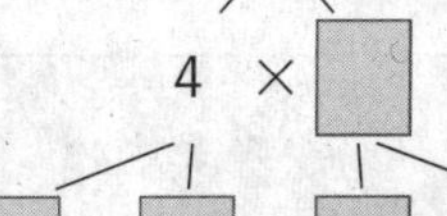

.

So, 52 is

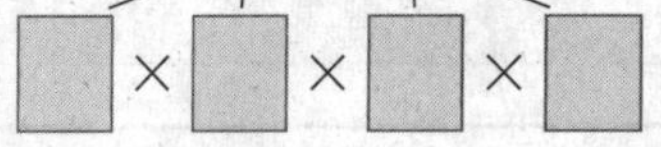

.

b. The factors of 17 are

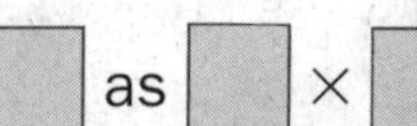

. So, 17 is [ ] .

Using a Factor Tree

Use a factor tree to write the prime factorization of 36.

One possible factor tree:

36

4 × [ ]

[ ] × [ ] × [ ] × [ ]

Write original number.

Factor 36 as 4 × [ ].

Factor 4 as [ ] × [ ] and [ ] as [ ] × [ ]

Another possible factor tree:

36

3 × 12

[ ] × 3 × [ ]

[ ] × [ ] × [ ] × [ ]

Write original number.

Factor 36 as 3 × 12.

Factor 12 as 3 × [ ].

Factor [ ] as [ ] × [ ].

Both trees give the same result: 36 = 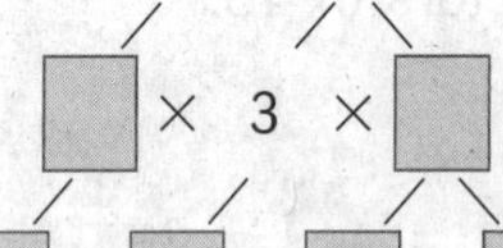 .

Answer: The prime factorization of 36 is  .

Use a factor tree to write the prime factorization of the number.

1. 20	**2.** 32	**3.** 52	**4.** 68

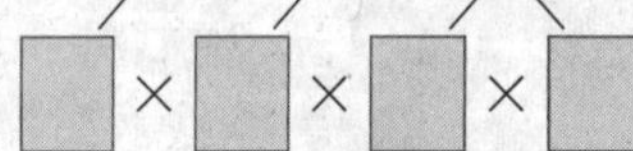

Greatest Common Factor

Goal: Find the greatest common factor of two or more numbers.

Vocabulary

Common factor:

Greatest common factor (GCF):

Relatively prime:

EXAMPLE 1 **Making a List to Find the GCF**

Flower Arranging A florist is making bouquets from 32 poppies, 40 irises, and 56 gerbera daisies. What is the greatest number of bouquets that the florist can make using the same number of each flower in the bouquets? How many poppies, irises, and gerbera daisies will be in each bouquet?

Factors of 32:

Factors of 40:

Factors of 56:

The common factors are   . The GCF is   .

Answer: The greatest common factor of 32, 40, and 56 is   . So, the greatest number of bouquets that can be made is   . Then each bouquet will have   poppies,   irises, and   gerbera daisies.

1. 20, 35	2. 28, 49	3. 45, 60
4. 10, 24, 36	5. 15, 40, 50	6. 54, 72, 99

EXAMPLE 2 Using Prime Factorization to Find the GCF

**Find the greatest common factor of 120 and 165 using prime
factorization.**

Begin by writing the prime factorization of each number.

Large
numbers may
have many factors,
and it may be difficult
to list all the factors.
It may be easier to
use prime factorization
to find the greatest
common factor of
large numbers.

120

□ × 12

□ × □ × 2 × □

□ × □ × 2 × □ × □

165

5 × □

□ × □ × □

120: ____________

165: ____________

Answer: The common prime factors of 120 and 165 are □ and □.
So, the greatest common factor is □ × □ = □.

7. 100, 140	**8.** 96, 160
9. 108, 172	**10.** 200, 280

EXAMPLE 3 **Identifying Relatively Prime Numbers**

Tell whether the numbers are relatively prime.

a. 16, 25

Factors of 16: ⬚   The GCF is ⬚.

Factors of 25: ⬚

Answer: Because the GCF is ⬚, 16 and 25 are ⬚.

b. 21, 54

Factors of 21: ⬚   The GCF is ⬚.

Factors of 54: ⬚

Answer: Because the GCF is ⬚, 21 and 54 are ⬚.

Equivalent Fractions

Goal: Write equivalent fractions.

Vocabulary

Fraction:

Numerator:

Denominator:

Equivalent fractions:

Simplest form:

EXAMPLE 1 Identifying Equivalent Fractions

Radio There are 12 songs played in one hour on a local radio station. Thre
of the songs are new releases. What *fraction* of the songs played in an hou
are new releases?

The songs in the problem are arranged in the diagram. Using the diagram,
you can write two equivalent fractions.

$$\frac{\text{Number of new releases}}{\text{Number of songs}} = \boxed{}$$

$$\frac{\text{Number of groups of 3 new releases}}{\text{Number of groups of 3 songs}} = \boxed{}$$

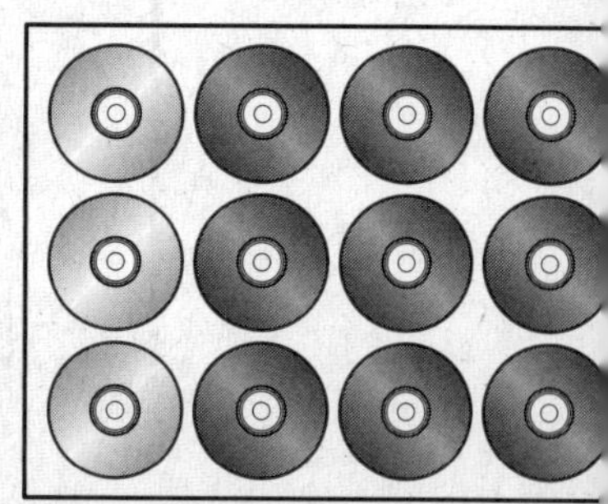

The fractions $\boxed{}$ and $\boxed{}$ are equivalent

equivalent fractions because they represent
the same part-to-whole relationship.

EXAMPLE 2 **Writing Equivalent Fractions**

Write two fractions that are equivalent to $\frac{3}{9}$.

Multiply or divide the numerator and denominator by the same nonzero number to find an equivalent fraction.

$$\frac{3}{9} = \frac{\boxed{} \times \boxed{}}{\boxed{} \times \boxed{}} = \frac{6}{18}$$

Multiply numerator and denominator by $\boxed{}$.

$$\frac{3}{9} = \frac{\boxed{} \div \boxed{}}{\boxed{} \div \boxed{}} = \frac{1}{3}$$

Divide numerator and denominator by $\boxed{}$, a common factor of $\boxed{}$ and $\boxed{}$.

EXAMPLE 3 **Simplifying Fractions**

Write the fraction in simplest form.

a. $\frac{10}{32}$ **b.** $\frac{9}{14}$

Solution

a. $\dfrac{10}{32} = \dfrac{\boxed{} \cdot \boxed{}}{\boxed{} \cdot \boxed{}}$

$= \boxed{}$

The GCF of $\boxed{}$ and $\boxed{}$ is $\boxed{}$.

b. $\frac{9}{14}$

The GCF of $\boxed{}$ and $\boxed{}$ is $\boxed{}$.

The fraction is in simplest form.

Your turn now **Write two fractions that are equivalent to the given fraction.**

1. $\frac{1}{5}$ **2.** $\frac{7}{15}$ **3.** $\frac{10}{12}$ **4.** $\frac{20}{25}$

5. $\dfrac{12}{18}$	6. $\dfrac{20}{36}$	7. $\dfrac{15}{60}$	8. $\dfrac{24}{40}$

EXAMPLE 4   Using Fractions in Simplest Form

Student Council Janet and Bob are both running for Student Council Representative in their homerooms. Janet received 18 out of 30 votes in her homeroom. Bob received 15 out of 25 votes in his homeroom. Write the fraction of votes received by each candidate in simplest form. Are the fractions equivalent?

Janet

$$\frac{\text{Votes received}}{\text{Total votes in the homeroom}} = \frac{18}{30} = \frac{\boxed{} \div \boxed{}}{\boxed{} \div \boxed{}} = \boxed{}$$

Bob

$$\frac{\text{Votes received}}{\text{Total votes in the homeroom}} = \frac{15}{25} = \frac{\boxed{} \div \boxed{}}{\boxed{} \div \boxed{}} = \boxed{}$$

Answer: $\boxed{}$, $\dfrac{18}{30}$ and $\dfrac{15}{25}$ $\boxed{}$ equivalent fractions.

Least Common Multiple

Goal: Find the LCM of two or more numbers.

Big Mu

Vocabulary

Multiple:

Common multiple:

Least common multiple:

EXAMPLE 1 Using the Least Common Multiple

Commercials One TV station shows commercials every 6 minutes. Another station shows commercials every 8 minutes. For the shows that air at 7:00 A.M., at what time will both stations first play a commercial?

You can determine when both stations will first play a commercial by finding the least common multiple of 6 and 8. Begin by writing the multiples of 6 and 8. Then identify any common multiples.

Multiples of 6: 6, 12, 18, 24

Multiples of 8: 8, 16, 24

[ ] and [ ] are common multiples. The LCM is [ ].

Answer: The television stations will first both show a commercial in [ ] minutes, or at [ ] A.M.

EXAMPLE 2 Finding the Least Common Multiple

Find the least common multiple of 5 and 9.

Multiples of 5: 5, 10, 15, 20, 25, 30, 35, 40, 45

Multiples of 9: 9, 18, 27, 36, 45

Answer: The least common multiple of 5 and 9 is [ ].

Use the prime factorization method to find the least common multiple of large numbers.

Find the LCM of 95 and 240 using prime factorization.

Begin by writing the prime factorization of each number.

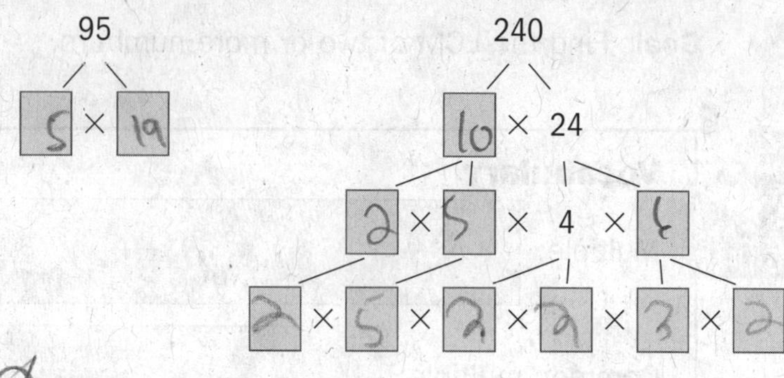

95: 5, 19

240: 2, 5, 2, 2, 3, 2

Circle the common factor. Then multiply the common factor and all the uncircled factors.

19 × 2 × 5 · 2 · 2 · 3 · 2 =

Answer: The least common multiple of 95 and 240 is 4,560.

Your turn now **Find the LCM of the numbers by listing the multiples.**

1. 4, 7 28	**2.** 10, 15
3. 3, 8, 12	**4.** 2, 6, 10 2 2 3 2 5 30 2 · 3 2 · 5

Find the LCM of the numbers using prime factorization.

5. 42, 70	**6.** 18, 27
7. 15, 20, 40	**8.** 45, 60, 72

Using the Least Common Multiple

Fitness Center All classes at the fitness center start at 6 A.M. The water aerobics class repeats every 60 minutes. The power yoga class repeats every 45 minutes. The circuit training class repeats every 90 minutes. What is the next time that all three classes start at the same time?

Solution

Find the least common multiple of 60, 45, and 90.

$$60 = \boxed{} \qquad 45 = \boxed{} \qquad 90 = \boxed{}$$

The least common multiple is $\boxed{} = \boxed{}$.

Answer: The classes start at the same time again in $\boxed{}$ minutes, or $\boxed{}$ hours, after 6 A.M., which is $\boxed{}$ A.M.

Comparing and Ordering Fractions

Goal: Compare and order fractions.

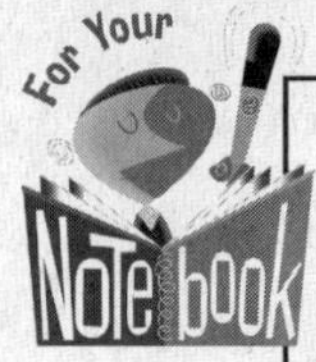

Vocabulary

Least common denominator:

Comparing Two or More Fractions

1. Find the ☐ of the fractions.

2. Use the ☐ to write ☐ fractions.

3. Compare the ☐.

EXAMPLE 1 Comparing Fractions Using the LCD

Sewing Tara is sewing a red shirt and a blue shirt. The pattern for the red shirt calls for $\frac{5}{8}$ yard of fabric. The pattern for the blue shirt calls for $\frac{7}{12}$ yard of fabric. Which shirt is made from more fabric?

Solution

1. Find the ☐ of the fractions.

Because the LCM of 8 and 12 is ☐, the ☐ is ☐.

2. Use the ☐ to write equivalent fractions.

Red: $\frac{5}{8} = \dfrac{\boxed{}}{\boxed{}} = \boxed{}$ **Blue:** $\frac{7}{12} = \dfrac{\boxed{}}{\boxed{}} = \boxed{}$

3. Compare the numerators: ☐, so $\frac{5}{8}$ ☐ $\frac{7}{12}$.

Answer: The ☐ shirt is made from more fabric.

Order the fractions $\frac{1}{4}$, $\frac{2}{5}$, $\frac{3}{10}$, and $\frac{5}{6}$ from least to greatest.

1. Find the LCD of the fractions.

Because the LCM of 4, 5, 10, and 6 is [ ], the LCD is [ ].

2. Use the LCD to write equivalent fractions.

$$\frac{1}{4} = \frac{\boxed{}}{\boxed{}} = \boxed{} \qquad \frac{2}{5} = \frac{\boxed{}}{\boxed{}} = \boxed{}$$

$$\frac{3}{10} = \frac{\boxed{}}{\boxed{}} = \boxed{} \qquad \frac{5}{6} = \frac{\boxed{}}{\boxed{}} = \boxed{}$$

3. Compare the numerators: [   ] , so [   ] .

Answer: From least to greatest, the fractions are [   ] .

  Copy and complete the statement using $<$, $>$, or $=$.

1. $\frac{3}{5}$? $\frac{8}{13}$	**2.** $\frac{7}{8}$? $\frac{11}{12}$	**3.** $\frac{3}{7}$? $\frac{4}{11}$

Order the fractions from least to greatest.

4. $\frac{5}{6}$, $\frac{3}{4}$, $\frac{1}{2}$, $\frac{7}{12}$	**5.** $\frac{2}{9}$, $\frac{1}{6}$, $\frac{2}{3}$, $\frac{7}{18}$	**6.** $\frac{4}{5}$, $\frac{19}{20}$, $\frac{3}{4}$, $\frac{7}{10}$

 Comparing Fractions Using Approximation

Use approximation to tell which fraction is greater, $\frac{15}{32}$ or $\frac{23}{42}$.

Notice that $\frac{15}{32}$ and $\frac{23}{42}$ are both approximately equal to [ ] because the numerator of each fraction is about [ ] the denominator.

Because $\frac{1}{2} = \frac{[\ ]}{32}$, you know that $\frac{15}{32}$ [ ] $\frac{1}{2}$.

Because $\frac{1}{2} = \frac{[\ ]}{42}$, you know that $\frac{23}{42}$ [ ] $\frac{1}{2}$.

Answer: So, $\frac{15}{32}$ [ ] $\frac{23}{42}$.

Mixed Numbers and Improper Fractions

Goal: Compare and order fractions and mixed numbers.

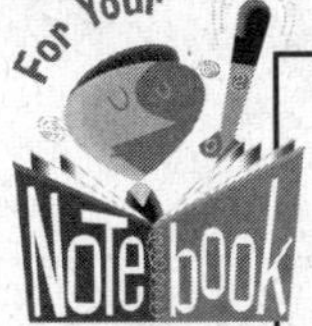

Vocabulary

Mixed number: $1\frac{1}{2}$

Proper fraction: $\frac{1}{2}$

Improper fraction: $\frac{31}{6}$

Writing Mixed Numbers as Improper Fractions

Words To write a mixed number as an improper fraction, multiply the

[   ] and the [   ] , add the

[   ] , and write the sum [ ] the denominator.

Numbers $2\frac{5}{6} = \dfrac{[\quad]\ +\ [\quad]}{[\quad]} = [\quad]$

The mixed number $2\frac{5}{6}$ is read "two and five sixths."

Writing Improper Fractions

Write (a) $4\frac{2}{5}$ and (b) $3\frac{1}{9}$ as improper fractions.

a. $4\frac{2}{5} = \dfrac{22\ +\ [\quad]}{5} = [\quad]$

b. $3\frac{1}{9} = \dfrac{[\quad]\ +\ [\quad]}{[\quad]} = [\quad]$

Writing Improper Fractions as Mixed Numbers

Words To write an improper fraction as a mixed number, divide the [____] by the [____] and write any remainder as a [____].

Numbers $\dfrac{17}{5} \rightarrow 17 \div$ [____] $=$ [____] , or [____]

EXAMPLE 2 **Writing Mixed Numbers**

Write $\dfrac{34}{5}$ as a mixed number.

[____] , or [____]

$5\overline{)34}$

30

Answer: $\dfrac{34}{5} =$ [____]

Your turn now Write the number as an improper fraction.

1. $2\dfrac{1}{3}$	2. 7	3. $3\dfrac{3}{4}$	4. $5\dfrac{2}{5}$
$\dfrac{7}{3}$	$\dfrac{7}{1}$	$\dfrac{5}{4}$	$\dfrac{27}{5}$

Write the improper fraction as a mixed number.

5. $\dfrac{17}{11}$	6. $\dfrac{19}{5}$	7. $\dfrac{22}{4}$	8. $\dfrac{27}{8}$
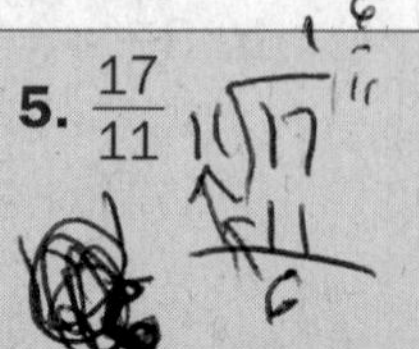	$3\dfrac{4}{5}$	$5\dfrac{1}{2}$	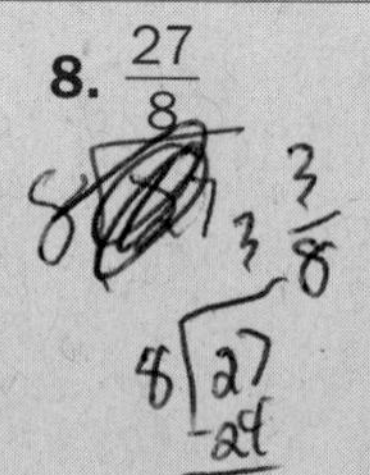

EXAMPLE 3 **Comparing Mixed Numbers and Fractions**

Compare $\frac{23}{8}$ and $2\frac{2}{3}$.

1. Write $2\frac{2}{3}$ as an improper fraction: $2\frac{2}{3} =$ .

2. Rewrite $\frac{23}{8}$ and $\frac{8}{3}$ using the least common denominator of ⬜.

$$\frac{23}{8} = \frac{\square}{\square} = \square \qquad \frac{8}{3} = \frac{\square}{\square} = \square$$

3. Compare the fractions: ⬜ , so $\frac{23}{8}$ ⬜ $2\frac{2}{3}$.

EXAMPLE 4 **Ordering Mixed Numbers and Fractions**

County Fair The county fair holds a pie eating contest. Participants are to eat as many pies as they can in 10 minutes. Joe ate $4\frac{1}{4}$ pies, Conan ate 5 pies, David ate $\frac{22}{5}$ pies, and Jonathan ate $4\frac{1}{2}$ pies. Order the amounts of pie the contestants ate from least to greatest.

Solution

The denominators are 4, 1 $\left(\text{because } 5 = \boxed{}\right)$, 5, and 2. Write the

numbers as improper fractions using the least common denominator of ⬜.

$$4\frac{1}{4} = \square = \frac{\square}{\square} = \square \qquad 5 = \square = \frac{\square}{\square} = \square$$

$$\frac{22}{5} = \frac{\square}{\square} = \square \qquad 4\frac{1}{2} = \square = \frac{\square}{\square} = \square$$

Answer: From least to greatest, the amounts of pie the contestants ate are

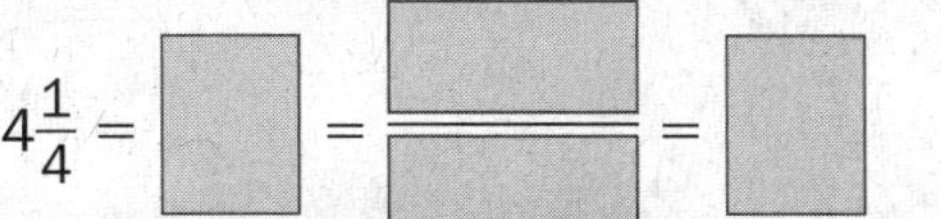 .

Fractions and Decimals

Goal: Write fractions as decimals and decimals as fractions.

Vocabulary

Terminating decimal:

Repeating decimal:

EXAMPLE 1 **Writing Fractions as Decimals**

Need help with dividing decimals? See page 67 of your textbook.

Write (a) $\frac{5}{8}$ and (b) $2\frac{3}{5}$ as decimals.

Solution

a.

$8\overline{)5.000}$ ← Write zeros in dividend as placeholders.

← Remainder is   .

b.

$5\overline{)3.0}$ ← Write a zero in divide as a placeholder.

← Remainder is

Answer: $\frac{5}{8} =$

Answer: $2\frac{3}{5} = + =$

 Write the fraction or mixed number as a decimal.

1. $\frac{7}{10}$	**2.** $\frac{25}{400}$	**3.** $4\frac{3}{4}$	**4.** $3\frac{1}{8}$

EXAMPLE 2 Writing Fractions as Repeating Decimals

Write (a) $\frac{11}{6}$ and (b) $\frac{14}{15}$ as decimals.

Solution

a.

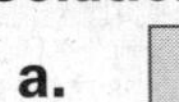

$6\overline{)11.000}$

The digit keeps repeating.

Remainder will never be .

b.

$15\overline{)14.000}$

The digit keeps repeating.

Remainder will never be .

Answer: $\frac{11}{6} =$ **Answer:** $\frac{14}{15} =$

EXAMPLE 3 Writing Decimals as Fractions

Write (a) 0.72 and (b) 3.875 as a fraction or mixed number.

Need help with place value? See page 52 of your textbook.

Solution

a. $0.72 = \dfrac{72}{}$

2 is in the   place.

$= \dfrac{ \cdot \frac{1}{4}}{ \cdot \frac{4}{1}}$

$=$

b. $3.875 = 3\dfrac{875}{}$

5 is in the   place.

$= 3\dfrac{ \cdot 1\overset{1}{\cancel{2}}5}{ \cdot \underset{1}{\cancel{12}}5}$

$= 3$

Veterinarian Jorja's cat gave birth to a litter of kittens. She took the kittens to the veterinarian for a check-up. The kitten's weights were recorded for their medical records. What is the order of the kittens from least to greatest weight?

Kitten 1: $\frac{5}{6}$ pound = [ ] pound

Kitten 2: $\frac{2}{5}$ pound = [ ] pound

Kitten 3: $\frac{1}{4}$ pound = [ ] pound

Kitten 4: $\frac{3}{8}$ pound = [ ] pound

Answer: Because [ ] < [ ] < [ ] < [ ], the kittens are, from least to greatest weight, Kitten [ ], Kitten [ ], Kitten [ ], and Kitten [ ].

Only the digit(s) under the bar should be repeated. In Example 4, Kitten 1's weight written as a decimal is $0.8\overline{3} = 0.8333...$, not $0.838383....$

Your turn now   Write the fraction or mixed number as a decimal.

5. $\frac{5}{12}$	6. $\frac{17}{8}$	7. $3\frac{2}{9}$	8. $6\frac{7}{16}$

Write the decimal as a fraction or mixed number.

9. 0.8	10. 3.35	11. 0.625	12. 1.175

Words to Review

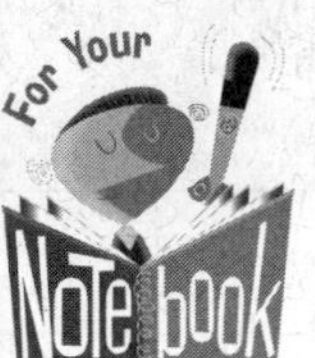

Give an example of the vocabulary word.

Prime number

Composite number

Prime factorization

Factor tree

Common factor

Greatest common factor

Relatively prime

Fraction

Numerator

Denominator

Equivalent fractions

Simplest form

Multiple

Common multiple

Least common multiple

Least common denominator

Mixed number

Proper fraction

Improper fraction

Terminating decimal

Repeating decimal

Review your notes and Chapter 4 by using the Chapter Review on pages 198–199 of your textbook.

Adding and Subtracting Fractions

Goal: Add and subtract fractions.

Fractions with Common Denominators

Words To add or subtract two fractions with a common denominator, write the [   ] or [   ] of the numerators over the [   ].

Numbers $\dfrac{1}{5} + \dfrac{2}{5} =$ [   ]

$\dfrac{4}{7} - \dfrac{1}{7} =$ [   ]

Algebra $\dfrac{a}{c} + \dfrac{b}{c} =$ [   ] $(c \neq 0)$

$\dfrac{a}{c} - \dfrac{b}{c} =$ [   ] $(c \neq 0)$

EXAMPLE 1 Adding Fractions

$\dfrac{2}{7} + \dfrac{3}{7} =$ [   ]   Add numerators.

$= $ [   ]   Simplify numerator.

EXAMPLE 2 Subtracting Fractions

$\dfrac{4}{9} - \dfrac{1}{9} =$ [   ]   Subtract numerators.

$= $ [   ]   Simplify numerator.

$= $ [   ]   Simplify fraction.

Need help with simplifying fractions? See page 169 of your textbook.

1. $\dfrac{3}{10} + \dfrac{1}{10}$	**2.** $\dfrac{2}{11} + \dfrac{8}{11}$	**3.** $\dfrac{6}{7} - \dfrac{4}{7}$	**4.** $\dfrac{8}{15} - \dfrac{3}{15}$

Fractions with Different Denominators

1. Rewrite the fractions using the ______ .

2. Add or subtract the ______ .

3. Write the result over the ______ .

4. ______ if possible.

EXAMPLE 3   **Adding Fractions**

$\dfrac{3}{4} + \dfrac{4}{5} = \boxed{}$ Rewrite the fractions using the LCD of $\dfrac{3}{4}$ and $\dfrac{4}{5}$.

$= \boxed{}$ Add numerators.

$= \boxed{}$, or $\boxed{}$ Simplify.

Need help with writing improper fractions as mixed numbers? See page 185 of your textbook.

✓ **Check**   You can use estimation to check that your answer is reasonable. Because $\dfrac{3}{4}$ is $\boxed{}$ $\dfrac{1}{2}$ and $\dfrac{4}{5}$ is $\boxed{}$ $\dfrac{1}{2}$, the sum of $\dfrac{3}{4}$ and $\dfrac{4}{5}$ should be $\boxed{}$ than 1.

Travel The usual flight from Houston to Dallas takes $\frac{5}{6}$ hour. Due to favorable weather conditions, today's flight only takes $\frac{3}{4}$ hour. How much faster was today's flight than usual?

Solution

To find how much faster today's flight was, subtract $\frac{3}{4}$ from $\frac{5}{6}$.

$\frac{5}{6} - \frac{3}{4} =$    Rewrite $\frac{5}{6}$ and $\frac{3}{4}$ using the LCD of the fractions.

$=$ 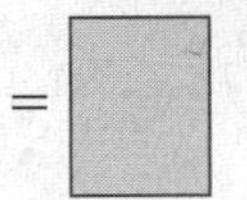   Subtract numerators.

$=$    Simplify numerator.

Answer: Today's flight was ___ hour faster.

Your turn now **Add or subtract. Simplify if possible.**

5. $\frac{1}{3} + \frac{4}{15}$	**6.** $\frac{5}{8} + \frac{11}{12}$	**7.** $\frac{5}{6} - \frac{2}{3}$	**8.** $\frac{7}{10} - \frac{1}{4}$

Adding and Subtracting Mixed Numbers

Goal: Add and subtract mixed numbers.

Adding and Subtracting Mixed Numbers

1. Find the [   ] of the fractions, if necessary.

2. [   ] the fractions, if necessary. Then add or subtract the fractions.

3. Add or subtract the [   ].

4. [   ] if possible.

EXAMPLE 1 **Adding with a Common Denominator**

Garden Javier bought $23\frac{1}{5}$ yards of humus to build a vegetable garden. He topped the garden with $25\frac{2}{5}$ yards of mulch. How much garden material did he put in the vegetable garden?

To solve the problem, you need to find the sum of $23\frac{1}{5}$ and $25\frac{2}{5}$.

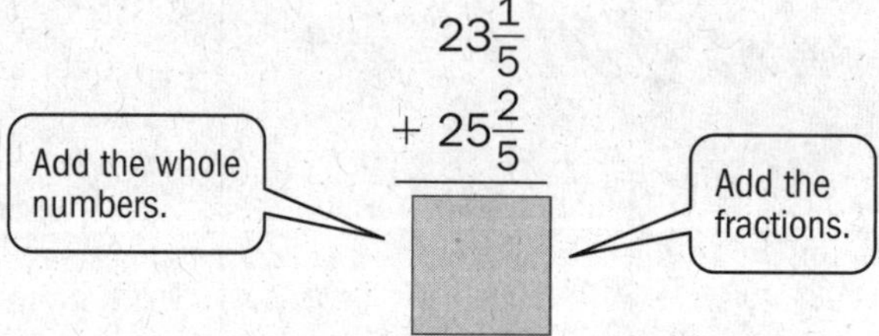

Answer: Javier put [   ] yards of garden material in the vegetable garden.

EXAMPLE 2 **Subtracting with a Common Denominator**

$4\frac{5}{8} - 2\frac{1}{8} =$ 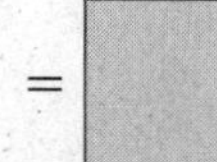   Subtract fractions and whole numbers.

$=$ [   ]   Simplify.

 Add or subtract. Simplify if possible.

1. $5\frac{3}{10} + 2\frac{1}{10}$	**2.** $6\frac{1}{6} + 1\frac{2}{6}$	**3.** $7\frac{4}{9} - 3\frac{1}{9}$	**4.** $15\frac{7}{8} - 7\frac{7}{8}$

In Example 3, you can estimate the answer by rounding each mixed number to the nearest whole number. By doing so, you have $4 + 6 = 10$, so your answer is reasonable.

EXAMPLE 3 Adding with Different Denominators

$3\frac{1}{2} + 5\frac{3}{4} = $ [ ] Rewrite fractions using the LCD of [ ] and [ ].

$= $ [ ] Add fractions and whole numbers.

$= $ [ ] Write [ ] as a mixed number.

$= $ [ ] Add whole numbers.

EXAMPLE 4 Renaming to Subtract Mixed Numbers

$8\frac{1}{10} - 5\frac{3}{5} = $ [ ] Rewrite fractions using the LCD of [ ] and [ ].

$= $ [ ] Rename [ ] as [ ].

$= $ [ ] Subtract fractions and whole numbers.

$= $ [ ] Simplify.

 Add or subtract. Simplify if possible.

5. $3\frac{1}{6} + 1\frac{2}{3}$	**6.** $7\frac{1}{2} + 2\frac{2}{3}$	**7.** $10 - 3\frac{2}{5}$	**8.** $7\frac{1}{5} - 6\frac{5}{6}$

Multiplying Fractions and Mixed Numbers

Goal: Multiply fractions and mixed numbers.

Multiplying Fractions

Words The product of two or more fractions is equal to the product of the [   ] over the product of the [   ].

Numbers $\dfrac{2}{9} \cdot \dfrac{4}{5} = $ [   ]

Algebra $\dfrac{a}{b} \cdot \dfrac{c}{d} = $ [   ] $(b, d \neq 0)$

EXAMPLE 1 **Multiplying Fractions**

Baking Eva's bread recipe calls for $\frac{1}{4}$ cup of olive oil. She only wants to make half of the recipe. How much olive oil does Eva need?

$\dfrac{1}{2} \cdot \dfrac{1}{4} = $ [   ]   Use rule for multiplying fractions.

$= $ [   ]   Multiply.

Answer: Eva needs [   ] cup of olive oil for half of the bread recipe.

Your turn now Find the product. Simplify if possible.

1. $\dfrac{3}{4} \cdot \dfrac{1}{2}$	2. $\dfrac{7}{10} \cdot \dfrac{1}{3}$	3. $\dfrac{2}{5} \cdot \dfrac{5}{8}$	4. $\dfrac{2}{3} \cdot \dfrac{3}{4}$

EXAMPLE 2 Multiplying Whole Numbers and Fractions

Bus At Jefferson Middle School, $\frac{2}{5}$ of the students ride the bus to and from school. If 750 students attend Jefferson Middle School, how many students take the bus to and from school?

Solution

$\frac{2}{5} \times 750 =$ [ ]   Write 750 as $\frac{750}{1}$.

$=$ [ ]   Use rule for multiplying fractions. Divide out the GCF of [ ] and [ ].

$=$ [ ] , or [ ]   Multiply.

Answer: There are [ ] students who take the bus to and from school.

EXAMPLE 3 Multiplying Mixed Numbers

$2\frac{4}{5} \times 2\frac{1}{12} =$ [ ]   Write [ ] and [ ] as improper fractions.

$=$ [ ]   Use rule for multiplying fractions. Divide out GCF of [ ] and [ ] and GCF of [ ] and [ ].

$=$ [ ]   Multiply.

$=$ [ ]   Write as a mixed number.

Your turn now Find the product. Simplify if possible.

5. $6 \times \frac{1}{4}$	6. $\frac{2}{3} \times 10$	7. $3\frac{9}{10} \times 2\frac{2}{3}$	8. $2\frac{1}{2} \times 7\frac{4}{15}$

Dividing Fractions and Mixed Numbers

Goal: Divide fractions and mixed numbers.

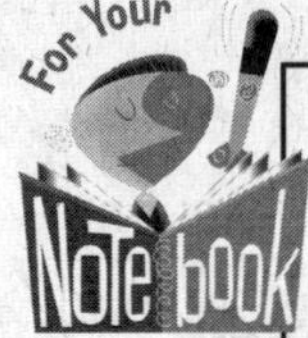

Vocabulary

Reciprocal:

Using Reciprocals to Divide

Words To divide by any nonzero number, multiply by its ______.

Numbers $\dfrac{3}{4} \div \dfrac{2}{3} = \boxed{} = \boxed{}$

Algebra $\dfrac{a}{b} \div \dfrac{c}{d} = \boxed{} = \boxed{}$ $(b, c, d \neq 0)$

EXAMPLE 1 **Dividing a Fraction by a Fraction**

$\dfrac{3}{5} \div \dfrac{9}{10} = \boxed{}$ Multiply by reciprocal.

$= \boxed{}$ Use rule for multiplying fractions. Divide out common factors.

$= \boxed{}$ Multiply.

EXAMPLE 2 **Dividing a Fraction by a Whole Number**

In Example 2, you can check your answer by multiplying the quotient and the divisor and comparing the result with the dividend: $\dfrac{1}{16} \times 6 = \dfrac{1}{16} \times \dfrac{6}{1} = \dfrac{3}{8}.$

$\dfrac{3}{8} \div 6 = \boxed{}$ Multiply by reciprocal.

$= \boxed{}$ Use rule for multiplying fractions. Divide out common factor.

$= \boxed{}$ Multiply.

  Find the quotient. Simplify if possible.

1. $\dfrac{5}{12} \div \dfrac{1}{10}$	**2.** $\dfrac{8}{3} \div \dfrac{4}{9}$	**3.** $\dfrac{3}{4} \div 9$	**4.** $\dfrac{2}{5} \div 8$

EXAMPLE 3   **Drawing a Diagram to Solve a Problem**

Craft Fair Organizers of a craft show have to place a cone on the sidewalk every $2\frac{1}{2}$ yards to mark where the craft vendors can set up their booths. One sidewalk that will be used in the craft show is 20 yards long. How many cones must be placed along this sidewalk?

Solution

Method 1 Draw a diagram on graph paper. Make the sidewalk 20 boxes long. Draw a point to mark off the location of a cone every $2\frac{1}{2}$ grid boxes.

Method 2 Use division.

$$20 \div 2\frac{1}{2} = \boxed{} \qquad \text{Write } \boxed{} \text{ as an improper fraction.}$$

$$= \boxed{} \qquad \text{Multiply by reciprocal.}$$

$$= \boxed{} \qquad \begin{array}{l}\text{Use rule for multiplying fractions.}\\ \text{Divide out common factor.}\end{array}$$

$$= \boxed{} \qquad \text{Multiply.}$$

The quotient $\boxed{}$ gives you the number of $2\frac{1}{2}$ yard *spaces*, not the number of *cones*. You have to $\boxed{}$ to get the number of cones: 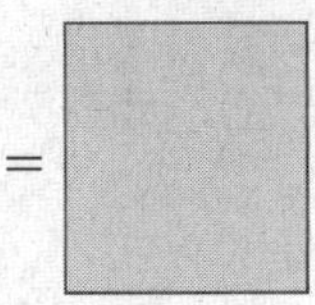 $\boxed{} = \boxed{}$.

Answer: 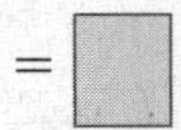 $\boxed{}$ cones can be set up along the sidewalk.

Divide $7\frac{1}{3}$ by $1\frac{8}{9}$.

In Example 4, you can estimate the answer by rounding each mixed number to the nearest whole number. You then have $7 \div 2 = 3.5$, so the answer is reasonable.

$$7\frac{1}{3} \div 1\frac{8}{9} = \boxed{}$$

Write $\boxed{}$ and $\boxed{}$ as improper fractions.

$$= \boxed{}$$

Multiply by reciprocal.

$$= \boxed{}$$

Use rule for multiplying fractions.
Divide out common factor.

$$= \boxed{}, \text{ or } \boxed{}$$

Multiply.

Your turn now Find the quotient. Then estimate to check the answer.

5. $5 \div \frac{10}{11}$

6. $8 \div 4\frac{4}{5}$

7. $3\frac{3}{5} \div \frac{1}{4}$

8. $1\frac{1}{6} \div 1\frac{1}{3}$

Measuring in Customary Units

Goal: Measure and estimate using customary units.

Vocabulary

U.S. customary system:

Inch:

Foot:

Yard:

Mile:

Ounce:

Pound:

Ton:

Fluid Ounce:

Cup:

Pint:

Quart:

Gallon:

To estimate the length of a playing card, think of small paper clips laid next to it. Then measure the playing card with a ruler to check your estimate.

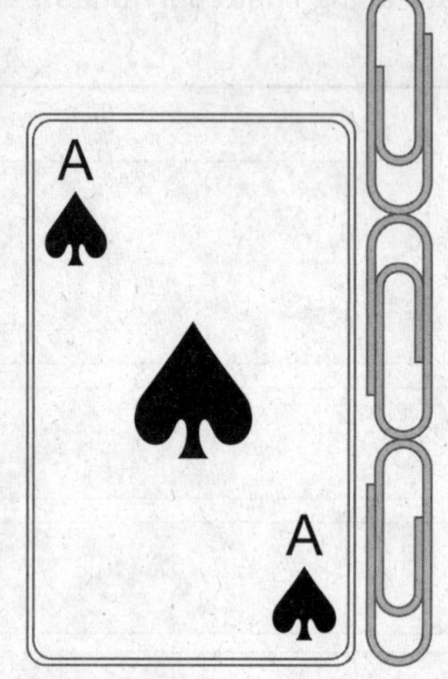

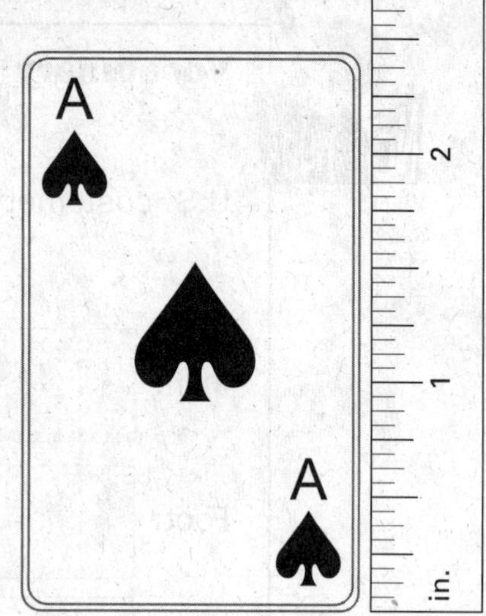

About ☐ paper clips fit alongside the card, so it is about ☐ inches long.

The ruler shows ☐ of an inch, so the playing card is ☐ inches long.

Be careful to distinguish between mass and weight. Your mass is the same wherever you are, but your weight depends on gravity. On the moon, for instance, you would weigh about $\frac{1}{6}$ of what you weigh on Earth.

EXAMPLE 2   **Measuring Weight**

Find the weight of the cantaloupe.

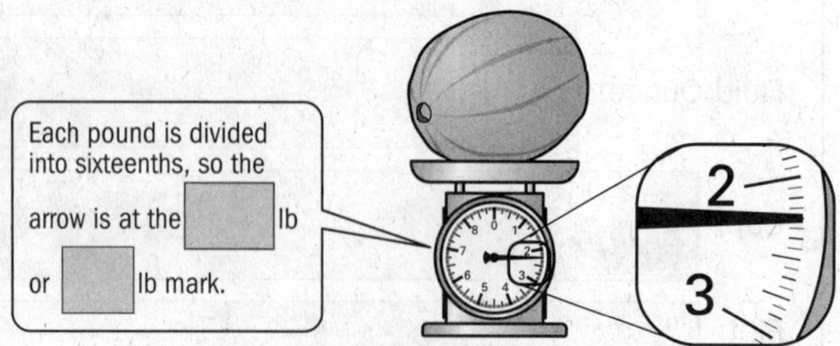

Copy and complete the statement with the appropriate customary unit:
The weight of a television is 56 __?__ .

The weight of a television is greater than [____] (56 [__]),

and it is certainly less than the weight of [____] (56 [__]).

Because a good estimate for the weight of a television is the weight of [____] , the appropriate customary unit is [____] .

Answer: The weight of a television is 56 [____] .

Your turn now **Complete the following exercises.**

1. Estimate the length of a CD case. Then use a ruler to check the estimate.

2. The weight of a kitchen chair is 15 __?__ .

Find the amount of liquid in the measuring cup.

Answer: There are about ☐ cups of liquid in the measuring cup.

WATCH OUT!

A fluid ounce is not the same as an ounce. Fluid ounces are a measure of the capacity of a container holding liquid, while an ounce measures the weight of the container.

EXAMPLE 5 — **Using Customary Units of Capacity**

What is the most reasonable capacity of a soup bowl?

A. 2 fl oz   **B.** 2 qt   **C.** 20 gal   **D.** 2 c

Solution

Both ☐ of water and ☐ of water are too much to fill the soup bowl. A soup bowl holds more than ☐ of water, so that capacity is too small. That leaves ☐ of water, which seems an appropriate capacity.

Answer: The most reasonable capacity of a soup bowl is ☐ .

Your turn now — **Match the object with the appropriate capacity.**

3. Large watering can	**4.** Spoon	**5.** Ladle
A. $\frac{3}{4}$ fl oz	**A.** $\frac{3}{4}$ fl oz	**A.** $\frac{3}{4}$ fl oz
B. 1 cup	**B.** 1 cup	**B.** 1 cup
C. $2\frac{1}{2}$ gal	**C.** $2\frac{1}{2}$ gal	**C.** $2\frac{1}{2}$ gal

Converting Customary Units

Goal: Convert between customary units.

Converting Units of Measure

Length

1 ft = ▢ in.

1 yd = ▢ ft = ▢ in.

1 mi = ▢ yd = ▢ ft

Weight

1 lb = ▢ oz

1 T = ▢ lb

Capacity

1 c = ▢ fl oz

1 pt = ▢ c

1 qt = ▢ pt

1 gal = ▢ qt

EXAMPLE 1 Converting Customary Units of Length

Farming The corn field on the Walters farm is made of 36 rows of the same length. Each row is 129 feet long. How many yards long is one row of corn?

Solution

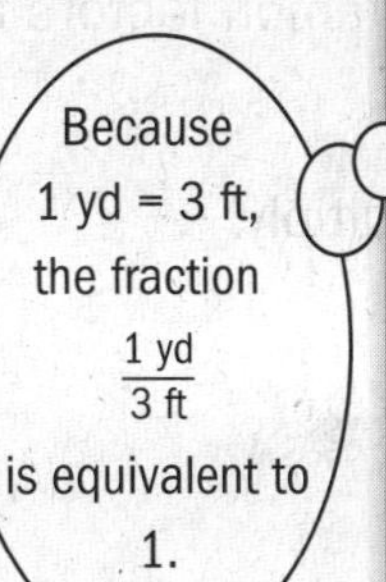

Because 1 yd = 3 ft, the fraction $\dfrac{1 \text{ yd}}{3 \text{ ft}}$ is equivalent to 1.

$129 \text{ ft} \times \dfrac{1 \text{ yd}}{3 \text{ ft}} =$ ▢   Use rule for multiplying fractions. Divide out common factor and unit.

$=$ ▢   Multiply.

Answer: A row of corn is ▢ yards long.

African Elephants The weight of an average African elephant is 6 tons. How many pounds is this?

Solution

Use the fact that 1 T = 2000 lb.

$$6\ T \times \frac{2000\ lb}{1\ T} = \boxed{}$$ Write 6 T as $\boxed{}$.

$$= \boxed{}$$ Use rule for multiplying fraction Divide out common unit.

$$= \boxed{}$$ Multiply.

Answer: The weight of an average African elephant is $\boxed{}$ pounds.

Convert 36 fluid ounces to pints. Use the fact that 1 c = 8 fl oz and 1 pt = 2 c.

$$36\ fl\ oz \times \frac{1\ c}{8\ fl\ oz} \times \frac{1\ pt}{2\ c} = \boxed{}$$ Use rule for multiplying fractions. Divide out common factors and u‸

$$= \boxed{}\ ,\ or\ \boxed{}$$ Multiply.

Your turn now **Copy and complete the statement.**

1. 2500 lb = __?__ T	**2.** 12 yd = __?__ in.	**3.** 9 c = __?__ fl oz

Convert 30 fluid ounces to cups and fluid ounces.

1. Convert 30 fluid ounces to cups.

$$30 \text{ fl oz} \times \frac{1 \text{ c}}{8 \text{ fl oz}} = \boxed{}$$

$$= \boxed{} \text{ , or } \boxed{}$$

2. Convert the fractional part from cups to fluid ounces.

$$\boxed{} = \boxed{}$$

$$= \boxed{}$$

Answer: So, 30 fl oz = $\boxed{}$ c $\boxed{}$ fl oz.

Your turn now **Copy and complete the statement.**

4. 19 oz = __?__ lb __?__ oz

5. 9 pt = __?__ qt __?__ pt

EXAMPLE 5 **Adding and Subtracting with Mixed Units**

Animals Two puppies are in the veterinarian's office. The terrier weighs 18 pounds 9 ounces. The poodle weighs 12 pounds 13 ounces.

a. Find the sum of the weights.

b. Find the difference of the weights.

Solution

a. Add. Then rename the sum.

```
   18 lb     9 oz
 + 12 lb    13 oz
 ___________________
   [  ] lb  [  ] oz
   [  ] lb  [  ] oz = [  ] lb  [  ] oz
```

Answer: $\boxed{}$ lb $\boxed{}$ oz

b. Rename. Then subtract.

```
   18 lb   9 oz       [  ] lb  [  ] oz
 − 12 lb  13 oz       [  ] lb  [  ] oz
 ________________________________________
                      [  ] lb  [  ] oz
```

Answer: $\boxed{}$ lb $\boxed{}$ oz

Words to Review

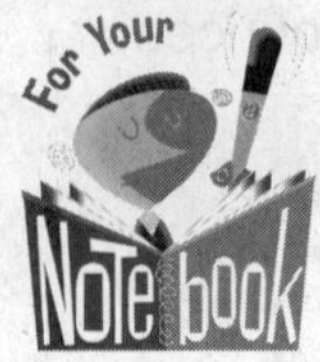

Give an example of the vocabulary word.

Reciprocal

U.S. customary system

Inch

Foot

Yard

Mile

Ounce

Pound

Ton

Fluid ounce

Cup

Pint

Quart

Gallon

Review your notes and Chapter 5 by using the Chapter Review on pages
242–243 of your textbook.

Comparing and Ordering Integers

Goal: Compare and order integers.

Vocabulary

Integer:

Negative integer:

Positive integer:

Opposite:

Integers and Their Opposites

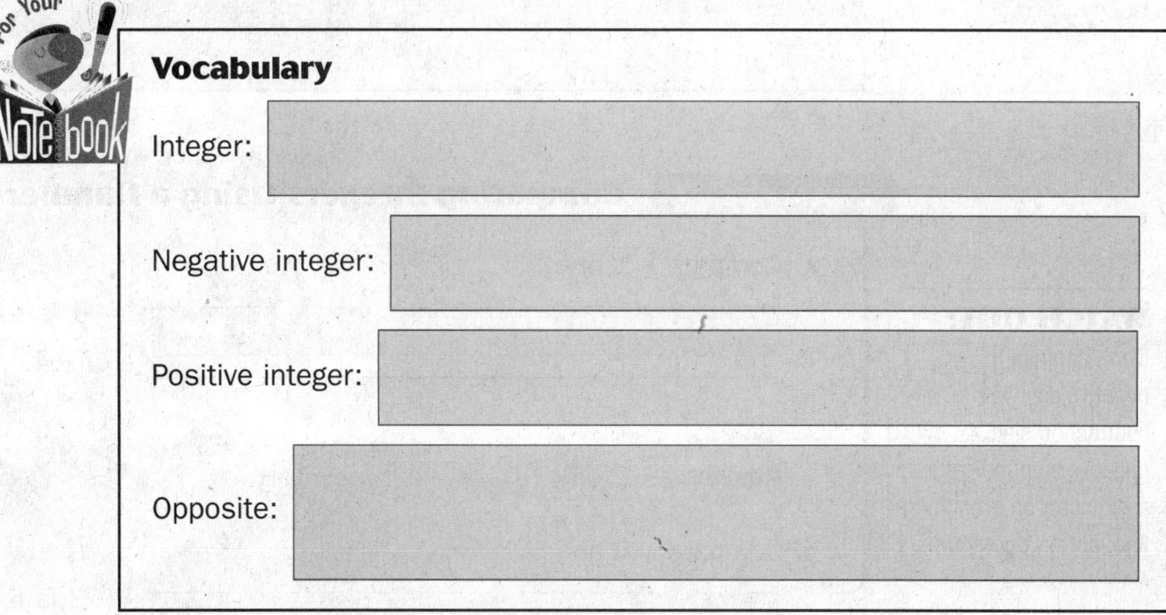

Two numbers are **opposites** if they are the [   ] from zero on a number line but are on [   ] of zero. For example, −3 is the opposite of [   ]. The opposite of 0 is [   ].

The integer −4 is read "negative four." A number other than 0 that has no sign is considered to be positive, so the integer 4 is read "positive four" or "four."

EXAMPLE 1 Writing Integers

Temperatures The temperature increased 12 degrees between 7 A.M. and 7 P.M. The temperature decreased 14 degrees between 7 P.M. and 7 A.M. You can use integers to represent the increase and decrease in the temperature.

Solution

12 degree increase: [   ]   14 degree decrease: [   ]

1. -17	2. 3	3. 41	4. -215

EXAMPLE 2 **Comparing Integers Using a Number Line**

WATCH OUT!
Don't confuse a negative sign with a subtraction sign. A negative sign indicates a direction on a number line, not an operation.

a. Compare -1 and -4.

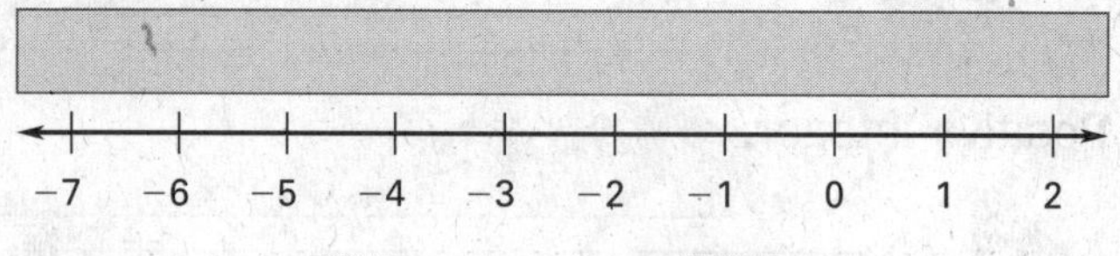

-1 is to the _____ of -4.

Answer: -1 ☐ -4, or -4 ☐ -1.

b. Compare -3 and 0.

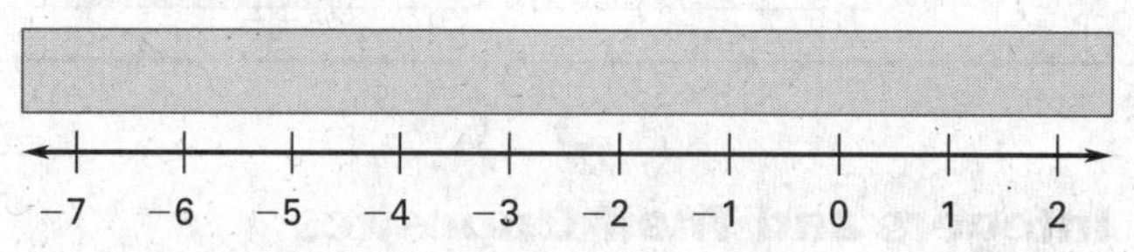

-3 is to the _____ of 0.

Answer: -3 ☐ 0, or 0 ☐ -3.

Your turn now Copy and complete the statement using $<$ or $>$.

5. 3 __?__ -5	6. -7 __?__ 2	7. -6 __?__ -8	8. -2 __?__ $-$

  Ordering Integers Using a Number Line

Football The table shows the number of yards gained by the West High School football team during the first play in each quarter during their first game of the season. Which quarter had the first play with the least yards gained?

Quarter	1	2	3	4	OT
Yards Gained During First Play	15	−7	−12	9	19

Solution

You can graph each integer on a number line to order the yards gained.

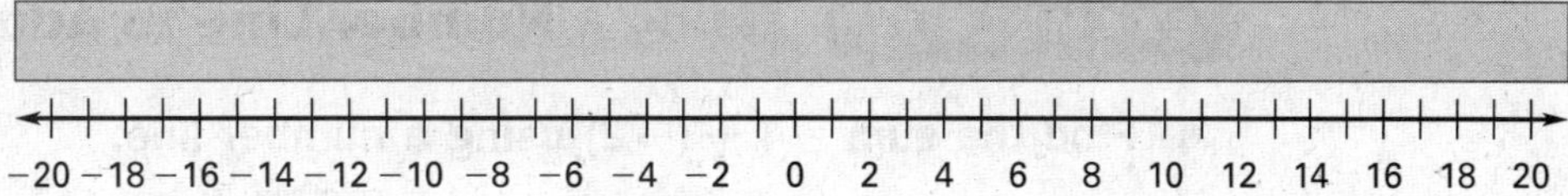

The yardages from least to greatest are: [   ].

Answer: At [   ] yards, the first play of the [   ] quarter had the least yards gained.

Adding Integers

Goal: Add integers.

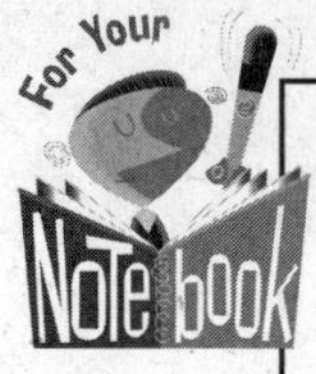

Vocabulary

Absolute value:

EXAMPLE 1 **Using a Number Line to Add Integers**

Find the sum −4 + (−2) using a number line.

Start at 0. Move ☐ units to the ☐.

Then move ☐ more units to the ☐.

$$-10 \quad -8 \quad -6 \quad -4 \quad -2 \quad 0 \quad 2 \quad 4$$

Answer: The final position is ☐ , so −4 + (−2) = ☐ .

EXAMPLE 2 **Using Integer Addition**

Glider A boy launched a glider that rose to an altitude of 14 feet above sea level. The glider then lost 8 feet of altitude. What is the glider's new altitude?

Solution

Start at 0. Move ☐ units to the ☐.

Then move ☐ units to the ☐.

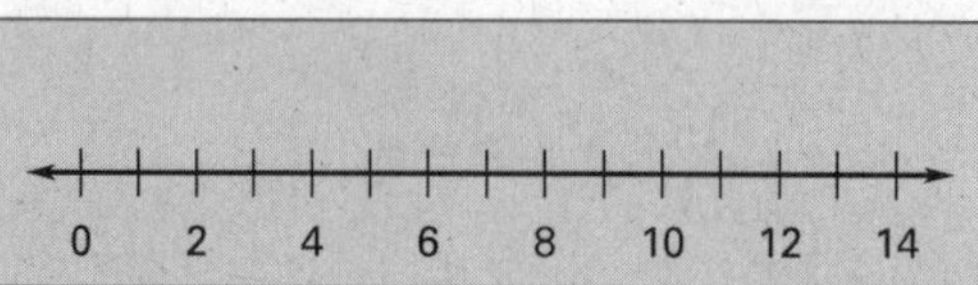

$$0 \quad 2 \quad 4 \quad 6 \quad 8 \quad 10 \quad 12 \quad 14$$

Answer: The final position is ☐ , so 14 + (−8) = ☐ . The altitude of the glider is ☐ feet above sea level.

 Use a number line to find the sum.

1. $-7 + (-2)$	**2.** $-9 + 5$	**3.** $7 + (-12)$	**4.** $18 + (-5)$

EXAMPLE 3 Finding Absolute Value

Find the absolute value of the number.

a. 4   **b.** -5 **c.** 1

Solution

a. The distance between 4 and 0 is ☐. So, $|4| =$ ☐.

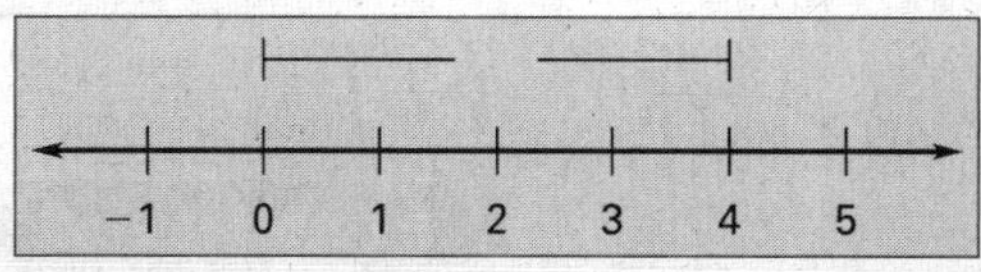

b. The distance between -5 and 0 is ☐. So, $|-5| =$ ☐.

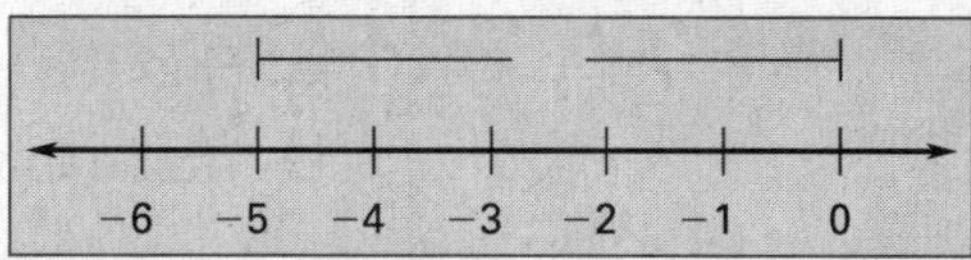

c. The distance between 1 and 0 is ☐. So, $|1| =$ ☐.

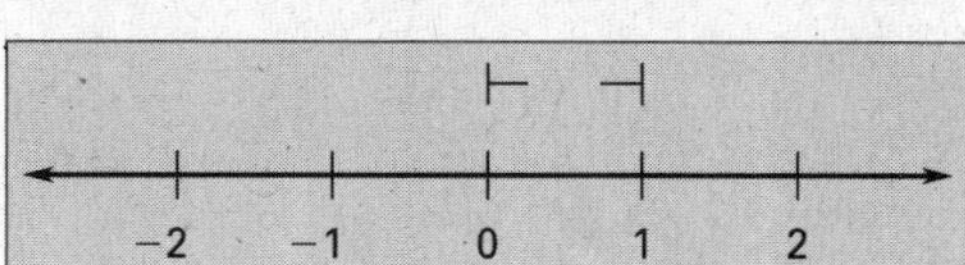

 Find the absolute value of the number.

5. 75	**6.** -10	**7.** -60	**8.** 36

Adding Integers with Absolute Value

Words   **Numbers**

Same Sign Add the [____] and use the [____] sign.

$$10 + 14 = \boxed{}$$
$$-7 + (-5) = \boxed{}$$

Different Signs Subtract the [____] from the [____] and use the sign of the integer with the [____].

$$13 + (-9) = \boxed{}$$
$$-11 + 6 = \boxed{}$$

Opposites The sum of an integer and its [____] is [__].

$$-4 + 4 = \boxed{}$$

EXAMPLE 4 **Adding Two Integers Using Absolute Value**

a. Find the sum $-2 + (-11)$.

These integers have [____].

Add $\left|\boxed{}\right|$ and $\left|\boxed{}\right|$.

$$-2 + (-11) = \boxed{}$$

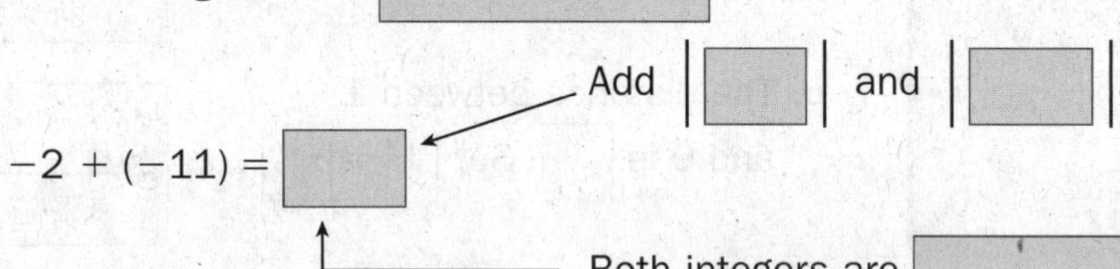

Both integers are [____], so the sum is [____].

b. Find the sum $-4 + 7$.

These integers have [____].

Subtract $\left|\boxed{}\right|$ from $\left|\boxed{}\right|$.

$$-4 + 7 = \boxed{}$$

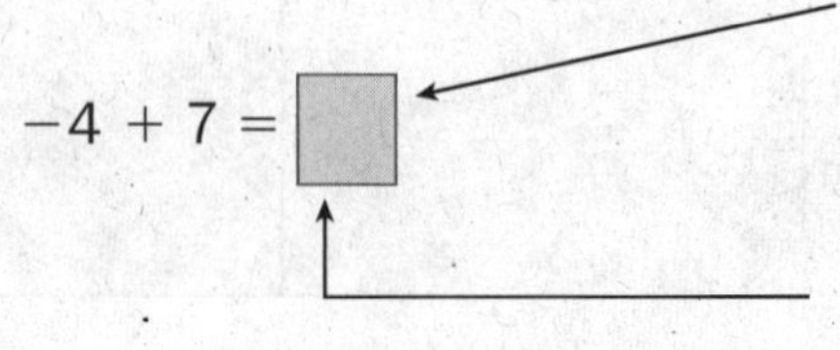

Because $\left|\boxed{}\right| \boxed{} \left|\boxed{}\right|$, the sum has the same sign as 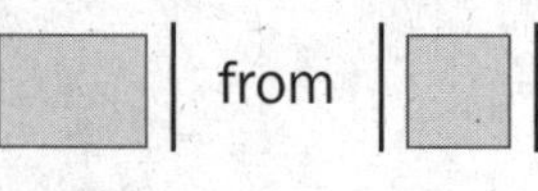 $\boxed{}$.

Your turn now Use absolute values to find the sum.

9. $-3 + (-9)$	**10.** $-8 + 4$	**11.** $0 + (-13)$
12. $-10 + 12$	**13.** $18 + (-10)$	**14.** $-25 + 25$

EXAMPLE 5 Adding Three or More Integers

Stock Market The stock price of the Morello Corporation changed every day this week. Find the value of the stock at the end of the week.

Starting Price:	$12
Monday	$4
Tuesday	$-\$5$
Wednesday	$-\$2$
Thursday	$1
Friday	$-\$3$

Solution

You can find the sum by adding the integers two at a time.

$12 + 4 + (-5) + (-2) + 1 + (-3)$

$= \boxed{} + (-5) + (-2) + 1 + (-3)$ Add 12 and 4.

$= \boxed{} + (-2) + 1 + (-3)$ Add $\boxed{}$ and -5.

$= \boxed{} + 1 + (-3)$ Add $\boxed{}$ and -2.

$= \boxed{} + (-3)$ Add $\boxed{}$ and 1.

$= \boxed{}$ Add $\boxed{}$ and -3.

Answer: The sum of the starting price and the changes in the stock price is $\boxed{}$. The stock was valued at $\$\boxed{}$ at the end of the week.

Your turn now Refer to Example 5.

15. During the next week, the stock changed value again.

$\$3, \$5, -\$2, -\$4, \$6$

Find the value of the stock at the end of the next week.

Subtracting Integers

Goal: Subtract integers.

Subtracting Integers

Words To subtract an integer, add its [____].

Numbers $5 - 7 = 5 + $ [____]   **Algebra** $a - b = a + $ [____]

EXAMPLE 1 Subtracting Integers

a. $4 - 9 = 4 + $ [____]   To subtract 9, add its opposite, [____].

  $= $ [____]   Use rule for adding integers.

b. $-3 - 7 = -3 + $ [____]   To subtract 7, add its opposite, [____].

  $= $ [____]   Use rule for adding integers.

c. $15 - (-4) = 15 + $ [____]   To subtract -4, add its opposite, [____].

  $= $ [____]   Use rule for adding integers.

d. $-12 - (-7) = -12 + $ [____]   To subtract -7, add its opposite, [____].

  $= $ [____]   Use rule for adding integers.

Your turn now Find the difference.

1. $7 - 2$	**2.** $-4 - (-7)$	**3.** $-2 - 1$	**4.** $12 - (-9)$

 Using Integer Subtraction

Diving A snorkeler explores the Great Barrier Reef at 3 feet below sea level. A diver explores the reef at 27 feet below sea level. What is the difference between these elevations?

Solution

1. Use integers to represent the two elevations.

   Snorkeler: ▢ feet   Diver: ▢ feet

2. Find the difference of ▢ and ▢ feet.

   ▢ − ▢ = ▢ + ▢   Rule for subtracting integers

        = ▢   Add.

Answer: The difference between the elevations is ▢ feet.

EXAMPLE 3 **Finding a Change in Temperature**

Weather In Spearfish, South Dakota, weather observers recorded the fastest change in temperature. In two minutes' time, the temperature changed from −20°C to 7°C. What was the change in temperature?

Solution

Change in temperature = ▢ temperature − ▢ temperature

        = ▢ − ▢   Substitute values.

        = ▢ + ▢   Rule for subtracting integers.

        = ▢   Add.

Answer: The change in temperature was ▢°C, so the temperature rose ▢°C.

Your turn now Solve the following problems.

5. Find the difference between an elevation of 620 feet above sea level and an elevation of 15 feet below sea level.

6. The temperature at 7 A.M. was −4°F. At 7 P.M. the temperature was −18°F. What was the change in temperature?

Multiplying Integers

Goal: Multiply integers.

Multiplying Integers

Words | **Numbers**

Same Sign The product of two integers with the same sign is ⬚.

$5 \cdot 3 =$ ⬚

$-5 \cdot (-3) =$ ⬚

Different Signs The product of two integers with different signs is ⬚.

$5 \cdot (-3) =$ ⬚

$-5 \cdot 3 =$ ⬚

Zero The product of an integer and 0 is ⬚.

$5 \cdot 0 =$ ⬚

$-5 \cdot 0 =$ ⬚

EXAMPLE 1 Multiplying Integers

a. $-4(-8) =$ ⬚
The product of two integers with the same sign is ⬚.

b. $-9(3) =$ ⬚
The product of two integers with different signs is ⬚.

c. $-1(0) =$ ⬚
The product of an integer and 0 is ⬚.

 Evaluating Variable Expressions

a. Evaluate a^2 when $a = -5$.

b. Evaluate xyz when $x = 3$, $y = -6$, and $z = 2$.

Solution

a. $a^2 = $ [ ] Substitute [ ] for a.

$ = $ [ ] Write [ ] as a factor [ ] times.

$ = $ [ ] Multiply [ ] and [ ].

b. $xyz = $ [ ] Substitute [ ] for x, [ ] for y, and [ ] for z.

$ = $ [ ] Multiply [ ] and [ ].

$ = $ [ ] Multiply [ ] and [ ].

Your turn now **Find the product.**

1. 7(5)	2. −2(−6)	3. 6(−6)	4. −8(8)	5. 0(−20)

EXAMPLE 3 **Using Integer Multiplication**

After-School Business Chris withdraws $5 from his savings account every day for 6 days to invest the money in his after-school business. Use multiplication to find the change in his balance after those 6 days.

Solution

You can find the total change in the account balance by multiplying the daily balance change by the number of days of withdrawals.

Change in balance $= $ [ ] ([ ]) $= $ [ ]

Answer: The account balance will decrease $[ ].

Dividing Integers

Goal: Divide integers.

Dividing Integers

Words

Same Sign The quotient of two integers with the same sign is ____.

Different Signs The quotient of two integers with different signs is ____.

Zero The quotient of 0 and any nonzero integer is ____.

Numbers

$14 \div 2 = \boxed{}$

$\dfrac{-16}{-4} = \boxed{}$

$25 \div (-5) = \boxed{}$

$\dfrac{-32}{8} = \boxed{}$

$0 \div 13 = \boxed{}$

$\dfrac{0}{-11} = \boxed{}$

EXAMPLE 1 Dividing Integers

a. $36 \div (-9) = \boxed{}$

The quotient of two integers with different signs is ____.

b. $\dfrac{-50}{-10} = \boxed{}$

The quotient of two integers with the same sign is ____.

c. $0 \div (-14) = \boxed{}$

The quotient of 0 and any nonzero integer is ____.

Your turn now Find the quotient.

1. $-18 \div 9$	**2.** $\dfrac{0}{-6}$	**3.** $\dfrac{-30}{-2}$	**4.** $22 \div (-1)$

Wall Street Stock brokers for a Wall Street firm tracked the changes in stock prices of the market over a 5-day period. Find the mean of the changes in the stock prices.

Day	Change in Market Value
Monday	$60
Tuesday	−$17
Wednesday	$23
Thursday	−$45
Friday	$19

Solution

1. Find the sum of the values.

$$60 + (-17) + 23 + (-45) + 19 = \boxed{}$$

2. Divide the sum of the numbers by the number of values, which is $\boxed{}$.

$$\boxed{} \div \boxed{} = \boxed{}$$

Answer: The mean change in stock prices is $\$\boxed{}$.

Your turn now Solve the following problem.

5. The low temperature was recorded over several hours' time. Find the mean of the temperatures.

$$-15°F, -8°F, 2°F, 0°F, -4°F, 19°F$$

Chemistry A chemical solution has a melting point of $-70°C$. Convert the temperature to degrees Fahrenheit.

Solution

$$F = \frac{9}{5}C + 32$$ 　Write formula for degrees Fahrenheit.

$$= \frac{9}{5}\left(\boxed{} \right) + 32$$ 　Substitute  for C.

$$= \frac{\boxed{}}{\boxed{}} + 32$$ 　Use rule for multiplying fractions.
Divide out common factor.

$$= \boxed{} + \boxed{}$$ 　Multiply.

$$= \boxed{}$$ 　Add.

Answer: The temperature $-70°C$ is equal to $\boxed{}$ °F.

 Convert the temperature from degrees Fahrenheit to degrees Celsius or from degrees Celsius to degrees Fahrenheit.

6. 40°C	**7.** 68°F	**8.** −58°F	**9.** −10°C

Rational Numbers

Goal: Perform operations on rational numbers.

Vocabulary

Rational number:

Additive inverse:

Multiplicative inverse:

Additive identity:

Multiplicative identity:

EXAMPLE 1 **Identifying Rational Numbers**

Show that the number is rational by writing it in $\frac{a}{b}$ form.

a. $12 =$

b. $-\frac{1}{2} =$

c. $0.6 =$

d. $-1\frac{1}{12} =$

The negative sign in a negative fraction usually appears in front of the fraction bar. However, it can also appear in the numerator or in the denominator.

Order -2, -2.4, $1\frac{4}{5}$, $-1\frac{1}{4}$, and $-2\frac{4}{5}$ from least to greatest.

Graph each number on a number line.

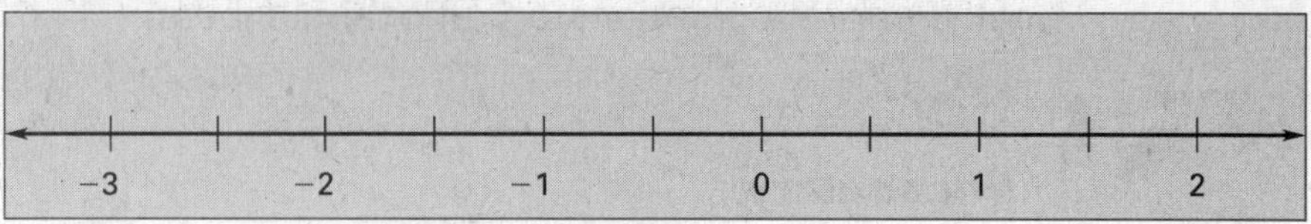

Answer: From least to greatest, the numbers are:

Your turn now Show that each number is rational by writing it in $\frac{a}{b}$ form. Then order the numbers from least to greatest.

1. 1.6, -6, $-\frac{6}{7}$, -0.7

2. $5\frac{1}{4}$, -4.5, $-4\frac{4}{5}$, 0

Commutative and Associative Properties

To remember the commutative property, remember that *commuters* are people who *move* or travel. To remember the associative property, remember that the people you *associate* with are the friends in your group.

Commutative Property of Addition

Words In a sum, you can add terms in any order.

Numbers $5 + (-6) = \boxed{} + \boxed{}$

Algebra $a + b = \boxed{} + \boxed{}$

Commutative Property of Multiplication

Words In a product, you can multiply factors in any order.

Numbers $4(-7) = \boxed{}\left(\boxed{}\right)$

Algebra $ab = \boxed{}$

Associative Property of Addition

Words Changing the grouping of terms will not change the sum.

Numbers

$(9 + 8) + 6 = \boxed{} + \left(\boxed{} + \boxed{}\right)$

Algebra

$(a + b) + c = \boxed{} + \left(\boxed{} + \boxed{}\right)$

Associative Property of Multiplication

Words Changing the grouping of factors will not change the product.

Numbers

$(2 \cdot 3) \cdot 4 = \boxed{} \cdot \left(\boxed{} \cdot \boxed{}\right)$

Algebra

$(ab)c = \boxed{}\left(\boxed{}\right)$

Evaluate the expression. Justify each step you take.

a. $-5.2 + 4 + (-6.8)$ **b.** $-20(12)(-5)$

Solution

a. $-5.2 + 4 + (-6.8)$

$= \boxed{} + \boxed{} + (-6.8)$ Commutative property of addition

$= \boxed{} + \boxed{}$ Associative property of addition

$= \boxed{} + \boxed{} = \boxed{}$ Add $\boxed{}$ and $\boxed{}$,

then $\boxed{}$ and $\boxed{}$.

b. $-20(12)(-5)$

$= \boxed{}(-5)$ Commutative property of multiplication

$= \boxed{}$ Associative property of multiplication

$= \boxed{} = \boxed{}$ Multiply $\boxed{}$ and $\boxed{}$, then $\boxed{}$

and $\boxed{}$.

> Remember that recording the steps you take in a multi-step calculation can help you perform similar calculations.

Your turn now Evaluate the expression. Justify each step you take.

3. $2.6 + [(-5) + 3.4]$

4. $5(-12)(2)$

5. $-8(9)(-5)$

<table>
<tr><td colspan="2">Inverse and Identity Properties</td></tr>
<tr><td>

Inverse Property of Addition

Words The sum of a number and its additive inverse, or opposite, is ☐.

Numbers $7 + (-7) = $ ☐

Algebra $a + (-a) = $ ☐

</td><td>

Inverse Property of Multiplication

Words The product of a number and its multiplicative inverse, or reciprocal, is ☐.

Numbers $\dfrac{2}{3} \cdot \dfrac{3}{2} = $ ☐

Algebra For nonzero integers a and b, $\dfrac{a}{b} \cdot \dfrac{b}{a} = $ ☐.

</td></tr>
<tr><td>

Identity Property of Addition

Words The sum of a number and the additive identity, 0, is ☐.

Numbers $-9 + 0 = $ ☐

Algebra $a + 0 = $ ☐

</td><td>

Identity Property of Multiplication

Words The product of a number and the multiplicative identity, 1, is ☐.

Numbers $3 \cdot 1 = $ ☐

Algebra $a \cdot 1 = $ ☐

</td></tr>
</table>

EXAMPLE 4 **Using Inverse and Identity Properties**

Evaluate the expression. Justify each step you take.

$$\frac{1}{7} + \frac{2}{3} + \left(-\frac{1}{7}\right) = \frac{1}{7} + \boxed{} + \boxed{} \qquad \text{Commutative property of addition}$$

$$= \boxed{} + \boxed{} \qquad \text{Inverse property of addition}$$

$$= \boxed{} \qquad \text{Identity property of addition}$$

6. $66 + 102 + (-66)$

7. $4 \cdot 18 \cdot \dfrac{1}{4}$

8. $-\dfrac{2}{5} + \dfrac{7}{8} + \dfrac{2}{5}$

The Distributive Property

Goal: Evaluate expressions using the distributive property.

Vocabulary

Equivalent expressions:

Distributive property:

EXAMPLE 1 Writing Equivalent Expressions

Tea Party A tea party has two rectangular tables: one that is 6 feet by 5 feet, and one that is 6 feet by 4 feet. What two expressions could be used to find the total area of the tables?

Solution

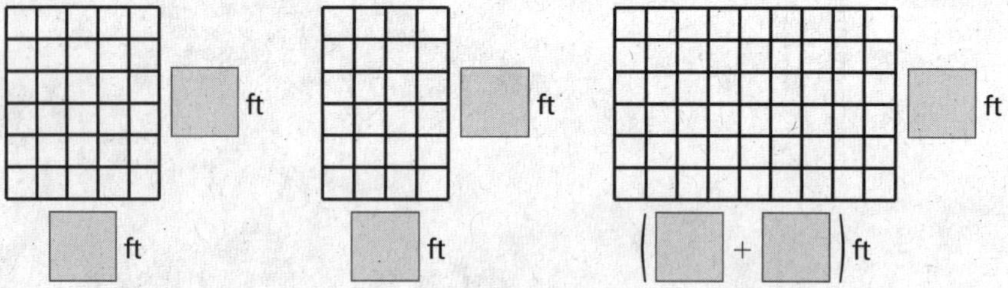

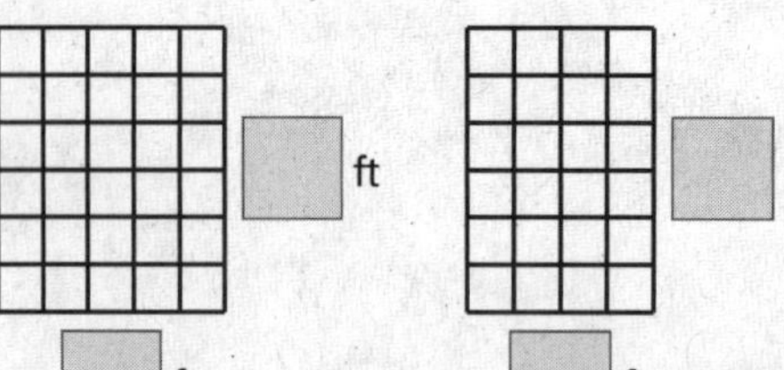

Area = ☐ + ☐

= ☐ + ☐ = ☐ ft^2

Area = ☐

= ☐ = ☐ ft^2

The Distributive Property

Algebra For all numbers a, b, and c, $a(b + c) =$ ☐ + ☐ and

$a(b - c) =$ ☐ − ☐ .

Numbers $8(10 + 4) =$ ☐ + ☐ and $3(4 - 2) =$ ☐ − ☐

Use the distributive property to write an equivalent expression.
Check your answer.

   a. $-6(2 + 7)$ **b.** $3(75 - 25)$ **c.** $8(2) + 8(9)$

Solution

a. $-6(2 + 7) = \boxed{} + \boxed{}$ Distributive property

     Check: $-6(9) \stackrel{?}{=} \boxed{} + \boxed{}$ Simplify.

            $-54 = \boxed{}$ ✓   Answer checks.

b. $3(75 - 25) = \boxed{} - \boxed{}$ Distributive property

     Check: $3(50) \stackrel{?}{=} \boxed{} - \boxed{}$ Simplify.

            $150 = \boxed{}$ ✓   Answer checks.

c. $8(2) + 8(9) = \boxed{}$ Distributive property

     Check: $16 + 72 \stackrel{?}{=} \boxed{}$ Simplify.

            $88 = \boxed{}$ ✓   Answer checks.

Your turn now   Use the distributive property to write an equivalent
expression. Check your answer.

1. $5\left(\dfrac{1}{4}\right) + 5\left(\dfrac{3}{4}\right)$	**2.** $-4(7 + 5)$
3. $9(15 - 8)$	**4.** $10(6) - 10(2)$

Scrapbooks Leslie is making a scrapbook for her mother's birthday. She bought 6 packs of stickers for $6.95 each. Use the distributive property to find the total cost of the stickers.

Solution

$6(6.95) = $ [ ]   Write 6.95 as a difference of a whole number and a decimal

$= $ [ ] $-$ [ ]   Distributive property

$= $ [ ] $-$ [ ] $=$ [ ]   Multiply. Then subtract.

Answer: The total cost of the stickers is $ [ ].

The Coordinate Plane

Goal: Identify and plot points in a coordinate plane.

Vocabulary

Coordinate plane:

x-axis:

y-axis:

Origin:

Quadrant:

Ordered pair:

x-coordinate:

y-coordinate:

Scatter plot:

Name the ordered pair that represents the point.

a. *A*　　　　　　　**b.** *B*

Solution

a. Point *A* is ☐ units to the ☐ of

the origin and ☐ units ☐ . So, the

x-coordinate is ☐ and the

y-coordinate is ☐ . Point *A* is

represented by the ordered pair (☐ , ☐).

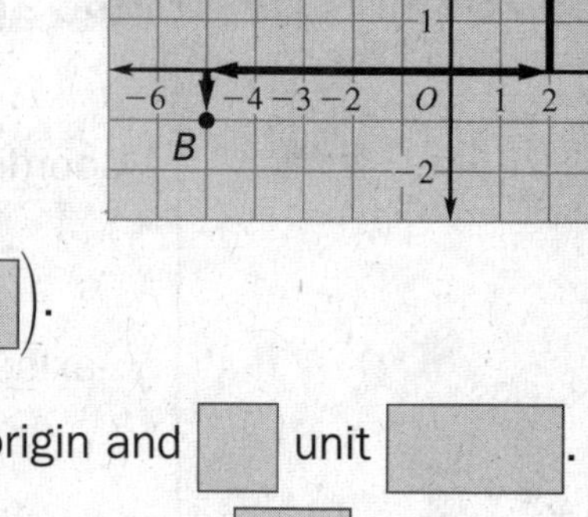

b. Point *B* is ☐ units to the ☐ of the origin and ☐ unit ☐ .

So, the *x*-coordinate is ☐ and the *y*-coordinate is ☐ . Point *B* is

represented by the ordered pair (☐ , ☐).

EXAMPLE **2** **Plotting Points in a Coordinate Plane**

Plot the point and describe its location.

a. $P(2, -3)$　　　　　**b.** $Q(-4, 3)$　　　　　**c.** $R(1, 0)$

Solution

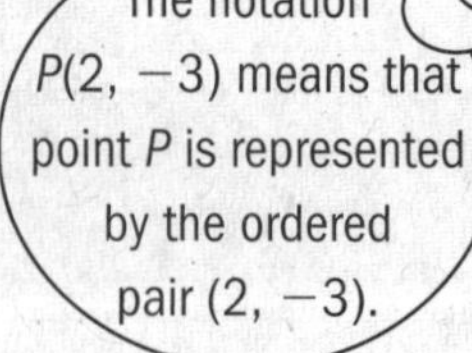

a. Begin at the origin. Move ☐ units to the

☐ , then ☐ units ☐ . Point *P* is

located in Quadrant ☐ .

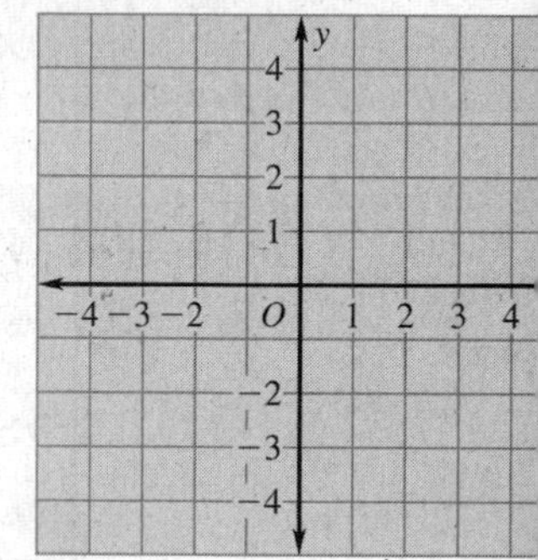

b. Begin at the origin. Move ☐ units to the

☐ , then ☐ units ☐ . Point *Q* is

located in Quadrant ☐ .

c. Begin at the origin. Move ☐ unit to the ☐ . Point *R* is

located ☐ .

1. $W(6, 1)$ **2.** $X(0, 4)$ **3.** $Y(-1, 3)$ **4.** $Z(-2, -4)$

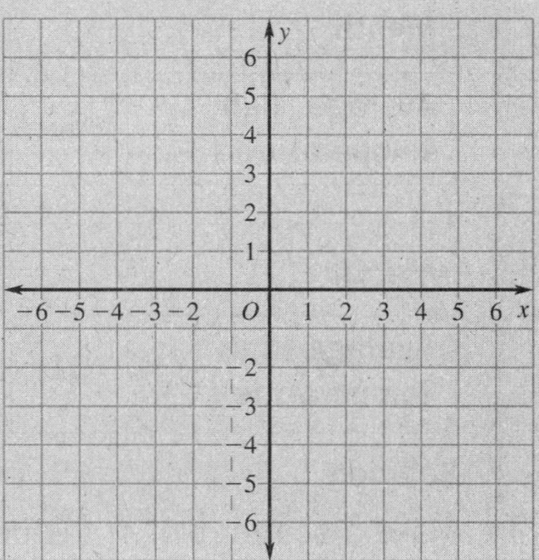

EXAMPLE 3   Finding Segment Lengths and Area

Find the length, width, and area of rectangle *ABCD* shown.

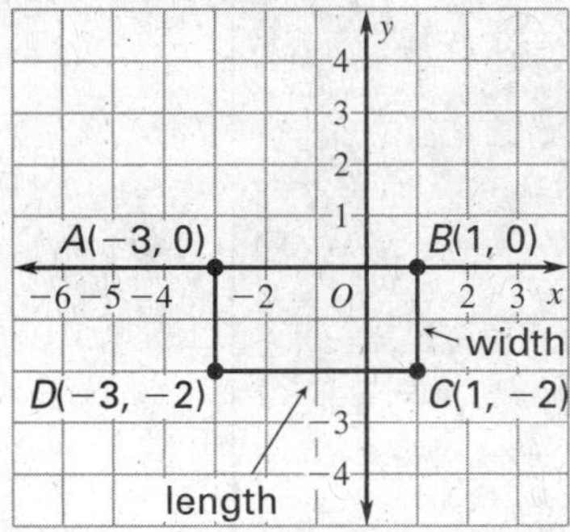

The length of the rectangle is the *horizontal* distance between *A* and *B*. To find this distance, find the absolute value of the difference between the *x*-coordinates of *A* and *B*.

Length $= |$*x*-coordinate of *A* $-$ *x*-coordinate of *B*$|$

$= \boxed{} = \boxed{} = \boxed{}$ units

The width of the rectangle is the *vertical* distance between *A* and *D*. To find this distance, find the absolute value of the difference between the *y*-coordinates of *A* and *D*.

Width $= |$*y*-coordinate of *A* $-$ *y*-coordinate of *D*$|$

$= \boxed{} = \boxed{} = \boxed{}$ units

The area of the rectangle is found by multiplying the length and width.

Area $= \ell w = \boxed{} = \boxed{}$ square units

Average High Temperature The monthly average high temperatures in Myrtle Beach are listed in the table below. Make a scatter plot of the data. Then make a conclusion about the data.

Month	1	2	3	4	5	6
Average High Temperature (°F)	56	60	68	76	83	88

Month	7	8	9	10	11	12
Average High Temperature (°F)	91	89	85	77	69	60

Solution

Make a scatter plot of the data pairs. Use the first quadrant of a coordinate plane, and show the month on the x-axis and the temperature on the y-axis.

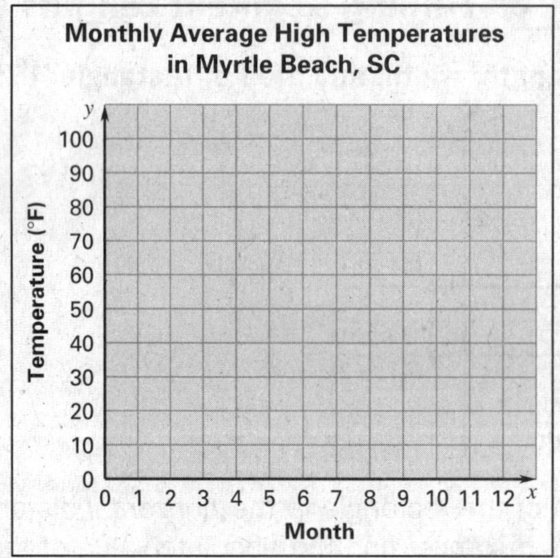

Because the points tend to rise from left to right from month 1 to month and then lower from left to right from month 7 to month 12, you can conclude that from January to July the monthly average high temperature
_______________ and from July to December the monthly average high

temperature _______________.

Words to Review

Give an example of the vocabulary word.

Integer

Negative integer

Positive integer

Opposite

Absolute value

Rational number

Additive inverse

Multiplicative inverse

Additive identity

Multiplicative identity

Equivalent expressions

Distributive property

Coordinate plane

x-axis

y-axis

Origin

Quadrant

Ordered pair

x-coordinate

y-coordinate

Scatter plot

Review your notes and Chapter 6 by using the Chapter Review on pages 302–303 of your textbook.

Writing Expressions and Equations

Goal: Write variable expressions and equations.

Vocabulary

Verbal model:

EXAMPLE 1 Translating Verbal Phrases

Verbal phrase	Expression
a. A number increased by 3	
b. 9 less than a number	
c. 1 more than three times a number	
d. 5 decreased by the quotient of a number and 2	

When translating verbal sentences into equations, look for the key words "is" and "equals," which can be represented by the symbol =.

EXAMPLE 2 Translating Verbal Sentences

Verbal sentence	Equation
a. 12 increased by a number is 18.	
b. The difference of a number and 6 equals -2.	
c. The product of $\frac{2}{3}$ and a number is 15.	
d. -2 is equal to five times the sum of a number and 3.	

1. 9 added to a number	**2.** $\frac{1}{4}$ of a number increased by 18
3. 24 divided by a number equals 6.	**4.** 26 minus 4 times a number is 1

EXAMPLE 3 Writing and Solving an Equation

Dinner The cost of a fish dinner is 3 times the cost of a chef salad. The fish dinner costs $21. Find the cost of the chef salad.

Solution

Write a verbal model.

Let *s* represent the cost of the salad.

3 times the cost of a [ ] = Cost of a [ ]

[ ] = [ ]

Use mental math: Because 3 times [ ] is 21, *s* = [ ].

Answer: The cost of a chef salad is $[ ].

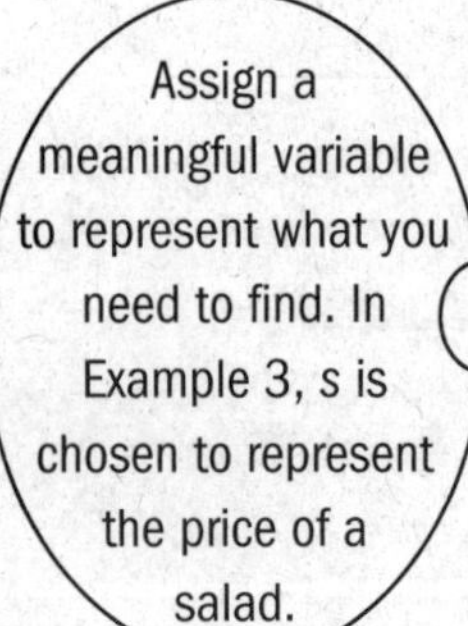

Your turn now Use mental math to solve the following problem.

5. This year, the enrollment at the local junior college dropped by 500 to 4250. Write and solve an equation to find the enrollment last year.

Simplifying Expressions

Goal: Simplify variable expressions.

Vocabulary

Term:

Like terms:

Equivalent variable expressions:

Coefficient:

Constant term:

EXAMPLE 1 Combining Like Terms

Simplify the expression $8x - 2 + 4x$.

After Example 1, the step of using the distributive property in order to combine like terms will not be shown.

$8x - 2 + 4x = $ ☐ Write expression as a sum.

$= 8x + $ ☐ Commutative property of addition

$= $ ☐ Distributive property

$= $ ☐ Simplify.

$= $ ☐ Rewrite without parentheses.

Identify the coefficients, constant terms, and like terms of the expression $x - 7 + 3x - 1$.

First, write the expression as a sum: $x + \left(\boxed{}\right) + 3x + \left(\boxed{}\right)$.

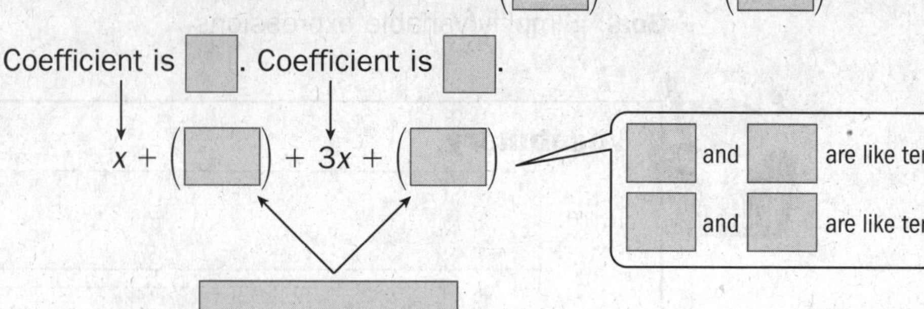

Simplify the expression $2(m - 1) + 6$.

$2(m - 1) + 6 = \boxed{}$ Distributive property

$ = \boxed{}$ Write as a sum.

$ = \boxed{}$ Combine like terms.

Your turn now Identify the coefficients, constant term(s), and like terms of the expression. Then simplify the expression.

1. $-2n + 4 - 3n$	**2.** $10 - 6p + 5p - 4$	**3.** $3\ell + 9 - \ell - 6$

Construction A rectangular skylight in an office building is 3 times as long as it is wide. Write and simplify an expression for the perimeter of the skylight in terms of the width w.

Solution

Because the skylight is 3 times as long as it is wide, its length is ☐ .

$$\text{Perimeter} = 2\ell + 2w \qquad \text{Formula for perimeter of a rectangle}$$

$$= 2\big(\ \square\ \big) + 2w \qquad \text{Substitute } \square \text{ for } \ell.$$

$$= \square + 2w \qquad \text{Multiply.}$$

$$= \square \qquad \text{Combine like terms.}$$

Answer: An expression for the perimeter of the skylight is ☐ .

Your turn now **Complete the following exercise.**

4. A rectangle is 4 inches longer than it is wide. Write and simplify an expression for the perimeter of the rectangle in terms of the width w.

Solving Addition and Subtraction Equations

Goal: Solve addition and subtraction equations.

Vocabulary

Inverse operations:

Equivalent equations:

Subtraction Property of Equality

Words Subtracting the same number from each side of an equation

produces an ___________ equation.

Algebra $x + a = b \longrightarrow x + a - a = b$ ☐ ☐

EXAMPLE 1 **Solving an Addition Equation**

Solve $x + 3 = -1$.

$x + 3 = -1$ Write original equation.

☐ ☐   ___________ from each side.

☐ = ☐   Simplify.

✓ **Check** $x + 3 = -1$ Write original equation.

☐ $\overset{?}{=}$ ☐   Substitute ☐ for x.

☐ ✓   Solution checks.

Addition Property of Equality
Words Adding the same number to each side of an equation produces an [ ] equation.
Algebra $x - a = b \longrightarrow x - a + a = b$ [ ][ ]

EXAMPLE 2 — Solving a Subtraction Equation

Solve $-4 = y - 9$.

$$-4 = y - 9 \qquad \text{Write original equation.}$$

[ ] = [ ]   [ ] to each side.

[ ] = [ ]   Simplify.

✓ **Check** $-4 = y - 9$ Write original equation.

[ ] $\overset{?}{=}$ [ ]   Substitute [ ] for y.

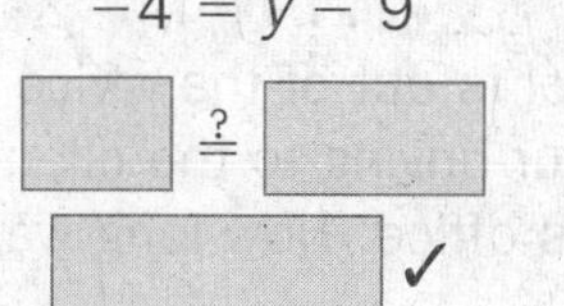 ✓   Solution checks.

EXAMPLE 3 — Combining Like Terms

Solve $7 = 4.1 + b + 1$.

$$7 = 4.1 + b + 1 \qquad \text{Write original equation.}$$

[ ] = $4.1 +$ [ ]   Commutative property of addition

[ ] = [ ]   Combine like terms.

[ ] = [ ]   [ ] from each side.

[ ] = [ ]   Simplify.

✓ **Check** $7 = 4.1 + b + 1$ Write original equation.

[ ] $\overset{?}{=}$ [ ]   Substitute [ ] for b.

[ ] ✓   Solution checks.

1. $t + 7 = 12$	**2.** $n + 8 = 0$	**3.** $6 = y - 4$
4. $r - 12 = 15$	**5.** $p - (-3.6) = 4.9$	**6.** $2.7 + s - 1.9 =$

EXAMPLE 4 **Writing and Solving an Equation**

Business Travel Carol is out of the office for 8 hours meeting with a clien
She spends 0.75 hour driving to the client's office, and 1.25 hours driving
back from the client's office. How long was Carol at the client's office?

Solution

Write a verbal model. Let h represent the number of hours Carol spent
at the client's office.

Time away from office = ☐ + ☐ + ☐

☐ = ☐   Write equation.

☐ = ☐   Combine like terms.

☐ = ☐ ☐   from each side.

☐ = ☐   Simplify.

Answer: Carol spent ☐ hours at the client's office.

Solving Multiplication and Division Equations

Goal: Solve multiplication and division equations.

Division Property of Equality

Words Dividing each side of an equation by the same nonzero number produces an ☐ equation.

Algebra $ax = b \ (a \neq 0) \longrightarrow \dfrac{ax}{a} = $ ☐

EXAMPLE 1 **Solving a Multiplication Equation**

Solve $-30 = 6x.$

$-30 = 6x$ Write original equation.

$\dfrac{-30}{\ \Box\ } = \dfrac{6x}{\ \Box\ }$ 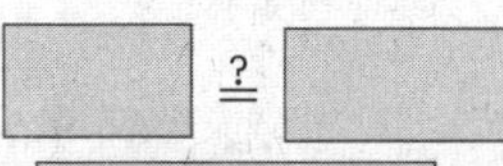 each side by ☐.

$\Box = \Box$ Simplify.

✓ **Check** $-30 = 6x$ Write original equation.

     $\Box \stackrel{?}{=} \Box$ Substitute ☐ for x.

     $\Box$ ✓   Solution checks.

Multiplication Property of Equality

Words Multiplying each side of an equation by the same nonzero number produces an ☐ equation.

Algebra $\dfrac{x}{a} = b \ (a \neq 0) \longrightarrow a \cdot \dfrac{x}{a} = $ ☐

EXAMPLE 2 **Solving a Division Equation**

Solve $\dfrac{x}{4} = 0.3$.

$$\dfrac{x}{4} = 0.3$$ Write original equation.

$$\boxed{} = \boxed{}$$ $\boxed{}$ each side by $\boxed{}$.

$$\boxed{} = \boxed{}$$ Simplify.

EXAMPLE 3 **Solving an Equation Using a Reciprocal**

Solve $\dfrac{3}{4}x = -6$.

$$\dfrac{3}{4}x = -6$$ Write original equation.

$$\boxed{} = \boxed{}$$ $\boxed{}$ each side by $\boxed{}$.

$$\boxed{} = \boxed{}$$ Simplify.

Your turn now   **Solve the equation. Check your solution.**

1. $9v = 36$	**2.** $-8b = 96$
3. $-1.7 = \dfrac{k}{3}$	**4.** $\dfrac{d}{4} = 15$

5. $6q - 4q = 16$	**6.** $\dfrac{5}{8}m = 10$
7. $12 = -v$	**8.** $-3 = \dfrac{3}{4}t$

EXAMPLE 4 Writing and Solving an Equation

Rollerblading A woman is rollerblading through the park. You measure a 75-foot stretch of sidewalk, and count that she skates that portion of the sidewalk in 12 seconds. Use the formula $d = rt$ to find the speed of the skater.

Solution

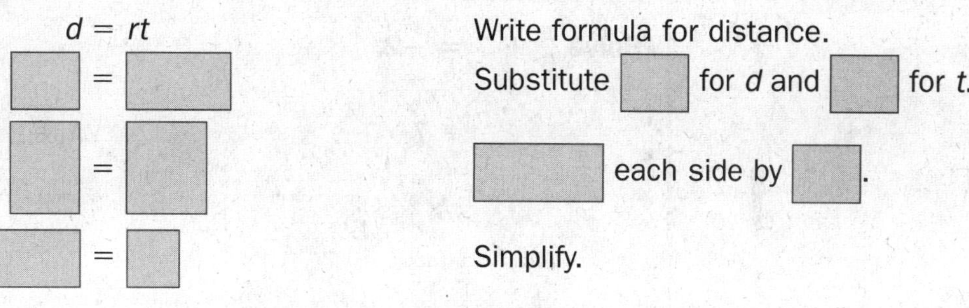

$$d = rt$$

Write formula for distance.

Substitute ☐ for d and ☐ for t.

☐ each side by ☐.

Simplify.

Answer: The speed of the skater is ☐ feet per second.

Your turn now Solve the following problem.

9. A filmmaker makes an edited version of his movie that is 120 minutes long. The unedited footage is 7 times as long as the edited version. Write and solve an equation to find the length of the unedited film.

Solving Two-Step Equations

Goal: Solve two-step equations.

EXAMPLE 1 Solving a Two-Step Equation

Solve $2m - 7 = -19$.

$$2m - 7 = -19$$ Write original equation.

$$\boxed{} = \boxed{}$$ $\boxed{}$ to each side.

$$\boxed{} = \boxed{}$$ Simplify.

$$\boxed{} = \boxed{}$$ $\boxed{}$ each side by $\boxed{}$.

$$\boxed{} = \boxed{}$$ Simplify.

EXAMPLE 2 Solving a Two-Step Equation

Solve $\dfrac{p}{5} + 7 = -2$.

$$\frac{p}{5} + 7 = -2$$ Write original equation.

$$\boxed{} = \boxed{}$$ $\boxed{}$ from each side.

$$\boxed{} = \boxed{}$$ Simplify.

$$\boxed{} = \boxed{}$$ $\boxed{}$ each side by $\boxed{}$.

$$\boxed{} = \boxed{}$$ Simplify.

1. $7q - 4 = 10$	**2.** $\dfrac{j}{6} + 2 = 0$	**3.** $\dfrac{y}{5} - 6 = -6$

EXAMPLE 3 Writing and Solving a Two-Step Equation

Long Distance Calls A long distance phone company charges customers a \$5 monthly fee plus \$3 per hour for long distance phone calls. One customer's bill was \$23. How many hours of long distance calls did the customer make?

Solution

Write a verbal model. Let h represent the number of hours of long distance the customer used.

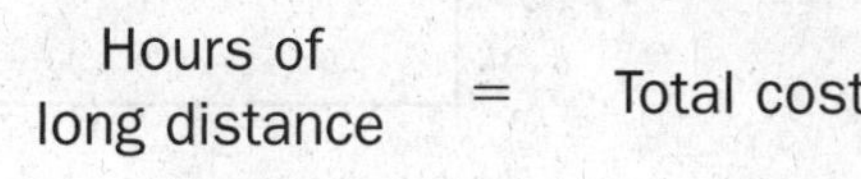

Monthly fee $+$ Hourly cost of long distance $\cdot$ Hours of long distance $=$ Total cost

☐ $+$ ☐ $\cdot$ ☐ $=$ ☐

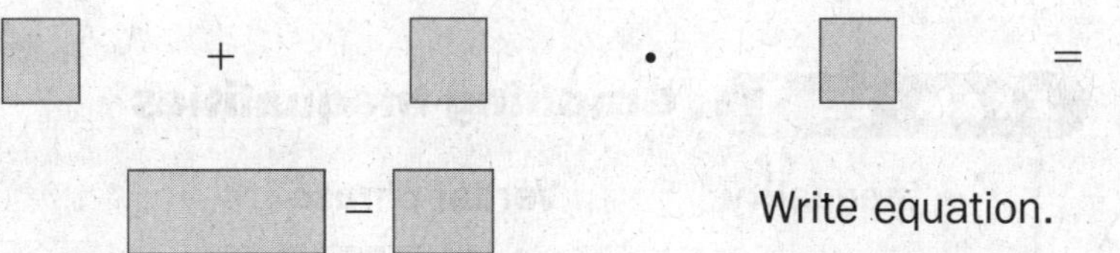

☐ $=$ ☐   Write equation.

☐ $=$ ☐   ☐ from each side.

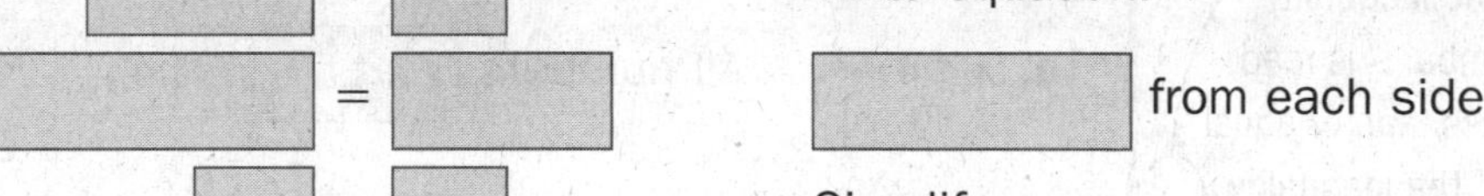

☐ $=$ ☐   Simplify.

☐ $=$ ☐   ☐ each side by ☐.

☐ $=$ ☐   Simplify.

Answer: The customer made ☐ hours of long distance phone calls.

Solving Inequalities

Goal: Write and solve inequalities.

Vocabulary

Inequality:

Solution of an inequality:

Graph of an inequality:

Equivalent inequalities:

EXAMPLE 1 Graphing Inequalities

> The inequality symbol ≤ is read "is less than or equal to." The inequality symbol ≥ is read "is greater than or equal to."

Inequality	Verbal phrase	Graph
a. $x < 4$	All numbers ______ 4	−5 −4 −3 −2 −1 0 1 2 3 4 5
b. $x \le -2$	All numbers ______ or ______ −2	−5 −4 −3 −2 −1 0 1 2 3 4 5
c. $x > 3$	All numbers ______ 3	−5 −4 −3 −2 −1 0 1 2 3 4 5
d. $x \ge -1$	All numbers ______ or ______ −1	−5 −4 −3 −2 −1 0 1 2 3 4 5

 Solving an Inequality

Solve $f - 3 \leq -1$. Then graph the solution.

$f - 3 \leq -1$ Write original inequality.

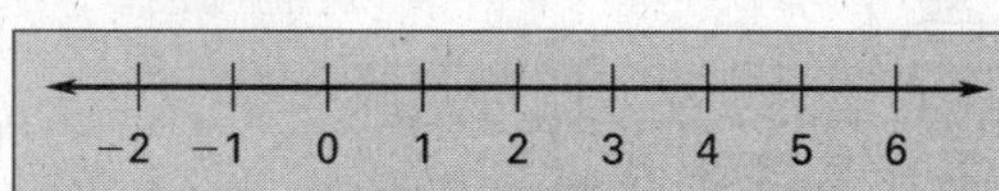   to each side.

Simplify.

To graph , use a(n)   dot and draw the arrow pointing

to the .

✓ Check To check the solution , choose any number

to substitute for f. Use $f = 1$ in the check below.

$f - 3 \leq -1$ Write original inequality.

$\boxed{} - 3 \overset{?}{\leq} -1$ Substitute for f.

$\boxed{} \leq -1$ Solution checks.

Your turn now **Solve the inequality. Then graph the solution.**

1. $s - 1 \geq 4$

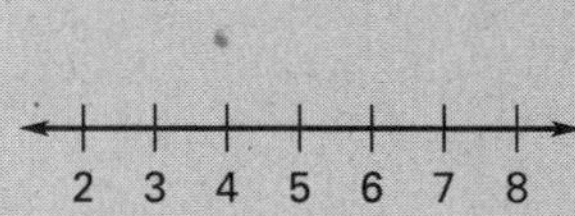

2. $4 < b - 3$

3. $w + 1 > -1$

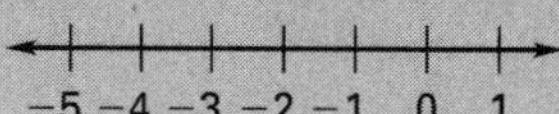

Solve $-3m < -12$. Then graph the solution.

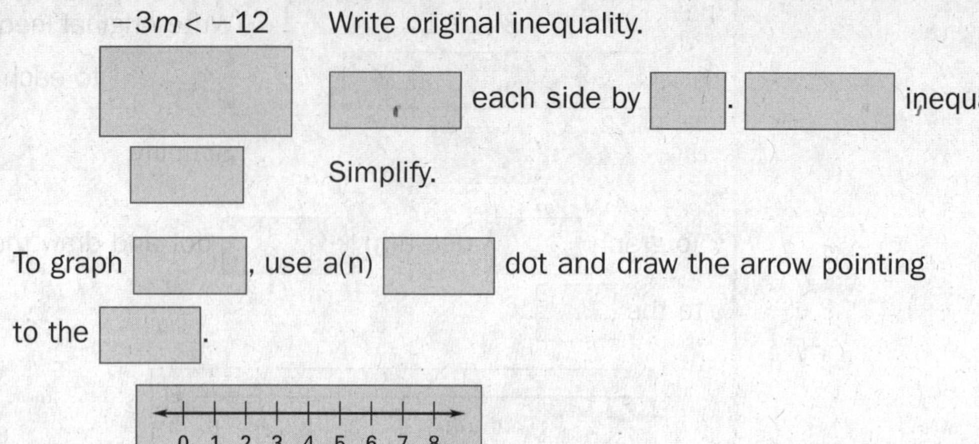

Your turn now   Solve the inequality. Then graph the solution.

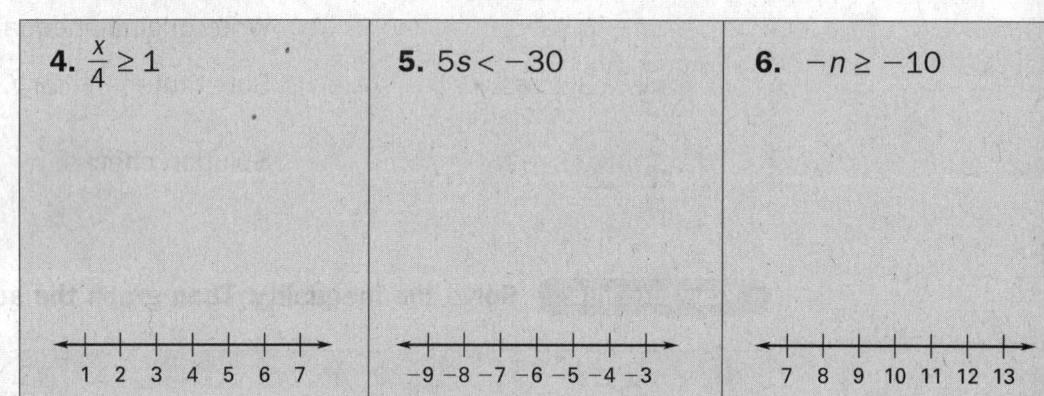

Functions and Equations

Goal: Write and evaluate function rules.

Vocabulary

Function:

Input:

Output:

Domain:

Range:

EXAMPLE 1 **Evaluating a Function**

Evaluate the function $y = 3x$ when $x = 8$.

$y = 3x$ Write rule for function.

$= $ Substitute for x.

$= $ Multiply.

 Making an Input-Output Table

Make an input-output table for the function $y = x - 4.2$ using the domain 0, 1, 2, and 3. Then state the range of the function.

Solution

Input x	0	1	2	3
Substitution	$y = \boxed{} - 4.2$	$y = \boxed{} - 4.2$	$y = \boxed{} - 4.2$	$y = \boxed{} - 4.2$
Output y	$\boxed{}$	$\boxed{}$	$\boxed{}$	$\boxed{}$

The range of the function is the set of outputs: $\boxed{}$, $\boxed{}$, $\boxed{}$,

and $\boxed{}$.

Your turn now Complete the following exercise.

1. Make an input-output table for the function $y = 4 - x$ using the domain
−2, −1, 0, 1, and 2. Then state the range of the function.

EXAMPLE 3 **Writing a Function Rule**

Write a function rule for the input-output table.

Input x	−2	−1	0	1	2	3	4
Output y	−3.5	−2.5	−1.5	−0.5	0.5	1.5	2.5

Solution

You can see that you obtain each output by $\boxed{}$
the input.

Answer: The function rule given by the table is $\boxed{}$.

Squares In the diagram of the squares, the input s is the length of each side of a square. The output P is the perimeter of the square. Write a rule for the function. Then use the rule to find the perimeter of a square with sides 9 units.

1 unit   2 units   3 units   4 units

Solution

1. Begin by making an input-output table.

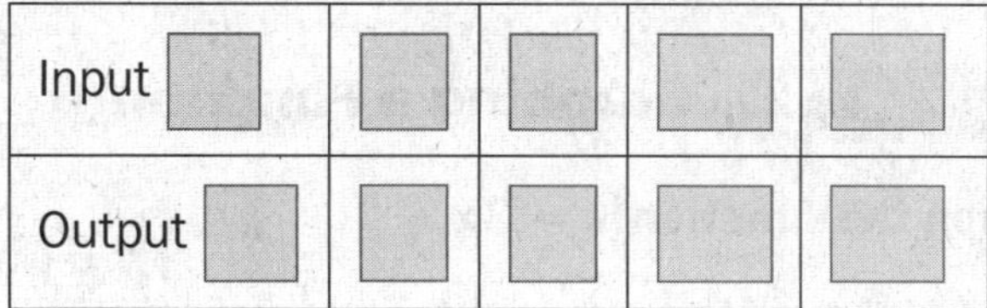

2. Notice that each output value is ⬚ the input value. So, a rule for the function is ⬚.

3. To find the perimeter of a square with sides 9 units, evaluate the function when $s = 9$. Because $P = $ ⬚ $= $ ⬚, the perimeter of the square is ⬚.

Your turn now Write a function rule for the input-output table.

2.

Input x	−1	0	1	2
Output y	−2	0	2	4

3.

Input x	2	4	6	8
Output y	$\frac{1}{2}$	1	$1\frac{1}{2}$	2

Graphing Functions

Goal: Graph functions in a coordinate plane.

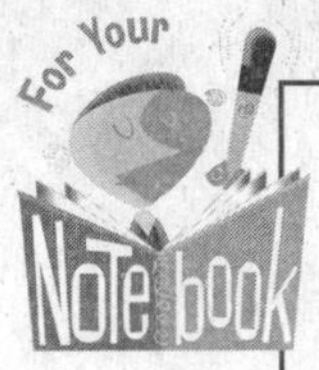

Vocabulary

Linear function:

EXAMPLE 1 **Graphing a Function**

Graph the function $y = 3x - 1$.

When the domain of a function is not given, assume that it includes every x-value for which the function can produce a corresponding y-value.

1. Make an input-output table by choosing several input values and evaluating the function for the output values.

2. Use the table to write a list of ordered pairs:

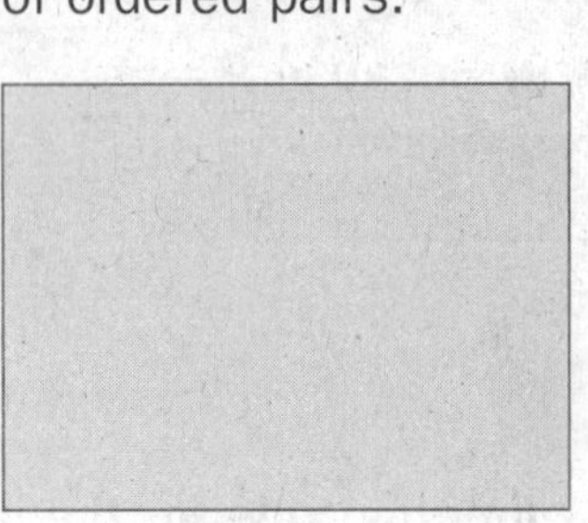

x	Substitution	y
−2		
−1		
0		
1		
2		

3. Plot the ordered pairs in a a coordinate plane.

4. Notice that all of the points lie on a line. Any other ordered pairs satisfying $y = 3x - 1$ would also lie on the line when graphed. The line represents the complete graph of the function $y = 3x - 1$.

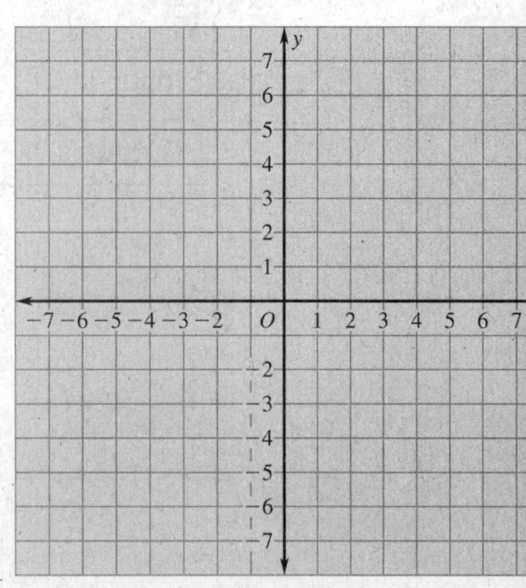

1. $y = x - 2$

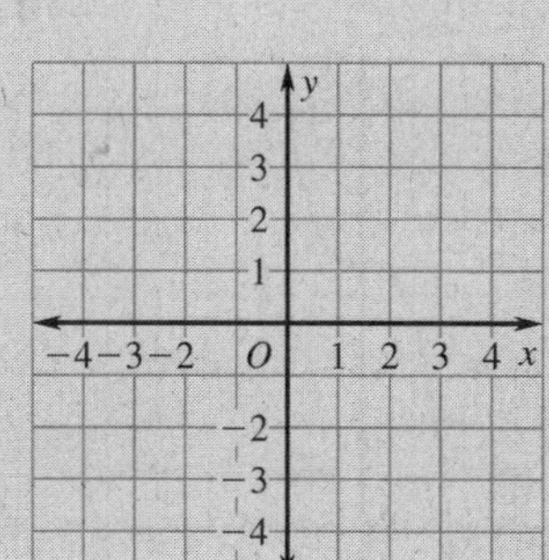

2. $y = \dfrac{x}{2}$

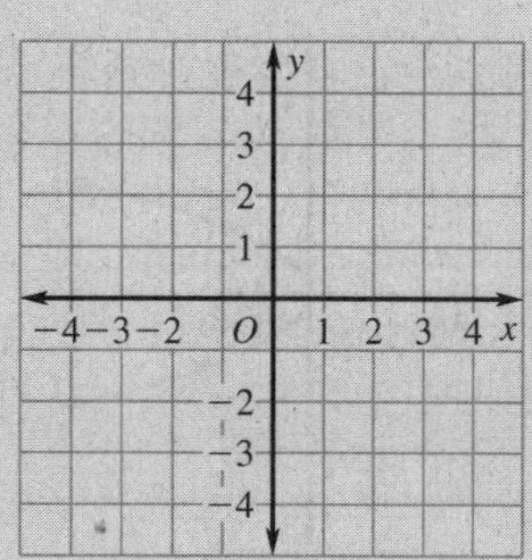

3. $y = 4x + 1$

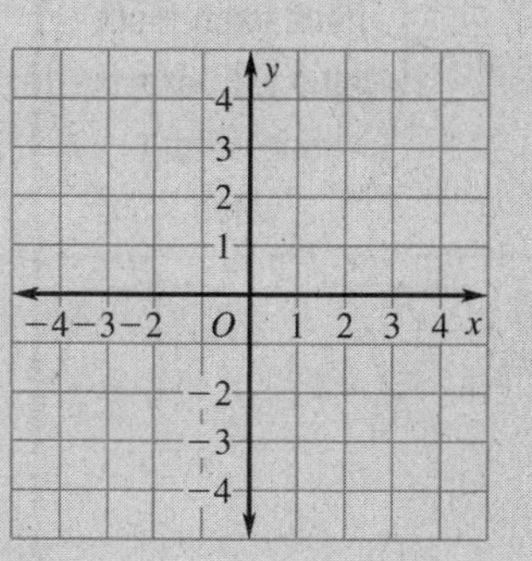

EXAMPLE 2 Writing and Graphing a Function

The cost of gasoline is \$1.50 per gallon. Write and graph a function that represents the cost y of x gallons of gasoline.

The situation can be represented by the function 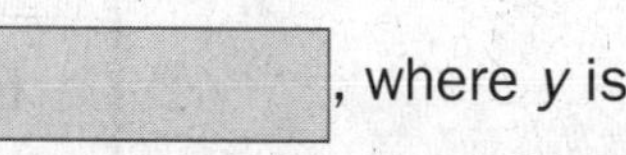, where y is the total cost of x gallons of gasoline.

1. Make an input-output table.

Input x	Output y
0	
1	
2	
3	
4	

2. Plot the ordered pairs and connect them.

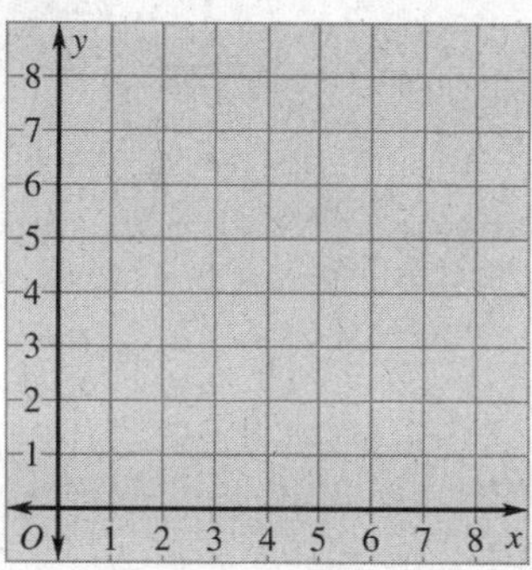

WATCH OUT!

In Example 2, note that you cannot have less than 0 gallons of gasoline, so you cannot use any numbers less than 0 in the domain.

EXAMPLE 3 **Identifying Linear Functions**

Tell whether each graph represents a function of *x*. If it does, tell whethe
the function is *linear* or *nonlinear*.

a.

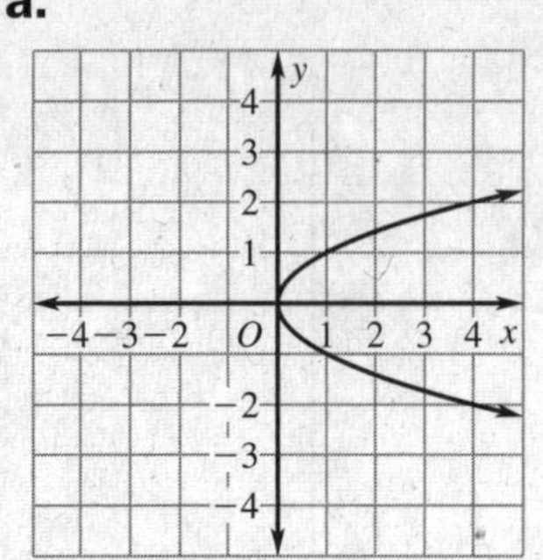

b.

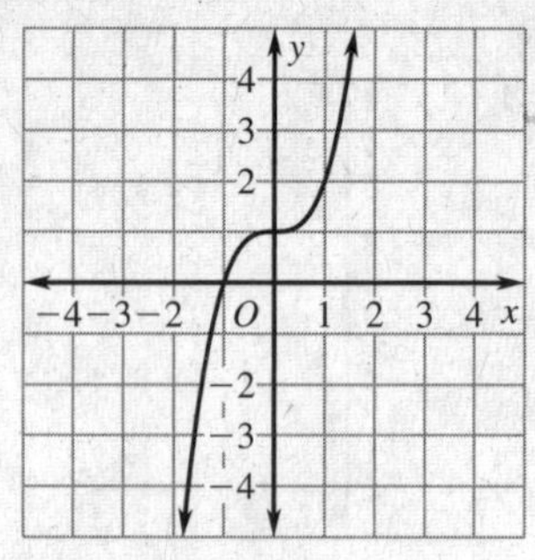

c.

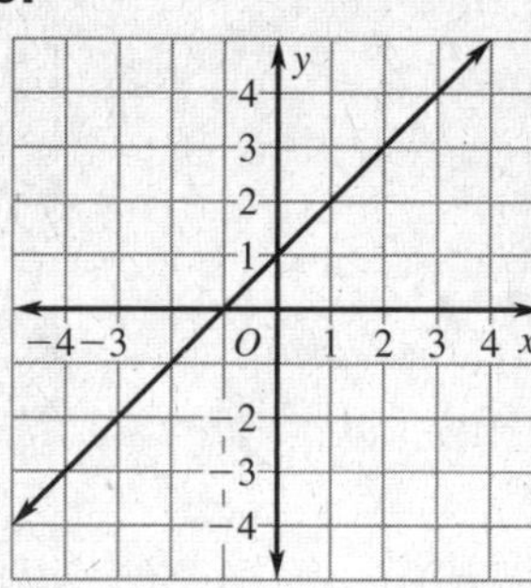

Solution

a.

b.

c.

Words to Review

Give an example of the vocabulary word.

Verbal model

Term

Like terms

Equivalent variable expressions

Coefficient

Constant term

Inverse operations

Equivalent equations

Inequality

Solution of an inequality

Graph of an inequality

Equivalent inequalities

Function

Input

Output

Domain

Range

Linear function

Review your notes and Chapter 7 by using the Chapter Review on pages 362–363 of your textbook.

Ratios

Goal: Write and compare ratios.

Vocabulary

Ratio:

Equivalent ratios:

Writing a Ratio

Words	Numbers	Algebra
wins to losses	16 to 10	a to b, where b is nonzero.
$\dfrac{\text{wins}}{\text{losses}}$		, where b is nonzero.
wins : losses		, where b is nonzero.

EXAMPLE 1   Writing a Ratio

You can make comparisons about 6th grade students in first period classes.

Silverlake Middle School's 6th Grade		
Teacher	**Students in 1st Period**	**Students in 2nd Period**
Ms. Black	29	23
Mr. Henderson	24	27
Ms. Solomon	25	26
Mr. O'Grady	24	25

a. Ms. Black's first period students to Mr. O'Grady's first period students

Ms. Black =   , Mr. O'Grady =

Answer: , or

b. Ms. Solomon's first period students to all first period students

Ms. Solomon = ◻ ; all = ◻ = ◻

Answer: ◻ , or ◻

Your turn now **Use the table on the previous page to write the ratios.**

1. Ms. Black's 1st period students to Ms. Black's 2nd period students

2. All 1st period students to all 2nd period students

3. Mr. O'Grady's 2nd period students to all other 2nd period students

EXAMPLE 2 **Writing Ratios in Simplest Form**

Holiday Dinner Mrs. Carr spends $4\frac{1}{2}$ hours cooking a holiday meal that her family eats in 30 minutes. Follow the steps below to find the ratio of time spent cooking to time spent eating.

1. Write hours as minutes so that the units are the same.

$$4\,h + \frac{1}{2}\,h = \boxed{} \text{ min} + \boxed{} \text{ min} \qquad \text{Write hours as minutes.}$$

$$= \boxed{} \text{ min} \qquad \text{Add.}$$

2. Write the ratio of time spent cooking to time spent eating.

$$\frac{\text{Time cooking}}{\text{Time eating}} = \boxed{} \qquad \text{Write ratio.}$$

$$= \boxed{} \qquad \text{Simplify fraction.}$$

Answer: The ratio of time spent cooking to time spent eating is ◻ : ◻

 Comparing Ratios

Books Kylie and Sophia compared their book collections. To determine who has the greater ratio of mysteries to biographies, write the ratios.

	Mystery	Fiction	Biography
Kylie	12	6	15
Sophia	7	15	10

Kylie: $\dfrac{\text{mysteries}}{\text{biographies}} =$ [ ]　　**Sophia:** $\dfrac{\text{mysteries}}{\text{biographies}} =$ [ ]　　Write ratios as fractions.

$=$ [ ]　　　　$=$ [ ]　　Write fractions as decimals.

Answer: Because [ ] > [ ], [ ] has the greater ratio of mysteries to biographies.

> Need help with writing fractions as decimals? See page 190 of your textbook.

Your turn now　Refer to Example 3.

4. Does Kylie or Sophia have a greater ratio of fiction to mystery books?

5. Does Kylie or Sophia have a greater ratio of biography to fiction?

Rates

Goal: Use rates to compare two quantities with different units.

Vocabulary

Rate:

Unit rate:

EXAMPLE 1 **Finding a Unit Rate**

Microwave Cooking A microwave oven increases the temperature of a cup water by 42°F in 14 seconds. What is the heating rate in degrees Fahrenhe per second?

Solution

First, write a rate comparing the temperature increase to the seconds it took to heat. Then rewrite the fraction so that the denominator is 1.

$$\frac{42°F}{14 \text{ sec}} = \frac{42°F \div \boxed{}}{14 \text{ sec} \div \boxed{}}$$ Divide numerator and denominator by $\boxed{}$

$$= \boxed{}$$ Simplify.

Answer: The heating rate is about $\boxed{}$°F per second.

Your turn now **Find the unit rate.**

1. $72 in 8 hours	**2.** 90 miles in 6 days	**3.** 4 cups in 10 servings

Family Vacation A family drove their car 429 miles in 8 hours and 15 minutes. What was the average speed of the car?

Solution

1. Rewrite the time so that the units are the same.

$$8 \text{ h} + 15 \text{ min} = 8 \text{ h} + \boxed{} \text{ h} = \boxed{} \text{ h}$$

2. Find the average speed.

$$\frac{429 \text{ miles}}{8.25 \text{ hours}} = \frac{429 \text{ miles} \div \boxed{}}{8.25 \text{ hours} \div \boxed{}} \qquad \text{Divide numerator and denominator by } \boxed{}.$$

$$= \boxed{} \qquad \text{Simplify.}$$

Answer: The car's average speed was $\boxed{}$ miles per hour.

EXAMPLE **3** **Comparing Unit Rates**

Cereal A store sells the same cereal the following two ways: a small 48-ounce package for $1.92 and a large 64-ounce package for $3.20. To determine which is the better buy, find the unit price for both types.

A unit price is a type of unit rate.

Small package: $\dfrac{\$1.92}{48 \text{ oz}} = \boxed{}$ $\qquad$ Write as unit rate.

Large package: $\dfrac{\$3.20}{64 \text{ oz}} = \boxed{}$ $\qquad$ Write as unit rate.

Answer: The $\boxed{}$ package of cereal is a better buy because it costs less per ounce.

Your turn now Solve the following problems.

4. It takes you 11 minutes and 40 seconds to ride your bike 2800 yards. What is your average speed in yards per second?

5. Which of the following is the better buy: 2 notebooks for $2.40 or 6 notebooks for $4.80?

Slope

Goal: Find the slope of a line.

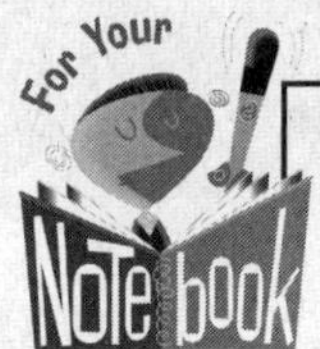

Vocabulary

Slope:

EXAMPLE 1 **Finding the Slope of a Line**

To find the slope of a line, find the ratio of the rise to the run between two points on the line.

Rise is positive when moving up and negative when moving down.

a.
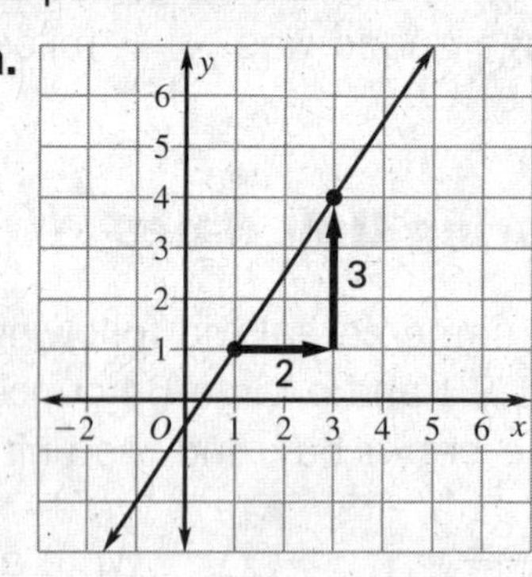

b.
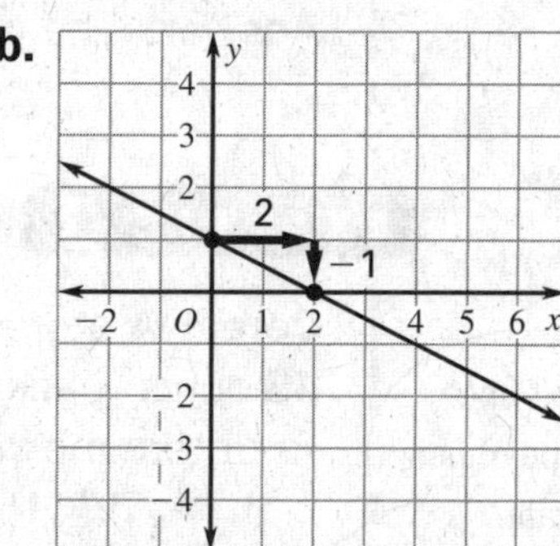

$$\text{slope} = \frac{\text{rise}}{\text{run}} = \boxed{}$$

$$\text{slope} = \frac{\text{rise}}{\text{run}} = \boxed{} = \boxed{}$$

EXAMPLE 2 **Interpreting Slope as a Rate**

Lemonade Stand The graph represents the cups of lemonade sold over time. To find the rate of sales, find the slope of the line.

$$\text{slope} = \frac{\text{rise}}{\text{run}} = \boxed{}$$ Write rise over run.

$$= \boxed{}$$ Find unit rate.

Answer: The lemonade sold at a rate of 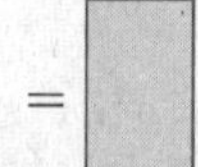 cups per hour.

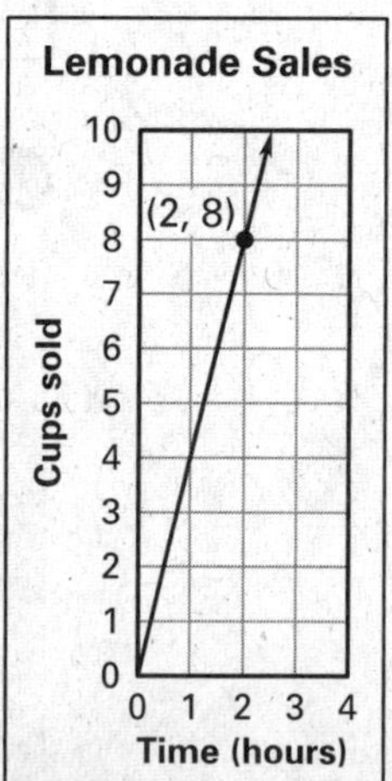

1. Plot the points (1, 5) and (0, 8). Then find the slope of the line that passes through the points.

2. In Example 2, suppose the line starts at the origin and passes through the point (2, 7). Find the rate of lemonade sales.

EXAMPLE 3 **Using Slope to Draw a Line**

Draw the line that has a slope of 4 and passes through (2, 1).

1. Plot (2, 1).

2. Write the slope as a fraction.

slope = ☐ = ☐

3. Move ☐ unit to the ☐ and ☐ units ☐ to plot the second point.

4. Draw a line through the two points.

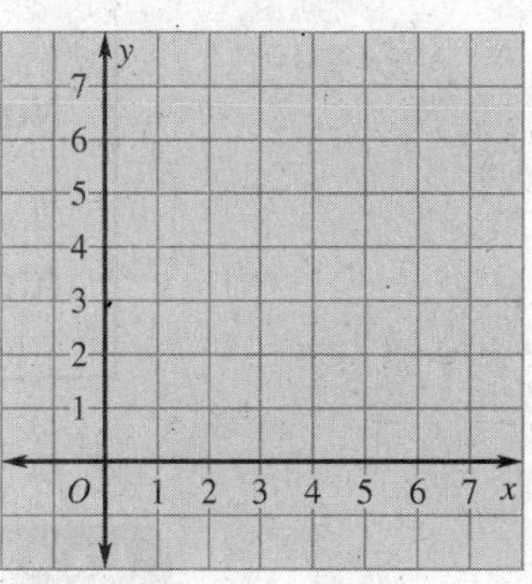

3. Draw the line that has a slope of $-\frac{2}{3}$ and passes through (5, 4).

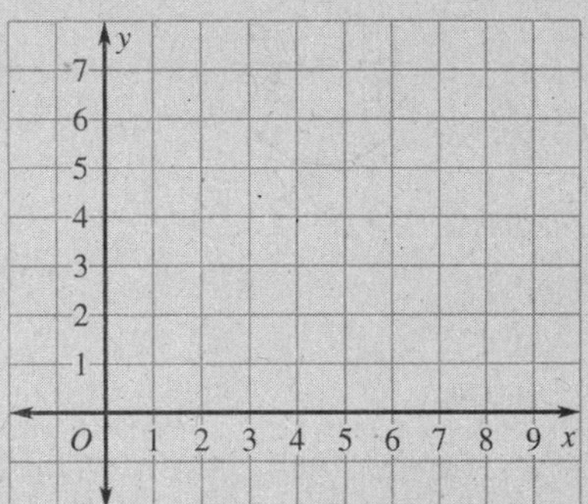

Writing and Solving Proportion

Goal: Solve proportions using equivalent ratios and algebra.

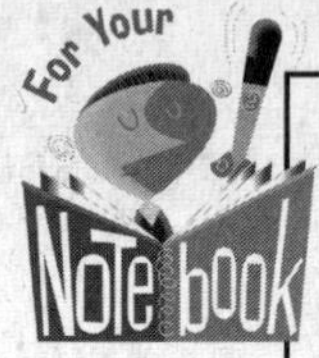

Vocabulary

Proportion:

Proportions

Words A **proportion** is an equation that states that two [   ] are [   ].

Numbers $\dfrac{}{} = \dfrac{}{}$ The proportion is read "4 is to 5 as 8 is to 10."

Algebra $\dfrac{a}{b} = \dfrac{c}{d}$, where b and d are nonzero numbers.

EXAMPLE 1 **Using Equivalent Ratios**

Skating Lessons A skating rink offers private skating lessons at a cost of $15 for 30 minutes. How much will it cost for 90 minutes of private lessons?

Solution

To find the price paid P for 90 minutes of lessons, solve the proportion $\dfrac{15}{30} = \dfrac{P}{90}$.

1. Ask yourself: What number can you multiply 30 by to get 90?

$$\frac{15}{30} = \frac{P}{90}$$

$\times\,?$

2. Because $30 \times \boxed{} = 90$, multiply the numerator by $\boxed{}$ to find P.

$$\times \boxed{}$$

$$\frac{15}{30} = \frac{P}{90}$$

$$\times \boxed{}$$

Answer: Because $15 \times \boxed{} = \boxed{}$, $P = \boxed{}$. So, the price of 90 minutes of private lessons is $\$\boxed{}$.

EXAMPLE 2 Solving Proportions Using Algebra

Solve the proportion $\dfrac{4}{14} = \dfrac{x}{21}$.

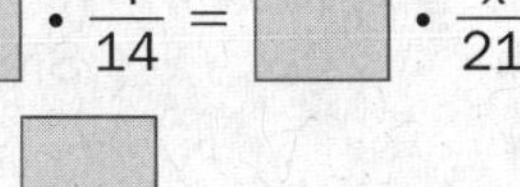

$$\frac{4}{14} = \frac{x}{21} \qquad \text{Write original proportion.}$$

$$\boxed{} \cdot \frac{4}{14} = \boxed{} \cdot \frac{x}{21} \qquad \text{Multiply each side by } \boxed{}.$$

$$\frac{\boxed{}}{\boxed{}} = x \qquad \text{Simplify.}$$

$$\boxed{} = x \qquad \text{Simplify fraction.}$$

Answer: The solution is $\boxed{}$.

As you learn different methods for solving a proportion, remember to write an example of each method in your notebook.

Your turn now Use equivalent ratios to solve the proportion.

1. $\dfrac{2}{3} = \dfrac{z}{12}$

2. $\dfrac{4}{3} = \dfrac{x}{18}$

3. $\dfrac{30}{c} = \dfrac{5}{8}$

4. $\dfrac{4}{n} = \dfrac{48}{12}$

Use algebra to solve the proportion.

5. $\dfrac{4}{6} = \dfrac{m}{15}$

6. $\dfrac{10}{15} = \dfrac{n}{9}$

7. $\dfrac{h}{20} = \dfrac{6}{8}$

8. $\dfrac{b}{12} = \dfrac{3}{18}$

Basketball Tyler scores an average of 10 points in 8 minutes of playing time. Follow the steps below to find the number of points that Tyler averages in 4 minutes of play.

1. Write a proportion. Let x represent the average number of points scored in 4 minutes.

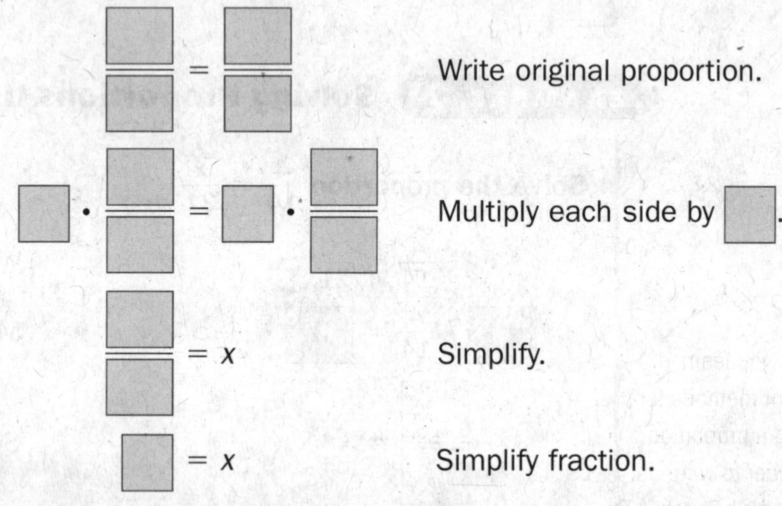

2. Solve the proportion.

Write original proportion.

Multiply each side by ☐.

= x Simplify.

= x Simplify fraction.

Answer: Tyler averages ☐ points in 4 minutes of playing time.

WATCH OUT!
You cannot write a proportion that compares points to minutes and minutes to points.
$$\frac{\text{points}}{\text{minutes}} \neq \frac{\text{minutes}}{\text{points}}$$

Solving Proportions Using Cross Products

Goal: Solve proportions using cross products.

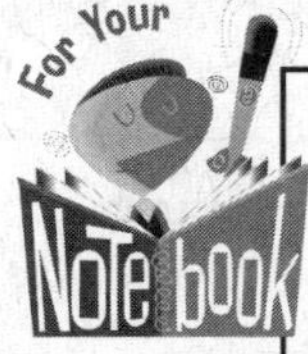

Vocabulary

Cross products:

Cross Products Property

Words The cross products of a proportion are [ ].

Numbers 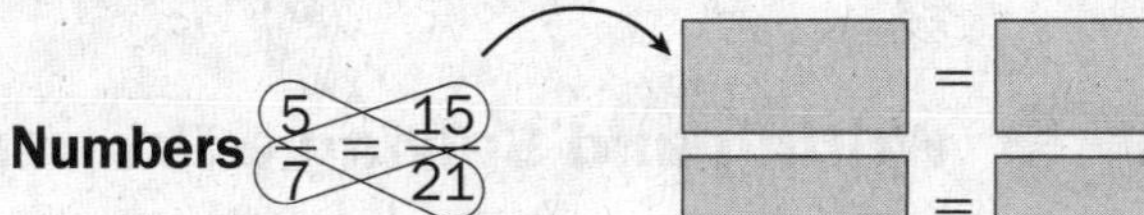

Algebra If $\dfrac{a}{b} = \dfrac{c}{d}$ where b and d are nonzero numbers, then [ ] = [ ].

EXAMPLE 1 **Solving a Proportion Using Cross Products**

The phrase *cross products* comes from the "X" shape formed by the diagonal numbers in a proportion.

Use the cross products property to solve $\dfrac{2}{5} = \dfrac{x}{7}$.

$\dfrac{2}{5} = \dfrac{x}{7}$ Write original proportion.

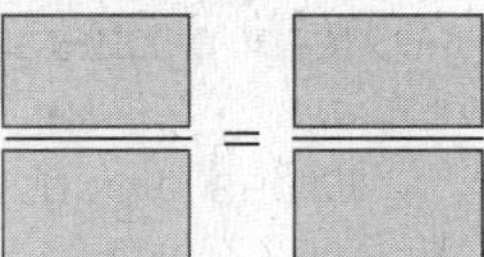 = [ ]   Cross products property

[ ] = [ ]   Divide each side by [ ].

[ ] = [ ]   Simplify.

 Writing and Solving a Proportion

Currency Exchange When Jake visited Canada, he exchanged 10 U.S. dollars and he received 14 Canadian dollars. Find how many U.S. dollars he exchanged when he received 35 Canadian dollars.

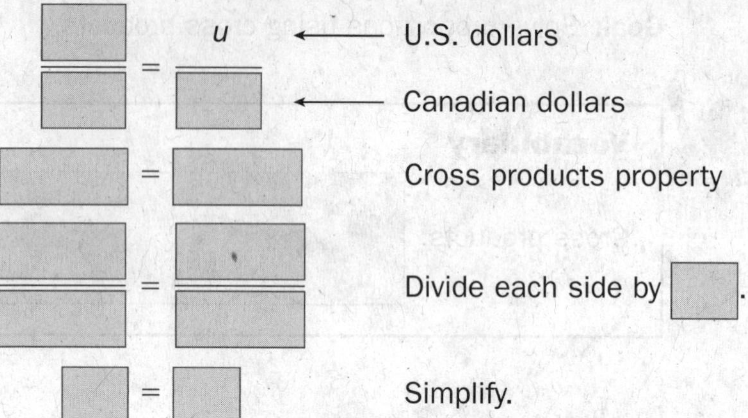

$$\frac{\boxed{}}{\boxed{}} = \frac{u}{\boxed{}} \quad \longleftarrow \quad \text{U.S. dollars}$$
$$\longleftarrow \quad \text{Canadian dollars}$$

$$\boxed{} = \boxed{} \qquad \text{Cross products property}$$

$$\frac{\boxed{}}{\boxed{}} = \frac{\boxed{}}{\boxed{}} \qquad \text{Divide each side by } \boxed{}.$$

$$\boxed{} = \boxed{} \qquad \text{Simplify.}$$

Answer: Jake exchanged $\boxed{}$ U.S. dollars when he received 35 Canadian dollars.

 Writing and Solving a Proportion

Baseball The ratio of left-handed pitchers to right-handed pitchers on a baseball team is 2 to 5. If the team has 14 pitchers, how many are left-handed?

Solution

First, determine the ratio of left-handed pitchers to total pitchers.

$$\frac{\boxed{}}{\boxed{} + \boxed{}} = \frac{\boxed{}}{\boxed{}} \qquad \text{For every } \boxed{} \text{ pitchers, } \boxed{} \text{ are left-handed.}$$

To find the number ℓ of left-handed pitchers, set up a proportion and solve

$$\frac{\boxed{}}{\boxed{}} = \frac{\boxed{}}{\boxed{}} \quad \longleftarrow \quad \text{left-handed pitchers}$$
$$\longleftarrow \quad \text{total pitchers}$$

$$\boxed{} = \boxed{} \qquad \text{Cross products property}$$

$$\frac{\boxed{}}{\boxed{}} = \frac{\boxed{}}{\boxed{}} \qquad \text{Divide each side by } \boxed{}.$$

$$\boxed{} = \boxed{} \qquad \text{Simplify.}$$

Answer: There are $\boxed{}$ left-handed pitchers on the team.

 Solve the following problems.

1. In Example 2, if Jake exchanged 45 U.S. dollars, how many Canadian dollars would he receive?

2. A baseball team has a ratio of wins to losses of 5 to 3. If they played 24 games, how many games did they lose?

Scale Drawings and Models

Goal: Use proportions with scale drawings.

Vocabulary

Scale drawing:

Scale:

Scale model:

EXAMPLE 1 **Using the Scale of a Map**

Maps Use the map of Nebraska to estimate the distance between the towns of Ogallala and Central City.

Solution

From the map's scale, 1.5 centimeters represent 100 miles. On the map, the distance between Ogallala and Central City is 3 centimeters.

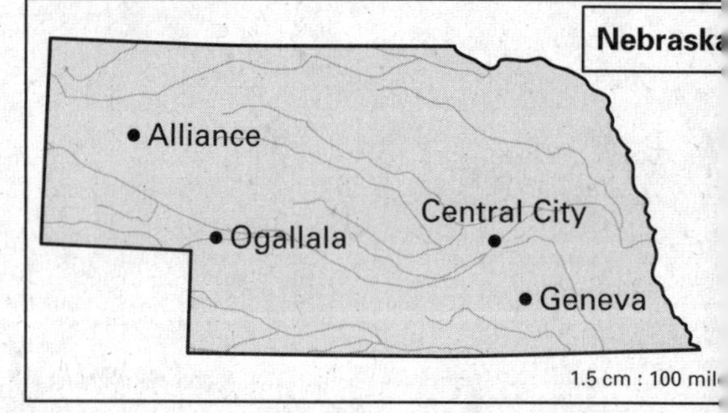

Write and solve a proportion to find the distance d between the towns.

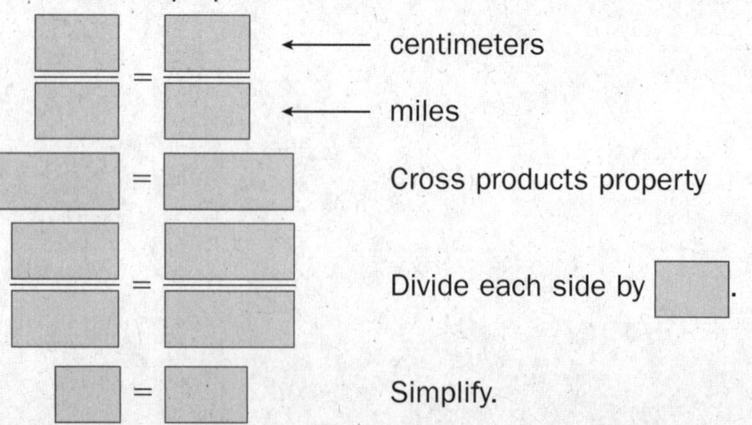

$$\frac{\qquad}{\qquad} = \frac{\qquad}{\qquad} \quad\longleftarrow \text{ centimeters}$$
$$\qquad\qquad\qquad\qquad \longleftarrow \text{ miles}$$

$\qquad = \qquad$ Cross products property

$$\frac{\qquad}{\qquad} = \frac{\qquad}{\qquad}$$ Divide each side by $\boxed{}$.

$\qquad = \qquad$ Simplify.

Answer: The actual distance between Ogallala and Central City is about $\boxed{}$ miles.

 Use a metric ruler and the map in Example 1.

1. Estimate the distance, in miles, between the towns of Alliance and Geneva.

EXAMPLE 2 Finding a Dimension on a Scale Model

Model Cars A scale model of an Austin Healy automobile is for sale at the local Hobby Shop. The scale used is $1 : 15$. The height of the actual car is 45 inches. Find the height of the model.

When a scale is written as a ratio, it usually takes the form shown below.

scale model:
actual object

Solution

Write and solve a proportion to find the height h of the model of the Austin Healy.

$$\frac{\boxed{}}{\boxed{}} = \frac{\boxed{}}{\boxed{}}$$ ⟵ scale model
⟵ car

$$\boxed{} = \boxed{}$$ Cross products property

$$\frac{\boxed{}}{\boxed{}} = \frac{\boxed{}}{\boxed{}}$$ Divide each side by $\boxed{}$.

$$\boxed{} = \boxed{}$$ Simplify.

Answer: The height of the model is $\boxed{}$ inches.

EXAMPLE 3 Finding the Scale

Architecture An architect is planning a theater complex. The model is 36 inches tall. The resulting theater complex will be 150 feet tall. What is the model's scale?

Solution

Write a ratio. Make sure that both measures are in feet. Then simplify the fraction.

$$\boxed{} = \boxed{} = \boxed{}$$ ⟵ scale model
⟵ full size

Answer: The model's scale is $\boxed{} : \boxed{}$.

2. The parking garage for the theater complex is 175 feet long. Find the length of the model.

Words to Review

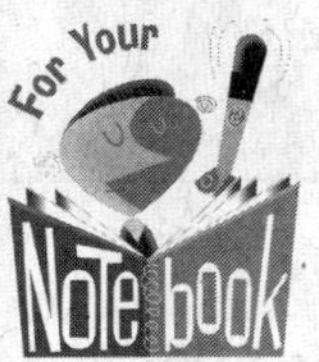

Give an example of the vocabulary word.

Ratio

Equivalent ratios

Rate

Unit rate

Slope

Proportion

Cross products

Scale drawing

Scale   Scale model

Review your notes and Chapter 8 by using the Chapter Review on pages 406–407 of your textbook.

Percents and Fractions

Goal: Use a fraction to find the percent of a number.

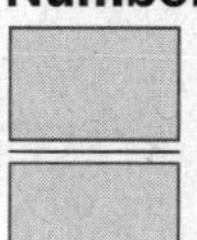

Vocabulary

Percent:

Understanding Percent

The model at the right has 22 out of 100 squares shaded. You can say that ☐ percent of the squares are shaded.

Numbers You can write 22 percent as

$$\frac{\boxed{}}{\boxed{}} \text{ or as } \boxed{}\%.$$

Algebra You can write p percent as

$$\frac{\boxed{}}{\boxed{}} \text{ or as } \boxed{}\%.$$

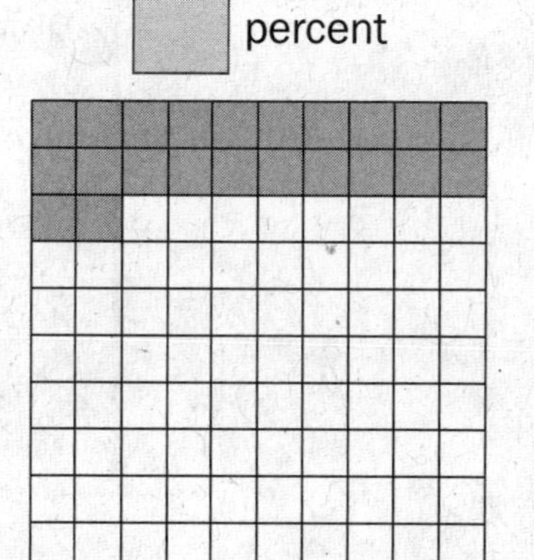

EXAMPLE 1 Writing Percents as Fractions

Write the percent as a fraction.

  a. 49%   **b.** 60%

Solution

  a. $49\% = \dfrac{\boxed{}}{\boxed{}}$ **b.** $60\% = \dfrac{\boxed{}}{\boxed{}} = \dfrac{\boxed{}}{\boxed{}}$

1. 18%	**2.** 45%	**3.** 41%	**4.** 70%

EXAMPLE 2 Writing Fractions as Percents

To write a fraction as a percent, rewrite the fraction with a denominator of 100.

a. $\dfrac{3}{10} = \dfrac{3 \times \boxed{}}{10 \times \boxed{}} = \dfrac{\boxed{}}{\boxed{}} = \boxed{}\%$

b. $\dfrac{4}{5} = \dfrac{4 \times \boxed{}}{5 \times \boxed{}} = \dfrac{\boxed{}}{\boxed{}} = \boxed{}\%$

EXAMPLE 3 Finding a Percent of a Number

To find 20% of 55, use the fact that $20\% = \frac{1}{5}$ and multiply.

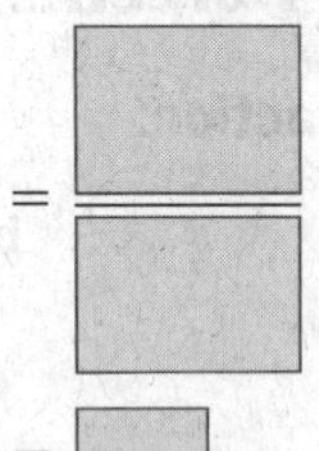

20% of $55 = \boxed{}$ Write percent as a fraction.

$= \boxed{}$ Use rule for multiplying fractions. Divide out common factor.

$= \boxed{}$ Simplify.

5. $\frac{7}{25}$	**6.** $\frac{11}{20}$	**7.** $\frac{9}{10}$	**8.** $\frac{13}{50}$
9. Find 30% of 400.		**10.** Find 75% of 280.	

EXAMPLE 4 Using Percents

Soccer According to the Smithville Athletic Club, 47 of the 100 children playing Pee Wee Soccer this year are boys. What percent of the players are girls?

Solution

You know that $\frac{47}{100} = \boxed{}$% of the soccer players are boys. To find the percent of soccer players who are girls, use the fact that the entire group of players represent 100%.

$$\boxed{}\% - \boxed{}\% = \boxed{}\%$$

Answer: $\boxed{}$% of the Pee Wee soccer players are girls.

Percents and Proportions

Goal: Use proportions to solve percent problems.

Solving Percent Problems

You can represent "*a* is *p* percent of *b*" with the proportion

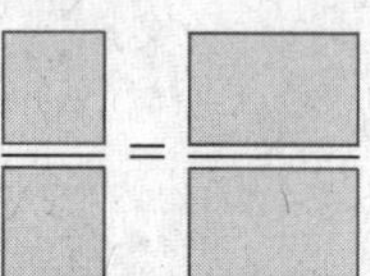

where *a* is a part of the base *b* and *p*% or $\dfrac{p}{100}$ is the percent.

EXAMPLE 1 Finding a Percent

What percent of 4 is 3?

In a percent problem, the word that follows "of" is usually the base *b*.

$$\dfrac{a}{b} = \dfrac{p}{100}$$

Write proportion.

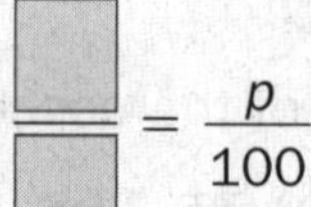 $= \dfrac{p}{100}$

Substitute ⬜ for *a* and ⬜ for *b*.

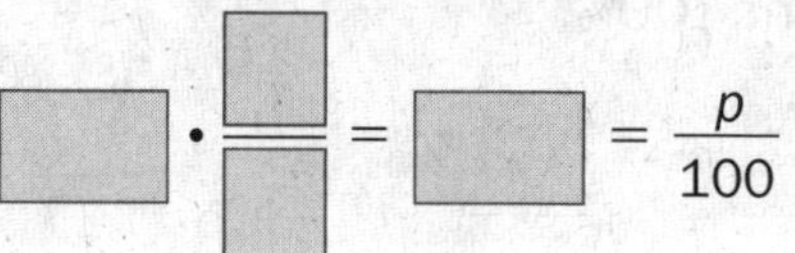 $= \dfrac{p}{100}$

Multiply each side by ⬜.

⬜ $=$ ⬜

Simplify.

Answer: 3 is ⬜ % of 4.

 Use a proportion to answer the question.

1. What percent of 25 is 10?	**2.** What percent of 300 is 9?

3. In a grocery store, 6 of the 30 breakfast cereals are generic brand. What percent of the breakfast cereals are generic brand?

EXAMPLE 2 Finding a Part of a Base

Tennis 328 fans attended a tennis tournament. In a survey, 25% of the fans wanted players to wear traditional white tennis clothes. How many fans wanted players to wear traditional white clothing?

$$\frac{a}{b} = \frac{p}{100}$$ Write proportion.

$$\frac{\boxed{}}{\boxed{}} = \frac{\boxed{}}{100}$$ Substitute $\boxed{}$ for b and $\boxed{}$ for p.

$$\boxed{} \cdot \frac{\boxed{}}{\boxed{}} = \boxed{} \cdot \frac{\boxed{}}{100}$$ Multiply each side by .

$$\boxed{} = 328 \cdot \frac{\overset{1}{\cancel{\boxed{}}}}{\underset{\underset{1}{4}}{\cancel{100}}}$$ Use rule for multiplying fractions. Divide out common factors.

$$\boxed{} = \boxed{}$$ Simplify.

Answer: In the survey,  of the fans wanted players in traditional white clothing.

4. What number is 85% of 120?	**5.** What number is 7% of 200?
6. What number is 21% of 80?	**7.** What number is 62% of 900?

EXAMPLE 3   Finding a Base

48 is 40% of what number?

$$\frac{a}{b} = \frac{p}{100}$$ Write proportion.

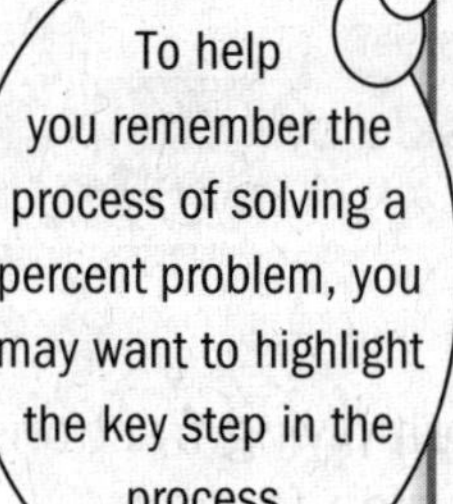

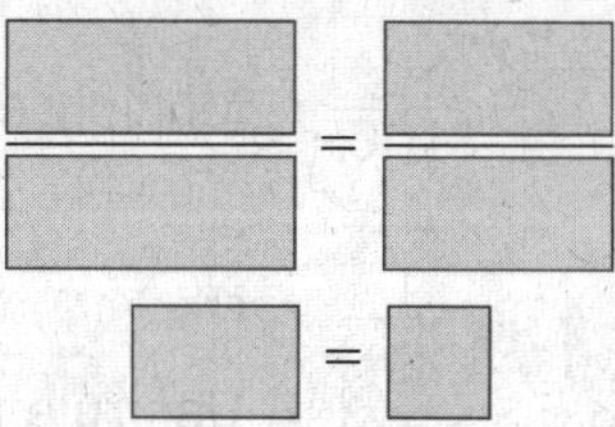

$$\frac{}{} = \frac{}{100}$$ Substitute.

$$\boxed{} = \boxed{}$$ Cross products property

$$\frac{\boxed{}}{\boxed{}} = \frac{\boxed{}}{\boxed{}}$$ Divide each side by $\boxed{}$.

$$\boxed{} = \boxed{}$$ Simplify.

Answer: 48 is 40% of $\boxed{}$.

To help you remember the process of solving a percent problem, you may want to highlight the key step in the process.

Percents and Decimals

Goal: Write percents as decimals and decimals as percents.

EXAMPLE 1 **Writing Percents as Decimals**

a. 52% = 52%

= [ ]

b. 4% = **0**4%

= [ ]

c. 18.4% = 18.4%

= [ ]

EXAMPLE 2 **Writing Decimals as Percents**

a. 0.27 = .27

= [ ]

b. 0.03 = .03

= [ ]

c. 0.091 = .091

= [ ]

Your turn now Write the percent as a decimal or the decimal as a percent.

1. 30%	2. 7%	3. 17.4%
4. 0.043	5. 0.01	6. 0.169

EXAMPLE 3 **Writing Fractions as Percents**

a. $\frac{5}{9} \approx$ [ ]   Write as a decimal rounded to the nearest thousandth.

= [ ]   Write as a percent.

b. $\frac{3}{11} \approx$ [ ]   Write as a decimal rounded to the nearest thousandth.

= [ ]   Write as a percent.

The symbol ≈ is read "approximately equal to." It indicates that a result has been rounded and is not exact.

Video Store A video store carries 0.8% of their videos in foreign languages. The store increased their inventory of DVDs by 500%. Write these percents as decimals.

Foreign language: 0.8% = 00.8%   DVDs: 500% = 500%

=   =

Your turn now Write the fraction as a percent. Round to the nearest tenth of a percent.

7. $\frac{1}{6}$	8. $\frac{7}{9}$	9. $\frac{6}{7}$	10. $\frac{9}{13}$

Write the percent as a decimal.

11. 0.36%	12. 740%	13. 0.0026%	14. 0.08%

EXAMPLE 5 Using a Percent Less Than 1%

Chemistry A chemical solution in a container has a volume of 85,000 milliliters. The solution contains 0.04% saline. How much of the solution is saline?

Solution

0.04% of 85,000 =   Write percent as a decimal.

=   Multiply.

Answer: The solution contains  milliliters of saline.

15. The enrollment at Little Angel's Preschool last year was 50 students. This year's enrollment is 220% of last year's. How many students enrolled this year?

The Percent Equation

Goal: Use equations to solve percent problems.

The Percent Equation

You can represent "*a* is *p* percent of *b*" with the equation

where *a* is part of the base *b* and *p*% is the percent.

EXAMPLE 1 **Finding a Part of a Base**

Pharmacy The pharmacy has 75% of the 300 tablets that Dr. Cole prescribed for her patient. How many tablets does the pharmacy have?

$a = p\% \cdot b$ Write percent equation.

$= \boxed{}\% \cdot \boxed{}$ Substitute $\boxed{}$ for *p* and $\boxed{}$ for *b*.

$= \boxed{} \cdot \boxed{}$ Write percent as a decimal.

$= \boxed{}$ Multiply.

Answer: The pharmacy has $\boxed{}$ of the tablets.

Your turn now   Use the percent equation to answer the question.

1. What is 30% of 250?	**2.** What is 32% of 65?

EXAMPLE 2   Finding a Percent

What percent of 240 is 72?

$a = p\% \cdot b$ Write percent equation.

[ ] $= p\% \cdot$ [ ]   Substitute [ ] for a and [ ] for b.

$\dfrac{[\ ]}{[\ ]} = \dfrac{p\% \cdot [\ ]}{[\ ]}$ Divide each side by [ ].

[ ] $= p\% =$ [ ] %   Simplify fraction. Then write as a percent.

Answer: The number 72 is [ ] % of 240.

EXAMPLE 3   Finding a Base

The number 80 is 32% of what number?

$a = p\% \cdot b$ Write percent equation.

[ ] $=$ [ ] $\% \cdot b$ Substitute [ ] for a and [ ] for p.

$\dfrac{[\ ]}{[\ ]} = \dfrac{[\ ] \cdot b}{[\ ]}$ Write percent as a decimal. Then divide each side by [ ].

[ ] $=$ [ ]   Simplify.

Answer: The number 80 is 32% of [ ].

Your turn now   Use the percent equation to answer the question.

3. 99 is what percent of 396?	**4.** 30 is 250% of what number?

Jewelry A jewelry salesperson sells a bracelet for $350. The salesperson earns an 8% commission on the sale. How much is the commission?

Solution

$a = p\% \cdot b$ Write percent equation.

$= \boxed{}\% \cdot \boxed{}$ Substitute $\boxed{}$ for p and $\boxed{}$ for b.

$= \boxed{} \cdot \boxed{}$ Write percent as a decimal.

$= \boxed{}$ Multiply.

Answer: The commission is $\$\boxed{}$.

Circle Graphs

Goal: Use percents to interpret and make circle graphs.

Vocabulary

Circle graph:

Ray:

Angle:

Vertex:

Degrees:

EXAMPLE 1 **Interpreting a Circle Graph**

Class Survey The results of a survey are displayed in the circle graph. What conclusions can you make about the data?

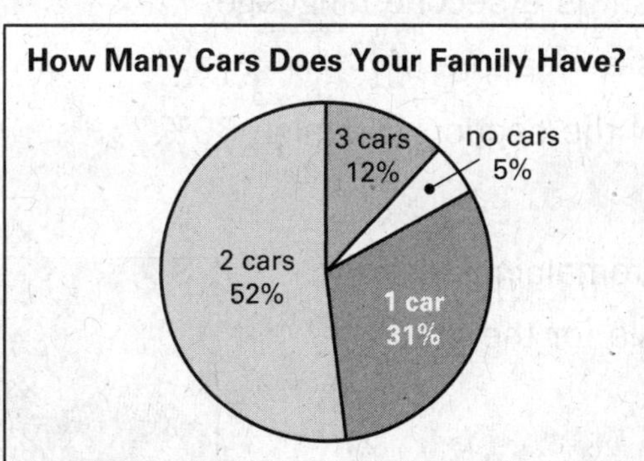

Solution

You can make conclusions about the data in the circle graph above.

- The largest section in the circle graph is labeled "   ." So, this is how many cars most families have.

- More families have "3 cars" than have "   cars".

Second Language The table shows the results of a survey that asked students what second language they speak. Display the data in a circle graph.

Language	Percent
Spanish	30%
Vietnamese	25%
Portuguese	5%
None	40%

Solution

1. Find the angle measure of each section.

Spanish

30% of 360° =

=

Vietnamese

25% of 360° =

=

Portuguese

5% of 360° =

=

None

40% of 360° =

=

2. Draw a circle using a compass.

3. Use a protractor to draw the angle for Spanish as a second language, which has a measure of   .
Then label the section "Spanish 30%."

4. Draw the remaining sections.

5. Write a title for the graph.

Need help using a compass? See page 700 of your textbook.

1. Can you determine from the circle graph the number of families that have three cars? Explain your reasoning.

2. The table shows the results of a survey that asked students to name their favorite pet. Display the data in a circle graph.

Pet	Percent
Dog	45%
Cat	30%
Rodent	15%
Amphibian	10%

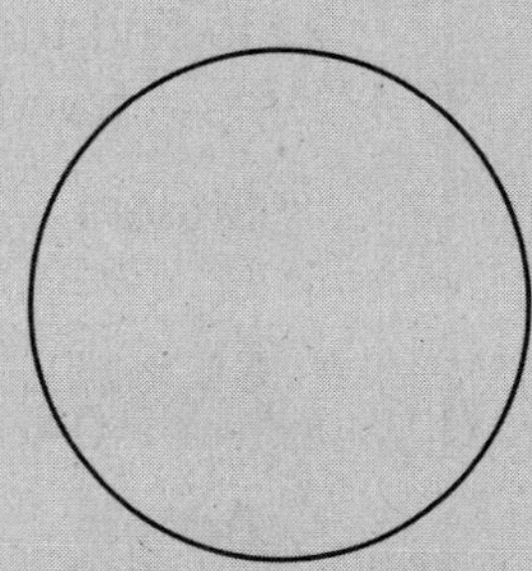

The table shows the results of a survey that asked people their favorite type of television show. Display the data in a circle graph.

Show	Sitcom	Drama	Cartoon	News
People	30	9	6	15

Solution

1. Find the total number of people surveyed.

$$30 + 9 + 6 + 15 = \boxed{}$$

2. To find the angle measure of each section, write each group of people as a fraction of all the people and multiply by $360°$.

Sitcom

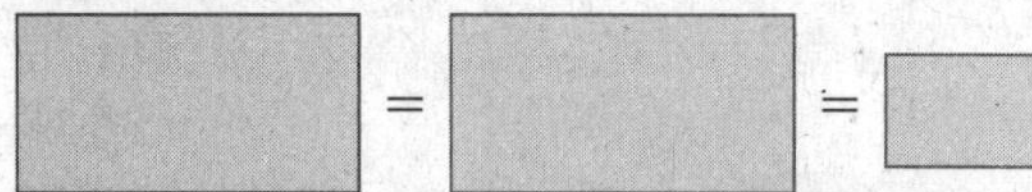

Drama

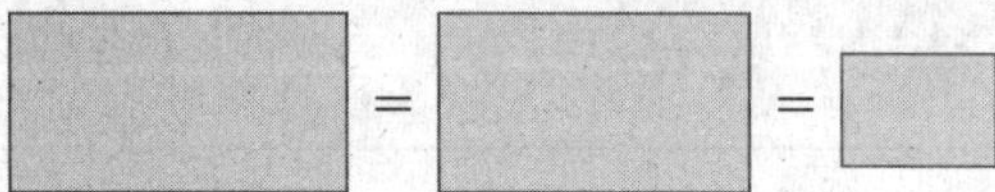

Cartoon

News

3. Draw and label the circle graph.

Percent of Increase and Decrease

Goal: Find a percent of change in a quantity.

Vocabulary

Percent of change:

Percent of increase:

Percent of decrease:

EXAMPLE 1 **Finding a Percent of Increase**

What is the percent of increase from 5 to 7?

$p\% = \dfrac{\text{Amount of increase}}{\text{Original amount}}$ Write percent of increase formula.

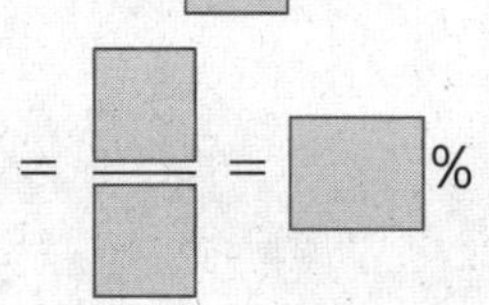   Substitute amount of increase and original amount.

$= \dfrac{\square}{\square} = \square\,\%$ Subtract. Then express fraction as a percent.

Answer: The percent of increase is $\square$%.

Need help with common percents? See pages 416 and 421 of your textbook.

Finding a Percent of Decrease

What is the percent of decrease from 30 to 25?

In Example 2, note that decreasing from 30 to 25 is about the same as decreasing from 30 to 24. Because $\frac{30-24}{30} = \frac{1}{5} = 20\%$, the answer is reasonable.

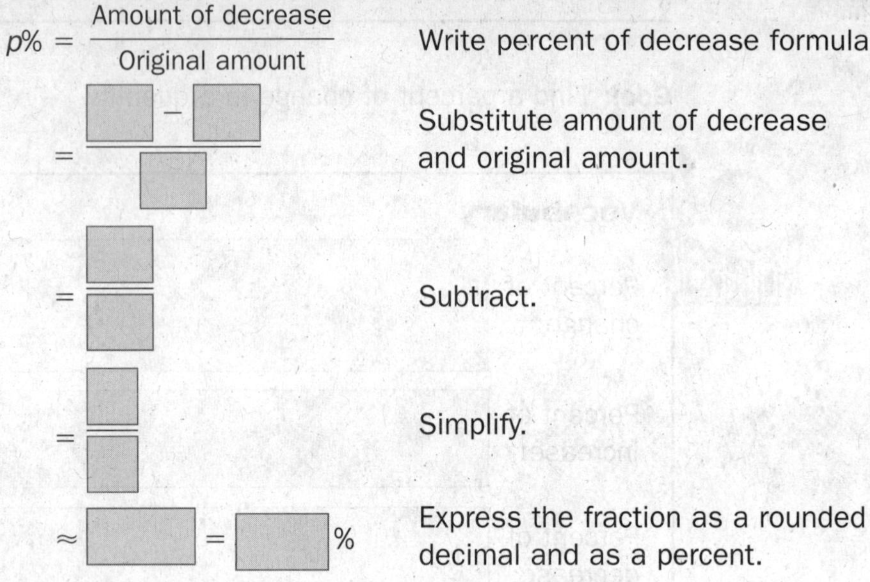

$$p\% = \frac{\text{Amount of decrease}}{\text{Original amount}}$$ Write percent of decrease formula.

$$= \frac{\boxed{} - \boxed{}}{\boxed{}}$$ Substitute amount of decrease and original amount.

$$= \frac{\boxed{}}{\boxed{}}$$ Subtract.

$$= \frac{\boxed{}}{\boxed{}}$$ Simplify.

$$\approx \boxed{} = \boxed{}\%$$ Express the fraction as a rounded decimal and as a percent.

Answer: The percent of decrease is about $\boxed{}$ %.

Your turn now Identify the percent of change as an *increase* or a *decrease*. Then find the percent of change. Use estimation to check your answer.

1. Original: 10 New: 12	**2.** Original: 125 New: 25	**3.** Original: 250 New: 150

Salary An employee's salary recently increased 15% from $28,000 per year. How much does the employee earn now?

Solution

Find the amount of increase, 15% of $28,000.

$$\text{Increase} = 15\% \times 28,000$$

$$= \boxed{} \qquad \text{Write percent as a decimal.}$$

$$= \boxed{} \qquad \text{Multiply.}$$

Add the increase to the original amount.

$$\text{New amount} = \text{Original amount} + \text{Increase}$$

$$= \boxed{} + \boxed{} = \boxed{}$$

Answer: The new salary is $\boxed{}$.

Discounts, Markups, Sales Tax, and Tips

Goal: Find discounts, markups, sales tax, and tips.

EXAMPLE 1 Finding a Sale Price

Music You buy a CD that is 40% off the original price of $12. What is the sale price?

Solution

1. Find the amount of the discount.

Discount = 40% of $12

= ☐   Write 40% as a decimal.

= ☐   Multiply.

2. Subtract the discount from the original price.

Sale Price = Original price − Discount

= ☐ − ☐ = ☐

Answer: The sale price is $☐.

EXAMPLE 2 Finding a Retail Price

Furniture A furniture store that sells sofas buys them from a manufacturer at a wholesale price of $350. The store's markup is 200%. What is the retail price of the sofa?

1. Find the amount of the markup.

Markup = 200% of $350

= ☐   Write 200% as a decimal.

= ☐   Multiply.

2. Add the markup to the wholesale price.

Retail Price = Wholesale price + Markup

= ☐ + ☐ = ☐

Answer: The retail price is $☐.

1. A store is selling all shoes at 20% off the original price. What is the sale price of a pair of shoes originally priced at $65?

2. A store buys software from a manufacturer at a wholesale price of $72. The store's markup is 75%. What is the retail price?

EXAMPLE 3   **Finding Sales Tax and Tip**

Diner At a diner, Maddie orders a meal that costs $8. She leaves a 15% tip. The sales tax is 6%. What is the total cost of the meal?

Solution

1. Find the tip.   15% of $8 =   =

2. Find the sales tax.   6% of $8 =   =

3. Add the food bill, tip, and sales tax.   =

Answer: The total cost of the meal is $.

Simple Interest

Goal: Calculate simple interest.

Vocabulary

Interest:

Principal:

Simple interest:

Annual interest rate:

Balance:

Simple Interest

Words Simple interest I is the product of the [ ] P, the [ ] r written as a decimal, and the [ ] t in years.

Algebra [ ]

Numbers A $1000 deposit earns 5% simple annual interest for 3 years.

$$I = (\quad)(\quad)(\quad) = \$\quad$$

 Finding a Balance

Carol deposits $30 in a bank account that pays 5% simple annual interest. What will be the total amount that she has in the account after 2 years?

$I = Prt$ Write simple interest formula.

$= (\quad)(\quad)(\quad)$ Substitute ___ for P, ___ for r, and ___ for t.

$= \quad$ Multiply.

To find the balance, add the interest to the principal.

Answer: Carol will have $30 + $___ , or $___ in her account.

 Finding an Interest Rate

You deposit $750 into an 8 month certificate of deposit. After 8 months the balance is $770. Find the simple annual interest rate.

To find the interest, subtract the principal from the balance.

$\quad - \quad = \quad$

Then use the simple interest formula and solve for r.

$I = Prt$ Write simple interest formula.

$\quad = (\quad)(\quad)\left(\quad\right)$ Substitute ___ for I, ___ for P, and $\frac{8}{12}$ for t.

$\quad = \quad$ Multiply.

$\dfrac{\quad}{\quad} = \dfrac{\quad}{\quad}$ Divide each side by ___.

$\quad = \quad$ Simplify.

$\quad \% = \quad$ Write decimal as a percent.

Answer: The simple annual interest rate is ___ %.

WATCH OUT!

When using the simple interest formula, make sure you write the number of months as a fraction of a year. For example, 7 months would be written as $\frac{7}{12}$.

1. If you deposit $1500 into an account that earns 5% simple annual interest, what will the account's balance be after 4 months?

2. You deposit $800 into a 9 month certificate of deposit. After 9 months the balance is $848. Find the simple annual interest rate.

EXAMPLE 3 **Finding an Amount of Time**

Mario borrows $500 from a bank to pay for car repairs. His simple annual interest rate is 10%. Mario pays a total of $100 in interest on the loan. How long did Mario have the loan?

$$I = Prt$$ Write simple interest formula.

$$\boxed{} = \left(\boxed{}\right)\left(\boxed{}\right)\boxed{}$$ Substitute $\boxed{}$ for I, $\boxed{}$ for and $\boxed{}$ for r.

$$\boxed{} = \boxed{}$$ Multiply.

$$\frac{\boxed{}}{\boxed{}} = \frac{\boxed{}}{\boxed{}}$$ Divide each side by $\boxed{}$.

$$\boxed{} = \boxed{}$$ Simplify.

Answer: Mario had the loan for $\boxed{}$.

Words to Review

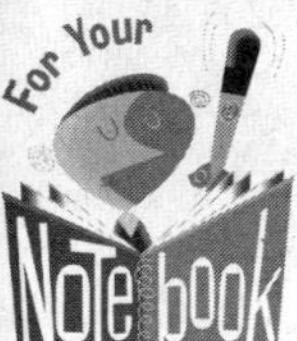

Give an example of the vocabulary word.

Percent

Circle graph

Ray

Angle

Vertex

Degrees

Percent of change

Percent of increase

Percent of decrease

Interest

Principal

Simple interest

Annual interest rate

Balance

Review your notes and Chapter 9 by using the Chapter Review on pages 460–461 of your textbook.

Angles

Goal: Classify angles by their measures.

Vocabulary

Acute angle:

Right angle:

Obtuse angle:

Straight angle:

Complementary:

Supplementary:

A quick way to check the size of an angle is to use the corner of a piece of paper. Because the corner forms a right angle, it is easy to determine whether the angle's measure is less than 90°, exactly 90°, or greater than 90°.

EXAMPLE 1 **Classifying an Angle**

Estimate to classify the angle as *acute*, *right*, *obtuse*, or *straight*.

a.

G

b.

D

Solution

a. Because $m\angle G$ is ______________ , $\angle G$ is ______ .

b. Because $m\angle D$ is ____________ , $\angle D$ is ______ .

Tell whether the angles are *complementary*, *supplementary*, or *neither*.

a.
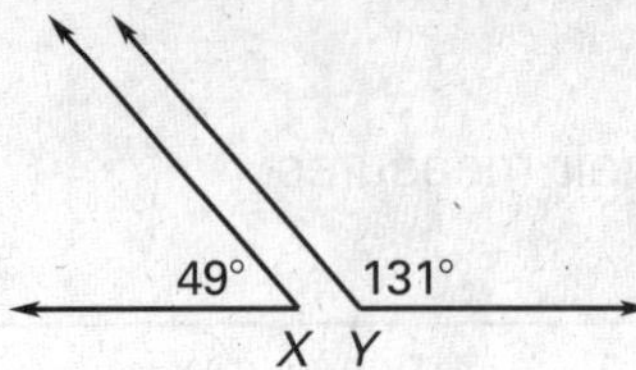

b.
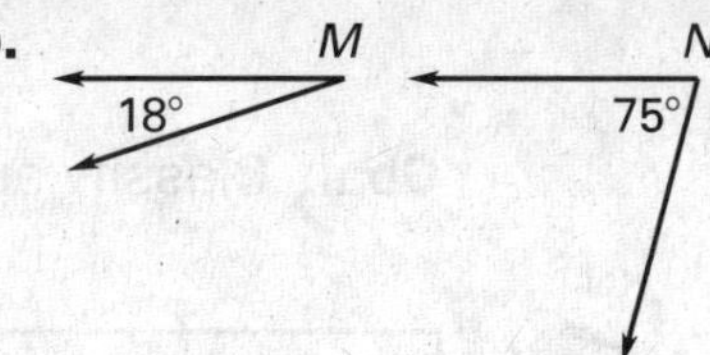

The angle above can be named in several ways: $\angle ABC$, $\angle CBA$, $\angle B$, and $\angle 1$. Notice that the vertex must be in the middle or the only letter used in the name of the angle.

Solution

a. $m\angle X + m\angle Y = \boxed{} + \boxed{} = \boxed{}$. So, $\angle X$ and $\angle Y$ are

$\boxed{}$.

b. $m\angle M + m\angle N = \boxed{} + \boxed{} = \boxed{}$. So, $\angle M$ and $\angle N$ are

$\boxed{}$.

Your turn now Classify the angle as *acute*, *obtuse*, *right*, or *straight*.

1. $m\angle D = 18°$	2. $m\angle V = 90°$	3. $m\angle S = 180°$	4. $m\angle J = 150°$

5. Give the measures of two angles that are complementary.

EXAMPLE 3 **Using Supplementary Angles**

For the two skateboard ramps at the right, $\angle 1$ and $\angle 2$ are complementary. If $m\angle 1 = 38°$, find $m\angle 2$.

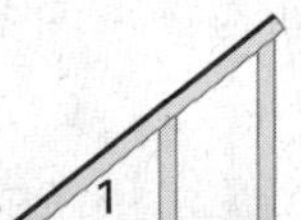
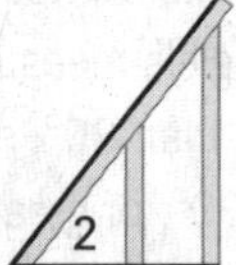
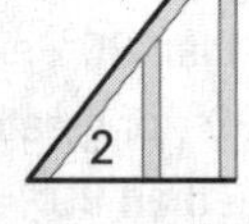

$m\angle 1 + m\angle 2 = \boxed{}$ Definition of $\boxed{}$ angles

$\boxed{} + m\angle 2 = \boxed{}$ Substitute $\boxed{}$ for $m\angle 1$.

$m\angle 2 = \boxed{}$ Subtract $\boxed{}$ from each side.

 Use the definitions of complementary and supplementary angles to find the measure of the angle.

6. $\angle P$ and $\angle Q$ are supplementary. If $m\angle P = 98°$, find $m\angle Q$.

7. $\angle T$ and $\angle U$ are complementary. If $m\angle T = 16°$, find $m\angle U$.

Special Pairs of Angles

Goal: Identify special pairs of angles and types of lines.

Vocabulary

Adjacent angles:

Vertical angles:

Congruent angles:

Plane:

Parallel lines:

Intersecting lines:

Perpendicular lines:

Corresponding angles:

EXAMPLE 1 Identifying Adjacent Angles

Name all pairs of adjacent, supplementary angles.

Adjacent, supplementary angles:

Given that $m\angle 1 = 68°$, find $m\angle 3$.

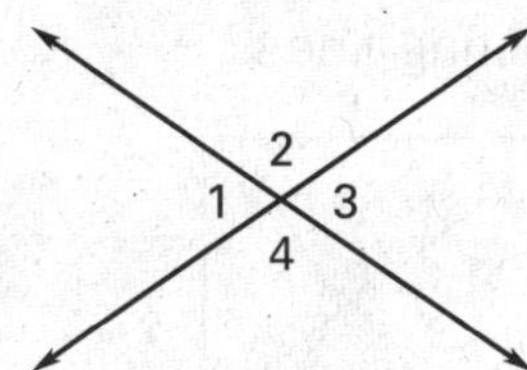

Because ☐ and $\angle 3$ are ☐ angles, they are ☐.

So, $m\angle 3 =$ ☐ $=$ ☐.

Your turn now   **Refer to the diagram in Example 2.**

1. Name all pairs of adjacent, supplementary angles.

2. Given that $m\angle 1 = 68°$, find $m\angle 2$.

3. Use your answer from Exercise 2 to find $m\angle 4$.

Maps The map shows a section of Houston. Streets shown on maps often appear to form parallel or intersecting lines.

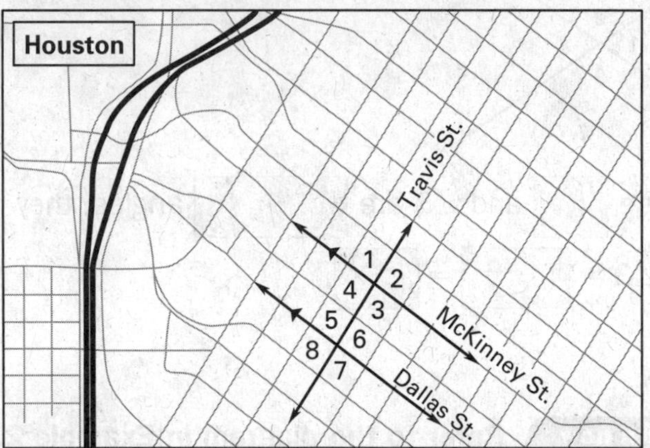

Arrowheads are used to indicate that lines are parallel.

a. Name two streets that are parallel and two streets that intersect.

b. If $m\angle 1 = 85°$, find $m\angle 7$.

Solution

a. [   ] is parallel to [   ]. [   ] intersects both [   ] and [   ].

b. Because $\angle$[ ] and $\angle$[ ] are [   ] angles, [   ] = [   ] = [   ]. Because McKinney Street and Dallas Stre[et] are [   ] lines, $\angle$[ ] and $\angle$[ ] are [   ] angles. So, [   ] = [   ] = [   ].

Your turn now   Refer to the map in Example 3.

4. Find $m\angle 2$ and $m\angle 6$. Explain your reasoning.

Triangles

Goal: Classify triangles.

Vocabulary

Acute triangle:

Right triangle:

Obtuse triangle:

Congruent sides:

Equilateral triangle:

Isosceles triangle:

Scalene triangle:

EXAMPLE 1 **Finding an Angle Measure in a Triangle**

Triangles are named by their *vertices*. The vertices of the triangle in Example 1 are *L, M,* and *N,* so the triangle can be named with the notation △*LMN.* This notation is read "triangle *LMN.*"

Find the value of *x* in the triangle shown.

$x° + \boxed{}° + \boxed{}° = \boxed{}°$ Sum of angle measures in a triangle is $\boxed{}$.

$x + \boxed{} = \boxed{}$ Add $\boxed{}$ and $\boxed{}$.

$x = \boxed{}$ Subtract $\boxed{}$ from each side.

Answer: The value of *x* is $\boxed{}$.

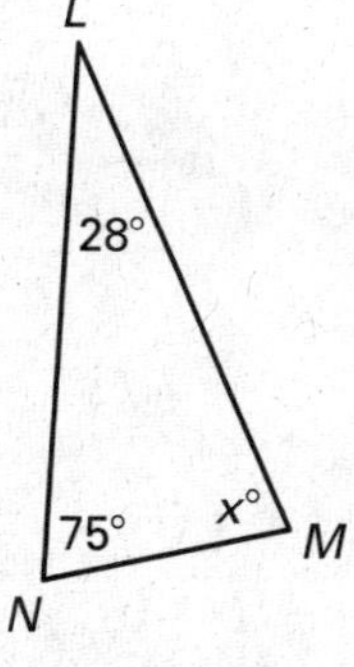

 Finding the Measure of an Exterior Angle

Find the value of _y_ in the figure.

To find the value of _y_, use the fact that adjacent interior and exterior angles of a triangle are supplementary.

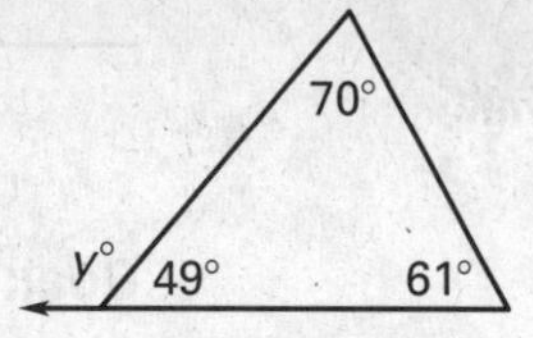

$y° +$ ▢ $° =$ ▢ $°$ Definition of ▢ angles

$y =$ ▢   Subtract ▢ from each side.

Answer: The value of _y_ is ▢ .

  Find the value of _y_.

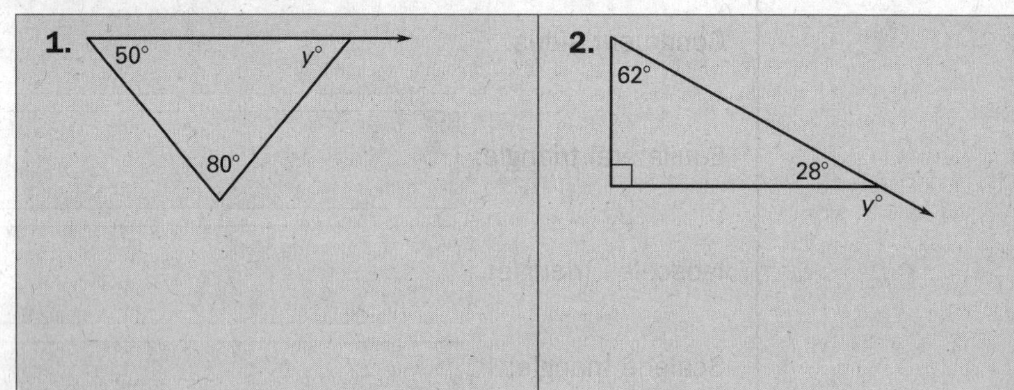

 Classifying a Triangle by Angle Measures

Classify the triangle by its angle measures.

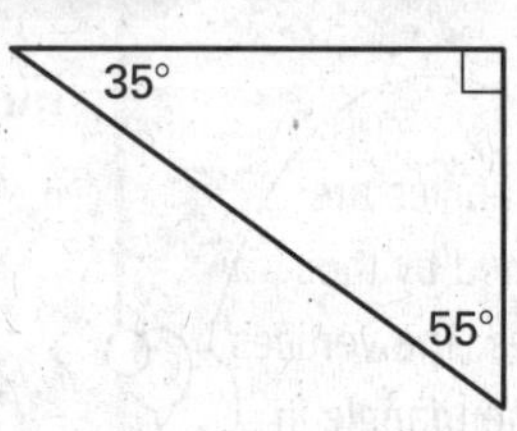

The triangle has ▢ angle, so it is a(n) ▢ triangle.

 Classifying a Triangle by Side Lengths

Classify the triangle by the lengths of its sides.

Two sides of the triangle are ▢ ,

so the triangle is ▢ .

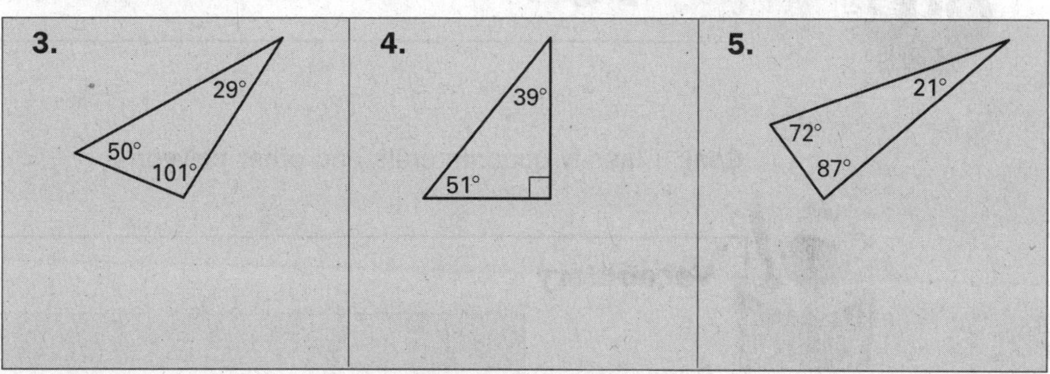

Classify the triangle by the lengths of its sides.

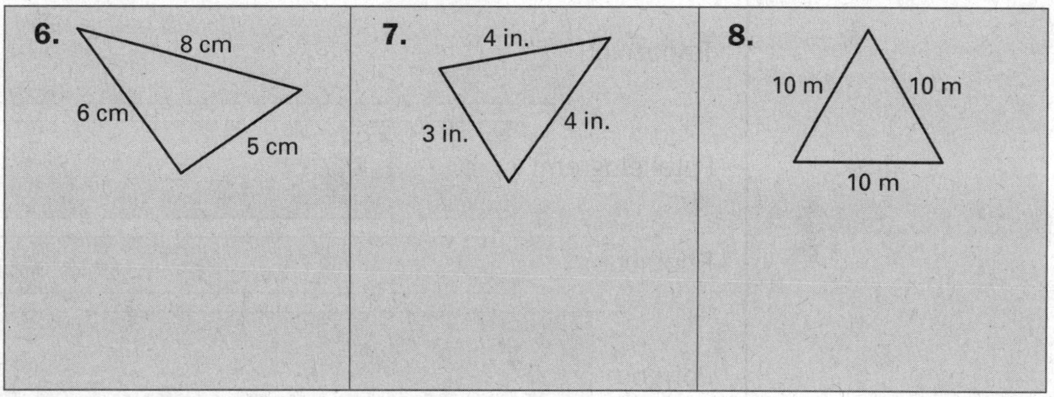

Polygons

Goal: Classify quadrilaterals and other polygons.

Vocabulary

Quadrilateral:

Trapezoid:

Parallelogram:

Rhombus:

Polygon:

Pentagon:

Hexagon:

Heptagon:

Octagon:

Regular polygon:

EXAMPLE 1 Classifying a Quadrilateral

Sketch and classify a quadrilateral with opposite sides parallel, and all four sides of length 2 centimeters.

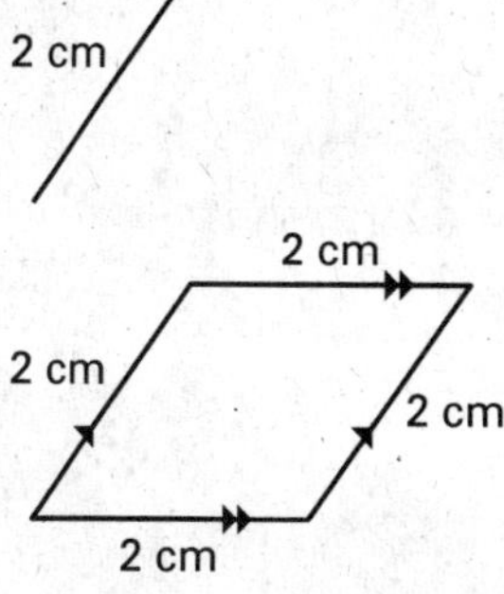

1. Draw two sides with a length of 2 centimeters. The angle between the two sides does not matter, except that it cannot be 0° or 180°.

2. Draw sides parallel to the first two sides to complete the figure.

Answer: The figure is a ▭ .

Your turn now Sketch and classify the quadrilateral described.

1. A quadrilateral with 4 right angles, 4 congruent sides of length 3 centimeters, and both pairs of opposite sides parallel.

EXAMPLE 2 Classifying Polygons

Tell whether the figure is a polygon. If it is, classify it. If it is not, explain why not.

a. 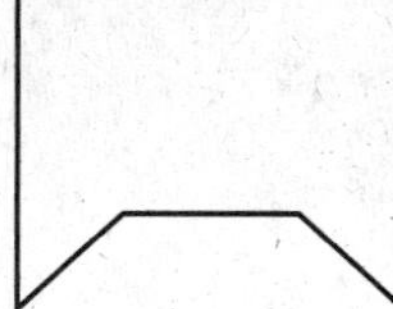

b. 

Solution

a.

b.

Your turn now Tell whether the figure is a polygon. If it is, classify it. If it is not, explain why not.

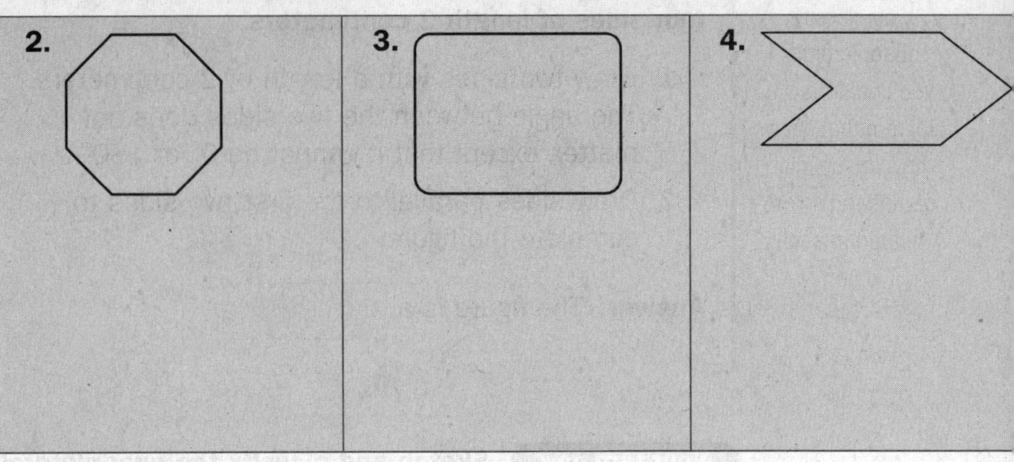

2.   **3.**   **4.**

EXAMPLE 3 Using a Regular Polygon

The hexagon shown is a regular hexagon. Find the perimeter of the hexagon. Then find the sum of the angle measures of the hexagon.

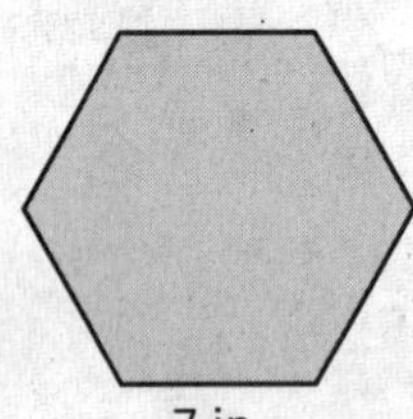

7 in.

WATCH OUT!

Just because a polygon has sides that are all congruent does not necessarily mean that it is a regular polygon. All angles must also be congruent.

1. A regular hexagon has ☐ sides of equal length,

so the perimeter of the hexagon is ☐(☐) = ☐ inches.

2. A hexagon can be divided into ☐ triangles. The sum of the angle

measures in a triangle is ☐ , so the sum of the angle measures

in any hexagon is ☐ + ☐ + ☐ + ☐ = ☐ .

Similar and Congruent Polygons

Goal: Use properties of similar and congruent polygons.

Vocabulary

Similar polygons:

Congruent polygons:

Similar Polygons	**Congruent Polygons**
$\triangle LMN \sim \triangle PQR$	$\triangle ABC \cong \triangle DEF$

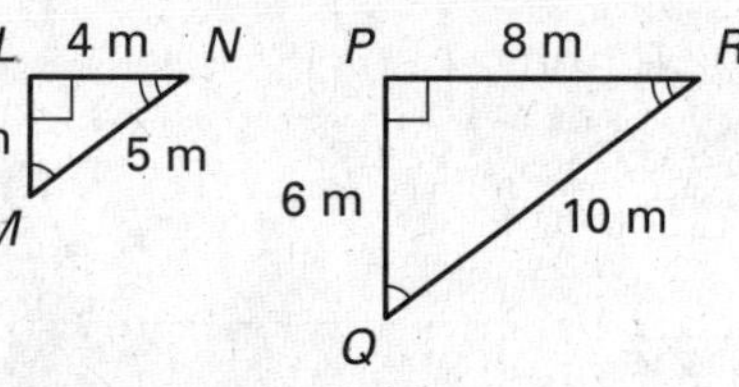

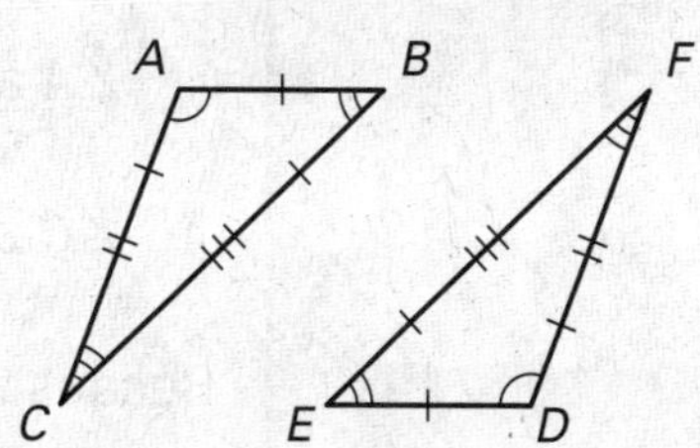

Similar Polygons	**Congruent Polygons**
Angles Corresponding angles are congruent:	**Angles** Corresponding angles are congruent:
$\angle L \cong \angle \boxed{}$, $\angle M \cong \angle \boxed{}$, and $\angle N \cong \angle \boxed{}$	$\angle A \cong \angle \boxed{}$, $\angle B \cong \angle \boxed{}$, and $\angle C \cong \angle \boxed{}$
Sides Ratios of lengths of corresponding sides are equal:	**Sides** Corresponding sides are congruent:
$\dfrac{LM}{\boxed{}} = \dfrac{MN}{\boxed{}} = \dfrac{LN}{\boxed{}}$	$\overline{AB} \cong \boxed{}$, $\overline{AC} \cong \boxed{}$, and $\overline{BC} \cong \boxed{}$

Finding Measures of Congruent Polygons

WATCH OUT!
When naming congruent or similar polygons, list the letters for the corresponding vertices in the same order. For instance, in Example 1, you cannot write $ABCD \cong XYZW$ because $\angle A$ and $\angle X$ are not corresponding angles.

Given that $ABCD \cong WXYZ$, name the corresponding sides and corresponding angles. Then find XY.

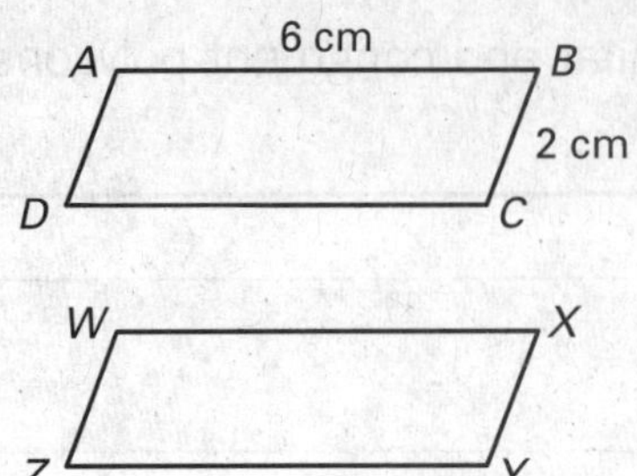

Solution

Corresponding Sides:

$\overline{AB}$ and ⬜ , $\overline{BC}$ and ⬜ ,

$\overline{CD}$ and ⬜ , $\overline{AD}$ and ⬜

Corresponding Angles:

$\angle A$ and $\angle$⬜ , $\angle B$ and $\angle$⬜ ,

$\angle C$ and $\angle$⬜ , $\angle D$ and $\angle$⬜

Because ⬜ and $\overline{XY}$ are ⬜ sides,

$\overline{XY}$ = ⬜ = ⬜ centimeters.

Your turn now Use the fact that $\triangle ABC \cong \triangle LMN$.

1. Name the corresponding sides and corresponding angles.

Corresponding Sides:

Corresponding Angles:

2. Find the unknown angle measures.

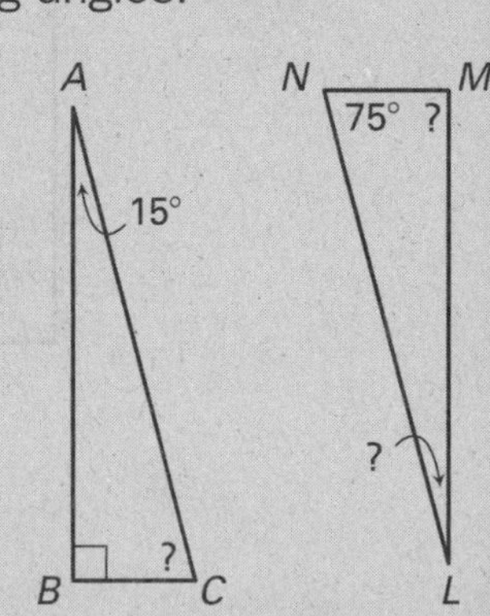

Given that $\triangle ABC \sim \triangle DEF$, find the ratio of the lengths of the corresponding sides of $\triangle ABC$ to $\triangle DEF$.

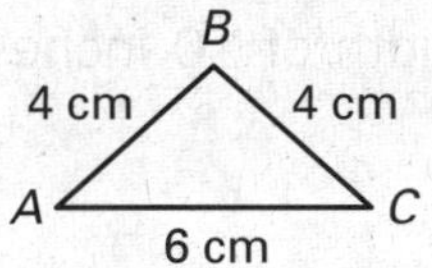

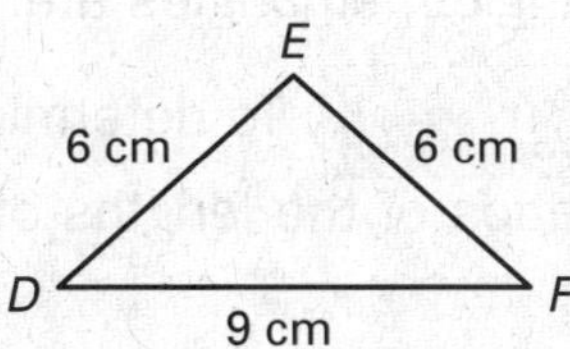

The ratios $\frac{DE}{AB}$, $\frac{EF}{BC}$, and $\frac{DF}{AC}$ are the ratios for the lengths of the corresponding sides of $\triangle DEF$ to $\triangle ABC$ in Example 2. Using these ratios, the ratio of the lengths of the corresponding sides is $\frac{3}{2}$.

Write the ratio for each pair of corresponding sides. Then substitute the lengths of the sides and simplify each ratio.

$$\frac{AB}{DE} = \boxed{} = \boxed{}$$

$$\frac{BC}{EF} = \boxed{} = \boxed{}$$

$$\frac{AC}{DF} = \boxed{} = \boxed{}$$

Answer: The ratio of the lengths of the corresponding sides is $\boxed{}$.

 Checking for Similarity

Landscape Design A landscape architect is planning a memorial garden at a local park. The rectangular garden will have a length of 18 feet and a width of 15 feet. A rectangular blueprint of the garden has a length of 12 inches and a width of 10 inches. Are the garden and the blueprint similar figures?

Solution

Because both figures are rectangles, all angles are [ ] angles, so corresponding angles are [ ]. To determine whether the figures are similar, see if the ratios of the lengths of the corresponding sides are [ ].

$$\frac{\text{Length of garden}}{\text{Length of } [\quad]} \overset{?}{=} \frac{\text{Width of } [\quad]}{\text{Width of } [\quad]}$$

Write ratios for lengths of corresponding sides

$$\frac{[\quad]}{[\quad]} \overset{?}{=} \frac{[\quad]}{[\quad]}$$

Substitute.

$$\frac{[\quad]}{[\quad]} \overset{?}{=} \frac{[\quad]}{[\quad]}$$

Convert all units to inches.

$$[\quad]$$

Simplify.

Answer: The corresponding angles [ ] and the ratios of the lengths of the corresponding sides [ ], so the figures [ ].

Using Proportions with Similar Polygons

Goal: Use similar triangles to find lengths indirectly.

EXAMPLE 1 Finding an Unknown Length

Quadrilaterals *LMNO* and *PQRS* are similar. Find *MN*.

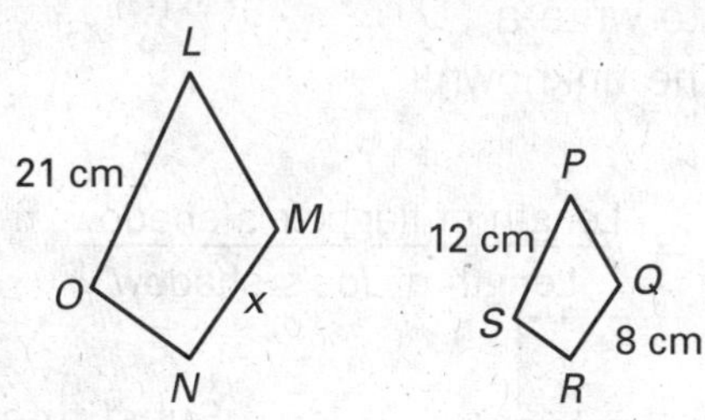

Need help writing and solving proportions? See pages 387 and 394 of your textbook.

Solution

Use the ratios of the lengths of corresponding sides to write a proportion involving the unknown length.

$$\frac{LO}{\boxed{}} = \frac{MN}{\boxed{}}$$ Write proportion involving *MN*.

$$\frac{\boxed{}}{\boxed{}} = \frac{x}{\boxed{}}$$ Substitute known values.

$$\boxed{} = \boxed{}$$ Cross products property

$$\boxed{} = \boxed{}$$ Divide each side by $\boxed{}$.

Answer: The length of $\overline{MN}$ is $\boxed{}$ centimeters.

Your turn now Find the unknown length *x* given that the polygons are similar.

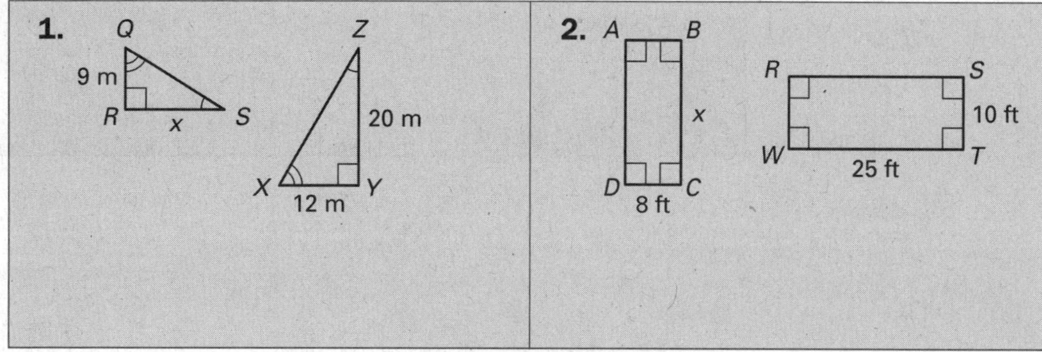

 Making an Indirect Measurement

Flagpole A flagpole casts a shadow that is 25 feet long. Joe is 4 feet tall and casts a shadow that is 5 feet long. How tall is the flagpole?

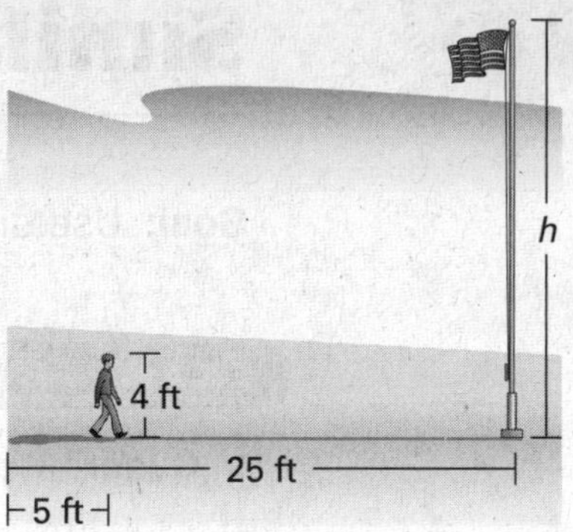

Solution

You can use indirect measurement to find the height of the flagpole. Use the ratios of the lengths of the corresponding parts to write a proportion involving the unknown height h.

$$\frac{\text{Height of flagpole}}{\text{Joe's height}} = \frac{\text{Length of flagpole's shadow}}{\text{Length of Joe's shadow}}$$

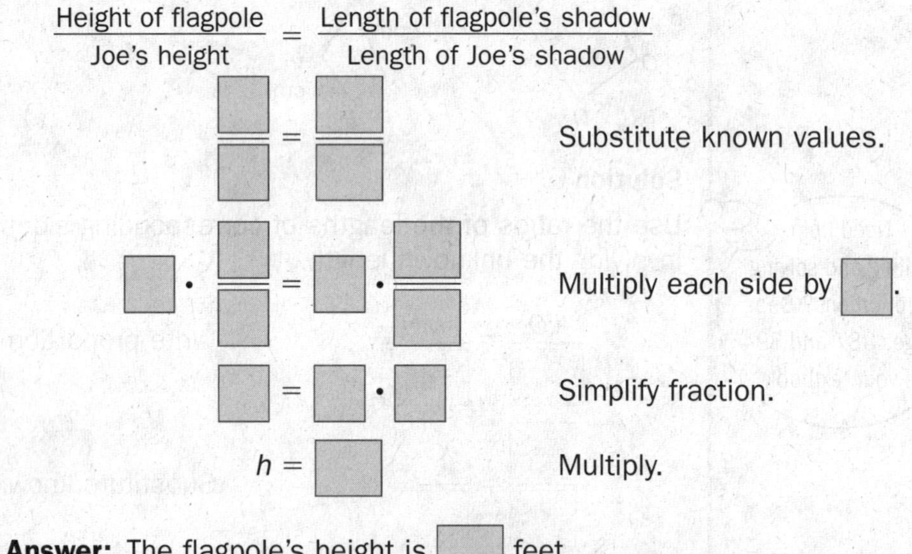

$$\frac{\boxed{}}{\boxed{}} = \frac{\boxed{}}{\boxed{}}$$ Substitute known values.

$$\boxed{} \cdot \frac{\boxed{}}{\boxed{}} = \boxed{} \cdot \frac{\boxed{}}{\boxed{}}$$ Multiply each side by $\boxed{}$.

$$\boxed{} = \boxed{} \cdot \boxed{}$$ Simplify fraction.

$$h = \boxed{}$$ Multiply.

Answer: The flagpole's height is $\boxed{}$ feet.

Your turn now   **Use indirect measurement to solve the problem.**

3. The shadow cast by a radio tower is 60 feet long. At the same time, the shadow cast by a 5-foot tall pole is 15 feet long. How tall is the radio tower?

Transformations and Symmetry

Goal: Identify transformations and symmetry in figures.

Vocabulary

Transformation:

Image:

Translation:

Reflection:

Line of reflection:

Rotation:

Center of rotation:

Angle of rotation:

Line symmetry:

Line of symmetry:

Rotational symmetry:

EXAMPLE 1 Identifying a Translation

Tell whether the dashed figure is a translation of the solid figure. Explain your reasoning.

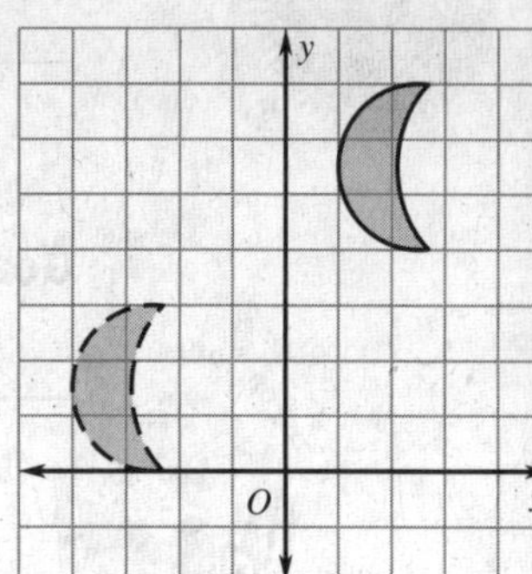

EXAMPLE 2 Identifying a Reflection

Tell whether the dashed figure is a reflection of the solid figure. If it is, identify the line of reflection.

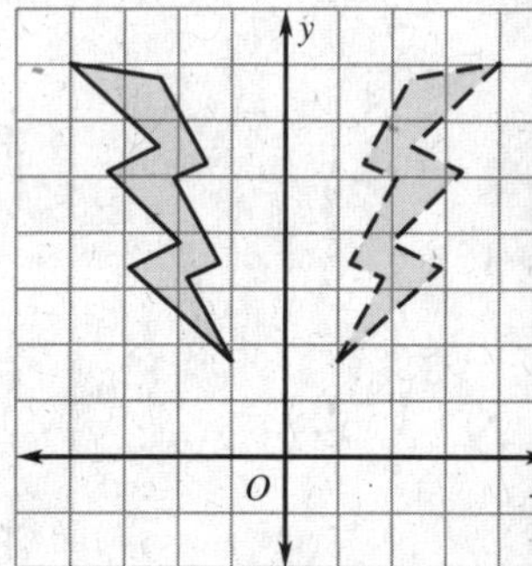

EXAMPLE 3 Identifying a Rotation

Tell whether the dashed figure is a rotation of the solid figure. If it is, give the angle and direction of rotation.

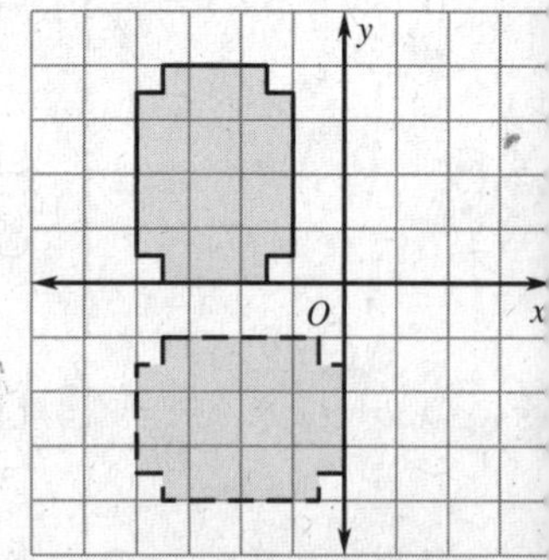

 Identify the transformation from the solid figure to the dashed figure. If it is a reflection, identify the line of reflection. If it is a rotation, give the angle and direction of rotation.

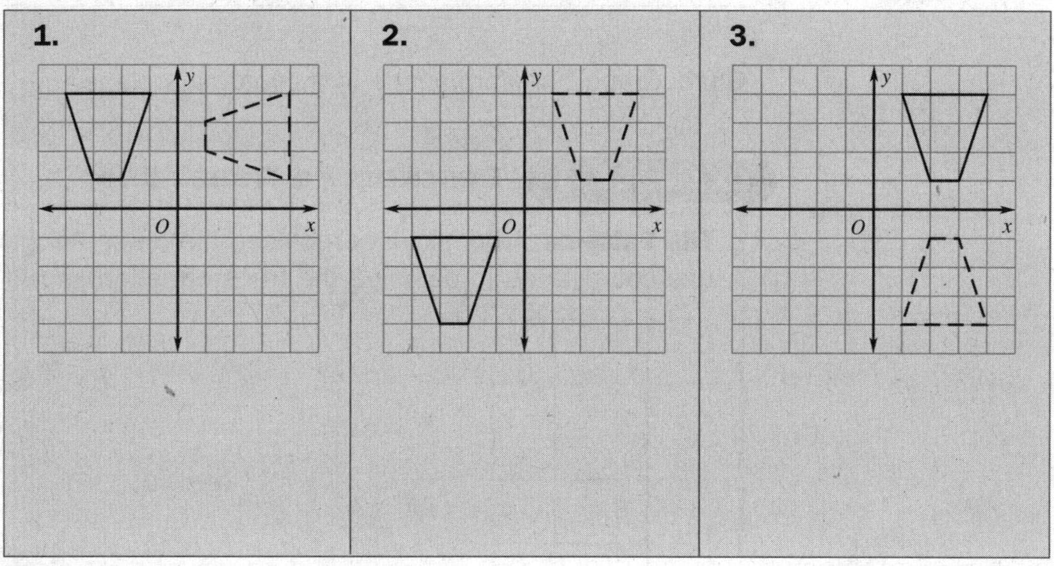

EXAMPLE 4 Identifying Symmetry

Tell whether a regular pentagon has (a) line symmetry and (b) rotational symmetry.

a. A regular pentagon [   ]. There are [ ] lines of symmetry.

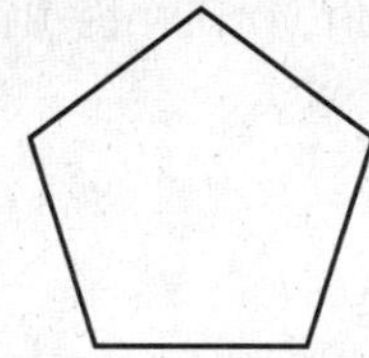

b. A regular pentagon [   ]. A turn of 72° or 144° clockwise (or counterclockwise) produces an image that fits exactly on the original figure.

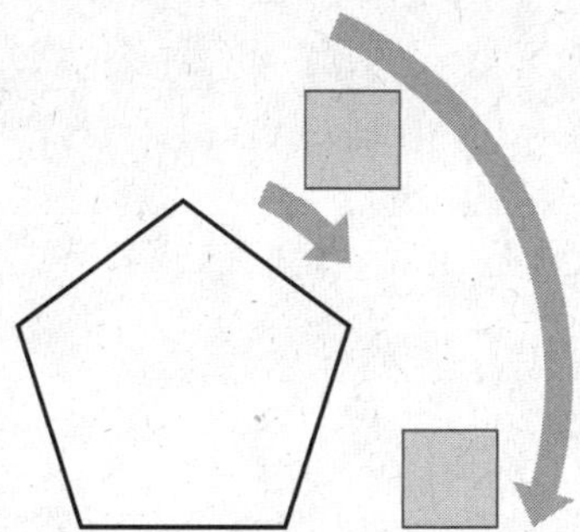

Transformations in the Coordinate Plane

Goal: Graph transformations in a coordinate plane.

EXAMPLE 1 **Describing a Translation**

Tile Patterns A homeowner replaced the tile in her bathroom. How can you use coordinates to describe the transformation shown?

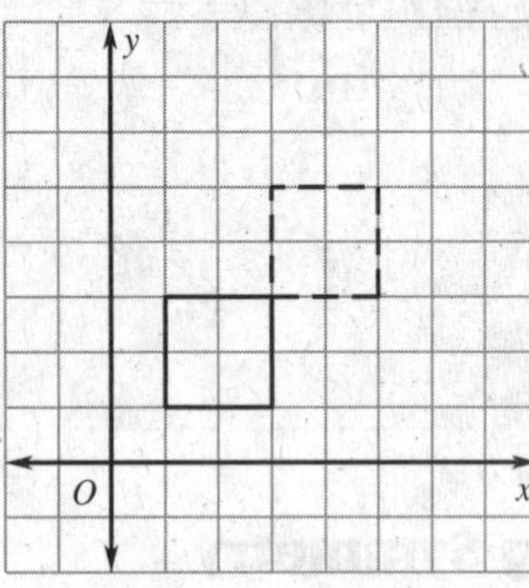

Solution

You can use coordinate notation to describe the translation shown above. Each point on the original figure is moved [   ] and [   ].

Answer: In coordinate notation you write this translation as:

$$(x, y) \rightarrow \left(\boxed{}, \boxed{} \right)$$

Your turn now Describe the translation using coordinate notation.

1. A figure is moved 3 units to the left and 1 unit up.

2. A figure is moved 5 units down.

 Translating a Figure

Draw triangle *FGH* with vertices F(−4, 4), G(−2, 6), and H(−1, 3). Then find the coordinates of the vertices of the image after the translation (*x*, *y*)→(*x* + 3, *y* − 4), and draw the image.

For each vertex of the original figure, [ ] to the *x*-coordinate and [ ] from the *y*-coordinate.

Original **Image**

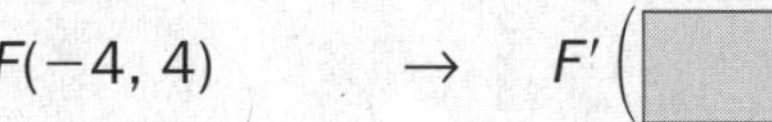

$F(-4, 4)$ → $F'\left(\boxed{}, \boxed{}\right)$

$G(-2, 6)$ → $G'\left(\boxed{}, \boxed{}\right)$

$H(-1, 3)$ → $H'\left(\boxed{}, \boxed{}\right)$

> Each point on an image is labeled with a *prime*. The notation *J'* is read "*J* prime."

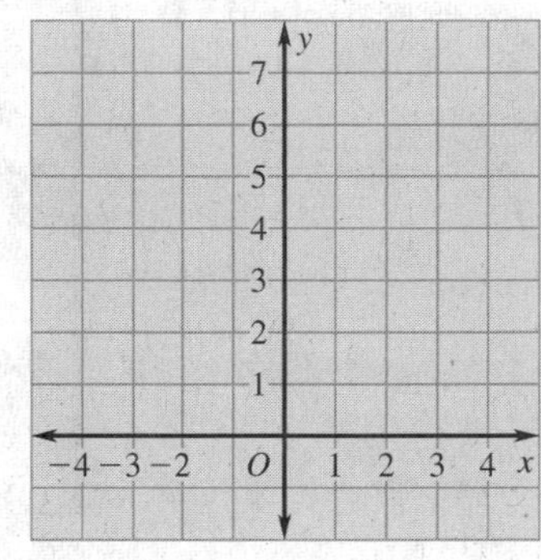

Each point on the original figure is translated [ ] and [ ]. The graph shows both figures.

 Complete the following exercise.

3. Draw quadrilateral *WXYZ* with vertices W(−1, 2), X(1, 2), Y(1, −1), and Z(0, −1). Then find the coordinates of the vertices of the image after the translation (*x*, *y*)→(*x* − 4, *y* + 2), and draw the image.

Original   Image

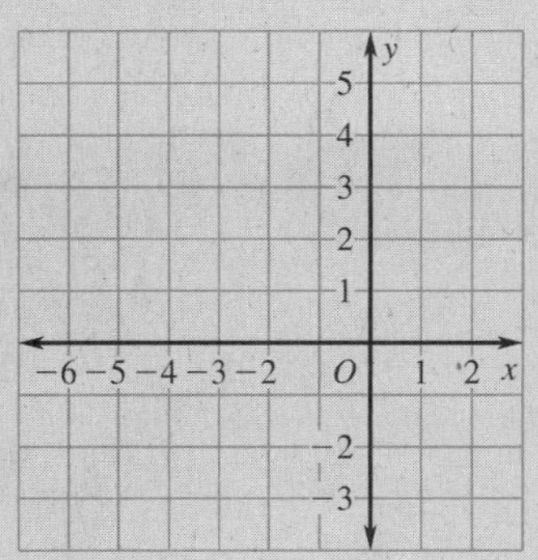

**Draw trapezoid *DEFG* with vertices *D*(3, 3), *E*(1, 4), *F*(1, 1), and
G(3, 1). Then find the coordinates of the vertices of the image
after a reflection in the *y*-axis, and draw the image.**

For each vertex of the original figure, multiply the ☐-coordinate by ☐

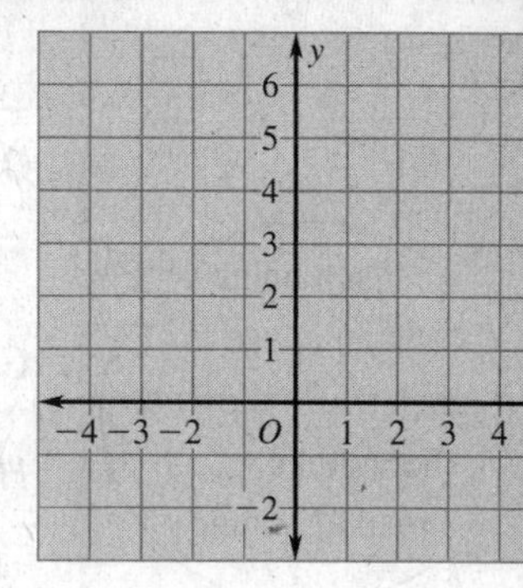

Original		Image
D(3, 3)	→	☐
E(1, 4)	→	☐
F(1, 1)	→	☐
G(3, 1)	→	☐

The graph shows both figures.

Words to Review

Give an example of the vocabulary word.

Acute angle

Right angle

Obtuse angle

Straight angle

Complementary

Supplementary

Adjacent angles

Vertical angles

Congruent angles

Plane

Parallel lines

Intersecting lines

Perpendicular lines

Corresponding angles

Acute triangle

Right triangle

Obtuse triangle

Congruent sides

Equilateral triangle

Isosceles triangle

Scalene triangle

Quadrilateral

Trapezoid

Parallelogram

Rhombus

Polygon

Pentagon

Hexagon

Heptagon

Octagon

Regular polygon

Similar polygons

Congruent polygons

Transformation

Image

Translation

Reflection

Line of reflection

Rotation

Center of rotation

Line symmetry

Line of symmetry

Angle of rotation

Rotational symmetry

Review your notes and Chapter 10 by using the Chapter Review on pages 526–527 of your textbook.

Square Roots

Goal: Evaluate expressions involving square roots.

Vocabulary

Square root:

Perfect square:

Radical expression:

EXAMPLE 1 **Finding Square Roots**

Find the two square roots of the number.

   a. 64   **b.** 100

Solution

  a. The square roots of 64 are $\boxed{}$ and $\boxed{}$ because $\boxed{}$ = 64

      and $\boxed{}$ = 64.

  b. The square roots of 100 are $\boxed{}$ and $\boxed{}$ because $\boxed{}$ = 100

      and $\boxed{}$ = 100.

EXAMPLE 2 **Evaluating Square Roots**

  a. $\sqrt{25} = \boxed{}$ because $\boxed{}$ = 25.

  b. You know that $\sqrt{4} = \boxed{}$ because $\boxed{}$ = 4. So, $-\sqrt{4} = \boxed{}$.

  c. $\sqrt{0} = \boxed{}$ because $\boxed{}$ = 0.

Flooring Pam has enough flooring to cover 196 square feet. If she lays the flooring on a square area, what is the side length of the largest square she can make?

Solution

$s = \sqrt{A}$ Write equation for side length of a square.

$= \boxed{}$ Substitute 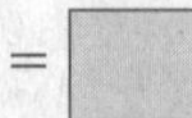 for A.

$= \boxed{}$ Evaluate square root.

Answer: The side length of the largest square Pam can make is $\boxed{}$

Your turn now   **Find the two square roots of the number.**

1. 16	**2.** 81	**3.** 121	**4.** 1

Evaluate the square root.

5. $\sqrt{9}$	**6.** $-\sqrt{9}$	**7.** $-\sqrt{25}$	**8.** $\sqrt{144}$

EXAMPLE 4 **Evaluating Radical Expressions**

Evaluate the expression when $z = 4$ and $m = -3$.

a. $\sqrt{21 + z}$ **b.** $\sqrt{z^2 + m^2}$

Need help with order of operations? See page 18 of your textbook.

Solution

a. $\sqrt{21 + z} = \boxed{}$ Substitute  for z.

$= \boxed{}$ Add.

$= \boxed{}$ Evaluate square root.

b. $\sqrt{z^2 + m^2} = $ ◻◻◻ Substitute ◻ for z and ◻ for m.

$= $ ◻◻ Evaluate powers.

$= $ ◻ Add.

$= $ ◻ Evaluate square root.

 Solving Equations Using Square Roots

Solve the equation.

  a. $x^2 = 100$ **b.** $g^2 - 4 = 45$

Solution

  a. $x^2 = 100$ Write original equation.

        ◻ $= \pm$ ◻◻   Use definition of square root.

        ◻ $= $ ◻◻   Evaluate square root.

  b. $g^2 - 4 = 45$ Write original equation.

    $g^2 - 4$ ◻ $= 45$ ◻   ◻ to each side.

        ◻ $= $ ◻   Simplify.

        ◻ $= $ ◻◻   Use definition of square root.

        ◻ $= $ ◻   Evaluate square root.

 Solve the equation.

9. $x^2 = 4$	**10.** $x^2 + 3 = 52$	**11.** $3x^2 = 75$	**12.** $x^2 - 15 = 1$

Approximating Square Roots

Goal: Approximate square roots of numbers.

Vocabulary

Irrational number:

Real number:

EXAMPLE 1 Approximating to a Whole Number

Approximate $\sqrt{18}$ to the nearest whole number.

Make a list of whole numbers that are perfect squares:
0, 1, 4, 9, 16, 25, ...

$\boxed{} < 18 < \boxed{}$ Identify perfect squares closest to 18.

$\boxed{} < \boxed{} < \boxed{}$ Take positive square root of each number.

$\boxed{} < \boxed{} < \boxed{}$ Evaluate square root of each perfect square.

Answer: Because 18 is closer to $\boxed{}$ than to $\boxed{}$, $\sqrt{18}$ is closer to

$\boxed{} = \boxed{}$. So, to the nearest whole number, $\sqrt{18} \approx \boxed{}$.

Approximate $\sqrt{18}$ to the nearest tenth.

You know from Example 1 that $\sqrt{18}$ is between ☐ and ☐. Make a list of squares. From the list, you can see that 18 is between ☐ and ☐. So, $\sqrt{18}$ is between ☐ and ☐.

Answer: Because 18 is closer to ☐ than to ☐, $\sqrt{18}$ is closer to ☐ = ☐. So, to the nearest tenth, $\sqrt{18} \approx$ ☐.

$4.0^2 =$ ☐

$4.1^2 =$ ☐

$4.2^2 =$ ☐

$4.3^2 =$ ☐

$4.4^2 =$ ☐

Once you find the approximation of a square root to the tenths' place, you can use the same method to find the approximation to the hundredths' place, thousandths' place, and so on.

Your turn now Approximate the square root to the nearest whole number and then to the nearest tenth.

1. $\sqrt{7}$	2. $\sqrt{30}$	3. $\sqrt{52}$	4. $\sqrt{125}$

EXAMPLE 3 **Using Square Roots**

Wolves The formula for an animal's maximum walking speed s, in inches per second, is $s = 19.6\sqrt{\ell}$ where ℓ is the animal's leg length, in inches. A wolf has 18-inch legs. Estimate the maximum walking speed of the wolf.

Solution

You can use the approximation the square root of 18 from Example 2 to estimate the maximum walking speed of the wolf.

$s = 19.6\sqrt{\ell}$ Write maximum walking speed formula.

$= 19.6$ ☐ Substitute ☐ for ℓ.

$\approx 19.6\left(\boxed{}\right)$ Use approximation of $\sqrt{18}$ to the nearest tenth.

$\approx$ ☐ Multiply.

Answer: The maximum walking speed is about ☐ inches per second.

 Identifying Rational and Irrational Numbers

Tell whether the number is *rational* or *irrational*. Explain.

a. $\sqrt{3}$ b. $-\dfrac{2}{5}$ c. $-\sqrt{225}$ d. 2.363663. . .

Solution

a. $\sqrt{3}$ is __________ because __________ __________.

b. $-\dfrac{2}{5}$ is __________ because __________ __________.

c. $-\sqrt{225}$ is __________ because __________ __________.

d. 2.363663. . . is __________ because __________ __________.

The Pythagorean Theorem

Goal: Find the length of a side of a right triangle.

Vocabulary

Hypotenuse:

Leg:

Pythagorean theorem:

Pythagorean Theorem

Words For any right triangle, the [ ] of the [ ] of the lengths of the [ ] equals the [ ] of the length of the [ ].

Algebra [ ] = [ ]

EXAMPLE 1 Finding the Length of a Hypotenuse

Find the length of the hypotenuse of the triangle shown.

To find c, the length of the hypotenuse, use the Pythagorean theorem. Let $a = 6$ and $b = 8$.

$$a^2 + b^2 = c^2$$ Write Pythagorean theorem.

[ ] + [ ] $= c^2$ Substitute [ ] for a and [ ] for b.

[ ] $= c^2$ Simplify.

[ ] = [ ] Take positive square root of each side.

[ ] = [ ] Evaluate square root.

Answer: The length of the hypotenuse is [ ] centimeters.

Take the positive square root in Example 1 because length is never negative.

 Approximating the Length of a Hypotenuse

For the right triangle shown, find the length of
the hypotenuse to the nearest tenth.

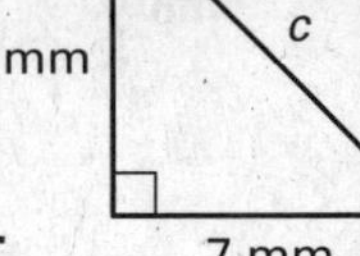

$$a^2 + b^2 = c^2$$ Write Pythagorean theorem.

$$\boxed{} + \boxed{} = c^2$$ Substitute $\boxed{}$ for a and $\boxed{}$ for b.

$$\boxed{} = c^2$$ Simplify.

$$\boxed{} = \boxed{}$$ Take positive square root of each side.

$$\boxed{} \approx \boxed{}$$ Approximate square root.

Answer: The length of the hypotenuse is about $\boxed{}$ millimeters.

Need help
with approximating
square roots? See
page 540 of your
textbook.

Your turn now Find the length of the hypotenuse. Round to the nearest
tenth if necessary.

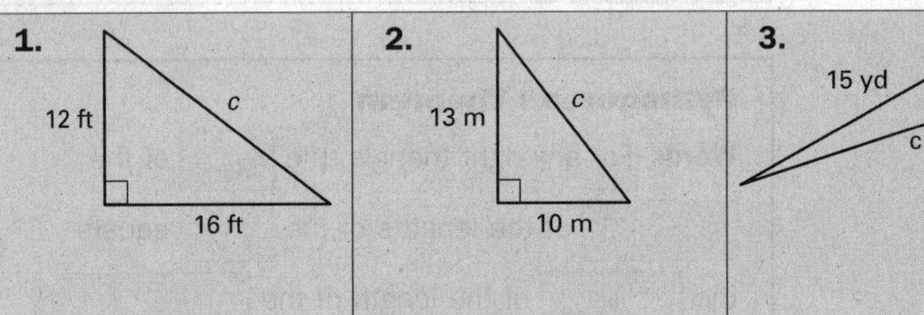

 Finding the Length of a Leg

House Painting A painter sets his 25 foot ladder against
the side of a house. The base of the ladder is 7 feet from
the house. At what height does the ladder touch the house?

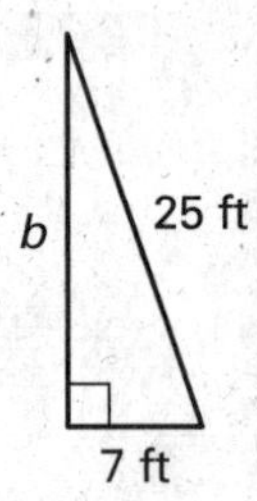

Solution

$$a^2 + b^2 = c^2$$ Write Pythagorean theorem.

$$\boxed{} + b^2 = \boxed{}$$ Substitute $\boxed{}$ for a and $\boxed{}$ for c.

$$\boxed{} + b^2 = \boxed{}$$ Evaluate powers.

$$b^2 = \boxed{}$$ Subtract $\boxed{}$ from each side.

$$\boxed{} = \boxed{}$$ Take positive square root of each side.

$$\boxed{} = \boxed{}$$ Evaluate square root.

Answer: The ladder touches the house $\boxed{}$ feet above the ground.

Area of a Parallelogram

Goal: Find the areas of parallelograms.

Vocabulary

Base of a parallelogram:

Height of a
parallelogram:

Area of a Parallelogram

Words The area A of a parallelogram is
the ___________ of a ___________ and the
corresponding ___________.

Algebra $\boxed{} = \boxed{}$

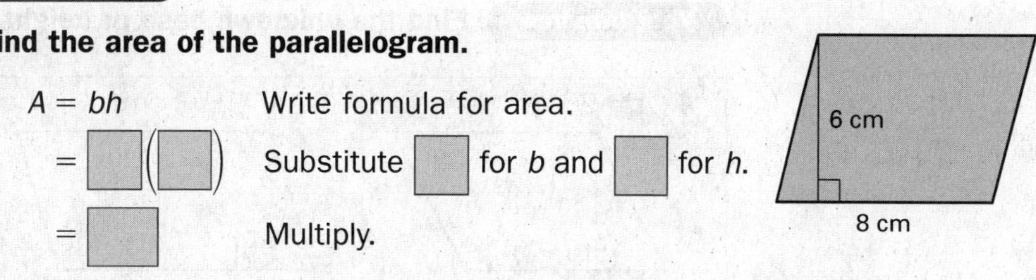

EXAMPLE 1 Finding the Area of a Parallelogram

WATCH OUT!
Area is measured in
square units, not linear
units.

Find the area of the parallelogram.

$A = bh$ .... Write formula for area.

$= \boxed{}(\boxed{})$ .... Substitute $\boxed{}$ for b and $\boxed{}$ for h.

$= \boxed{}$ .... Multiply.

Answer: The area of the parallelogram is ___________.

Your turn now Find the area of the parallelogram with the given base and height.

1. $b = 12$ m, $h = 7$ m	**2.** $b = 7$ mm, $h = 7$ mm	**3.** $b = 10.5$ ft, $h = 8$ ft

---

EXAMPLE 2 **Finding the Base of a Parallelogram**

Glass Cutting A window in an office building is a parallelogram. The height of the window is 12 inches. The window covers 180 square inches. Find the base of the window.

Solution

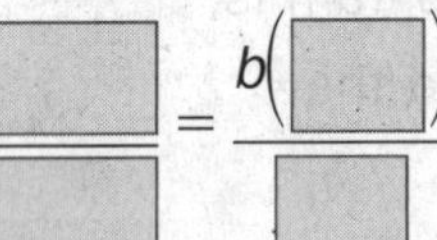

$A = bh$ — Write formula for area of a parallelogram.

$\boxed{} = b\left(\boxed{}\right)$ — Substitute $\boxed{}$ for A and $\boxed{}$ for h.

$\dfrac{\boxed{}}{\boxed{}} = \dfrac{b\left(\boxed{}\right)}{\boxed{}}$ — Divide each side by $\boxed{}$.

$\boxed{} = b$ — Simplify.

Answer: The base of the window is $\boxed{}$.

Your turn now Find the unknown base or height or the parallelogram.

4. $A = 96$ m^2	**5.** $A = 153$ cm^2	**6.** $A = 121$ in.^{2}
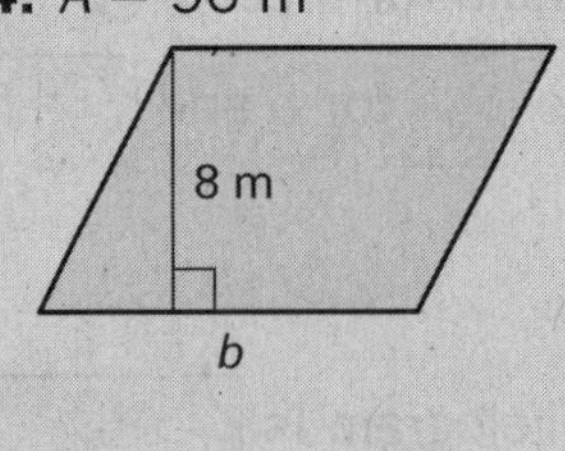	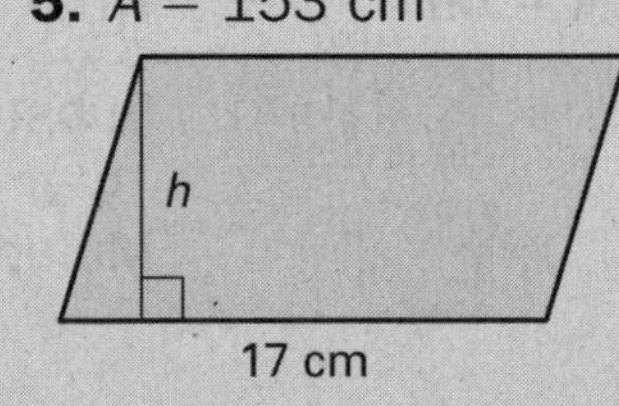	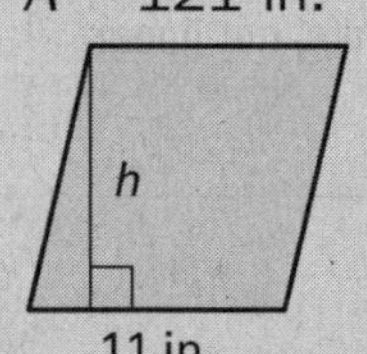

Areas of Triangles and Trapezoids

Goal: Find the areas of triangles and trapezoids.

Vocabulary

Base of
a triangle:

Height of
a triangle:

Bases of a
trapezoid:

Height of
a trapezoid:

Area of a Triangle

Words The area A of a triangle is ☐ the product

of a ☐ and the ☐ .

Algebra ☐ = ☐

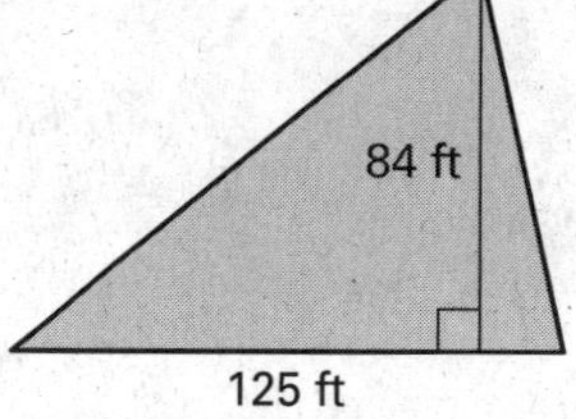

EXAMPLE 1   Finding the Area of a Triangle

Sculpture An artist is creating a sculpture that includes a triangular face that has a base 125 feet long and a height of 84 feet. Find the area of the triangular face.

Solution

$A = \frac{1}{2}bh$ Write formula for area of a triangle.

$= \frac{1}{2}(\boxed{})(\boxed{})$ Substitute ☐ for b and ☐ for h.

$= \boxed{}$ Multiply.

Answer: The area of the face is ☐ .

A triangle has a height of 15 centimeters and an area of 202.5 square centimeters. Find the base of the triangle.

$A = \frac{1}{2}bh$ Write formula for area of a triangle.

[   ] = [   ] Substitute [   ] for A and [   ] for h.

[   ] = [   ] Simplify.

[   ] = b Divide each side by [   ].

Answer: The base of the triangle is [   ].

Your turn now **Find the unknown area or height of the triangle.**

1. $A = \underline{\ ?\ }$, $b = 7$ ft, $h = 12$ ft

2. $A = 52$ m^2, $b = 8$ m, $h = \underline{\ ?\ }$

Because a trapezoid has more than one base, the bases of a trapezoid are usually labeled b_1 and b_2. b_1 is read "b sub one."

Area of a Trapezoid

Words The area A of a trapezoid is [   ] the product of the [   ] and the [   ].

Algebra [ ] = [   ]

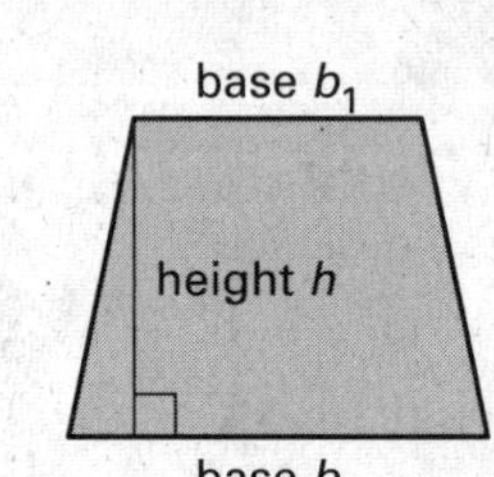

 Finding the Area of a Trapezoid

Find the area of the trapezoid shown.

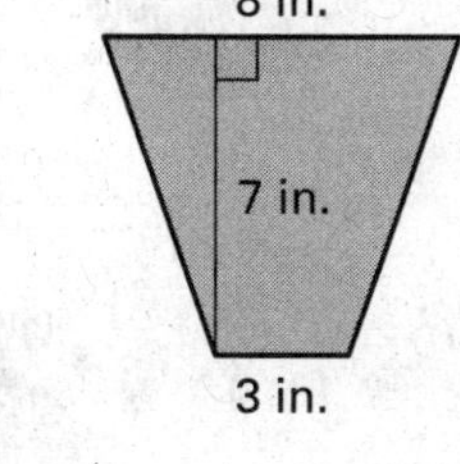

$A = \frac{1}{2}(b_1 + b_2)h$ Write formula for area of a trapezoid.

$= \frac{1}{2}\left(\boxed{} + \boxed{}\right)\left(\boxed{}\right)$ Substitute $\boxed{}$ for b_1, $\boxed{}$ for b_2, and $\boxed{}$ for h.

$= \boxed{}$ Simplify.

Answer: The area of the trapezoid is $\boxed{}$.

EXAMPLE 4 **Finding the Height of a Trapezoid**

A trapezoid has an area of 82 square meters. The bases are 11 meters and 9 meters. Find the height.

$A = \frac{1}{2}(b_1 + b_2)h$ Write formula for area of a trapezoid.

$\boxed{} = \frac{1}{2}\left(\boxed{} + \boxed{}\right)h$ Substitute $\boxed{}$ for A, $\boxed{}$ for b_1, and $\boxed{}$ for b_2.

$\boxed{} = \frac{1}{2}\left(\boxed{}\right)h$ Add.

$\boxed{} = \boxed{}h$ Multiply.

$\boxed{} = h$ Divide each side by $\boxed{}$.

Answer: The height of the trapezoid is $\boxed{}$.

 **Your turn now**   Find the unknown area, base, or height of the trapezoid.

3. $A = \underline{\ ?\ }$, $b_1 = 12$ ft, $b_2 = 8$ ft, $h = 4$ ft

4. $A = 22$ m^2, $b_1 = 7$ m, $b_2 = \underline{\ ?\ }$, $h = 4$ m

5. $A = 15$ cm^2, $b_1 = 3$ cm, $b_2 = 7$ cm, $h = \underline{\ ?\ }$

Circumference of a Circle

Goal: Find the circumferences of circles.

Vocabulary

Circle:

Center:

Radius:

Diameter:

Circumference:

Circumference of a Circle

Words The circumference C of a circle is the product of [ ] and the [ ] , or [ ] the product of [ ] and the [ ] .

Algebra [ ] = [ ]   [ ] = [ ]

EXAMPLE 1   Finding the Circumference of a Circle

Find the circumference of the sundial. Use 3.14 for π.

$C = \pi d$ Write formula for circumference.

$\approx$ [ ]([ ])   Substitute [ ] for π and [ ] for d.

$=$ [ ]   Multiply.

Answer: The circumference of the sundial is about [ ] .

WATCH OUT!
The circumference of a circle is measured in linear units, not square units.

EXAMPLE 2 Finding the Circumference of a Circle

Find the circumference of the circle. Use $\frac{22}{7}$ for π.

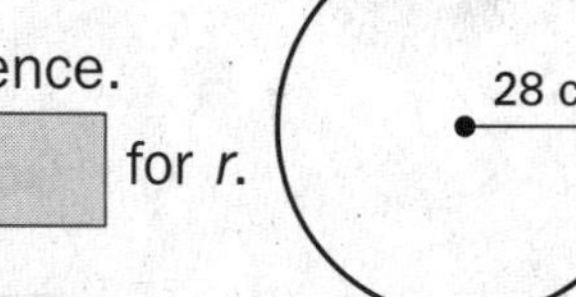

$C = 2\pi r$ Write formula for circumference.

$\approx 2(\ \boxed{}\ )(\ \boxed{}\ )$ Substitute $\boxed{}$ for π and $\boxed{}$ for r.

$= \boxed{}$ Multiply.

Answer: The circumference is about $\boxed{}$.

Your turn now   Find the circumference of the circle. Use $\frac{22}{7}$ or 3.14 for π.

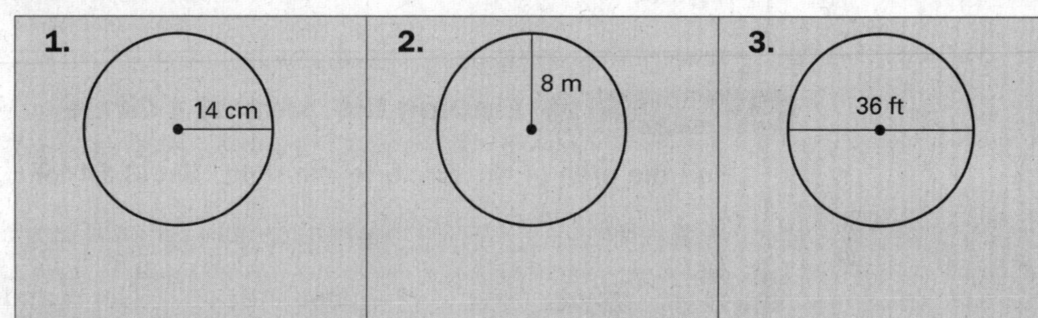

EXAMPLE 3 Finding the Diameter of a Circle

Needlework Amelia is making a rug for her dining room floor. The rug will have a circumference of 44 feet. What will the diameter of the rug be?

Solution

$C = \pi d$ Write formula for circumference.

$\boxed{} \approx \frac{22}{7}d$ Substitute $\boxed{}$ for C and $\frac{22}{7}$ for π.

$\boxed{}\left(\ \boxed{}\ \right) \approx \boxed{}\left(\frac{22}{7}\right)d$ Multiply each side by $\boxed{}$.

$\boxed{} \approx d$ Simplify.

Answer: The diameter of the rug will be about $\boxed{}$.

Your turn now   Solve the following problem.

4. The circumference of a circle is 100.48 meters. Find the circle's diameter.

Area of a Circle

Goal: Find the areas of circles.

Area of a Circle

Words The area A of a circle is the product of [ ]

and [   ]

Algebra [ ] $=$ [ ]

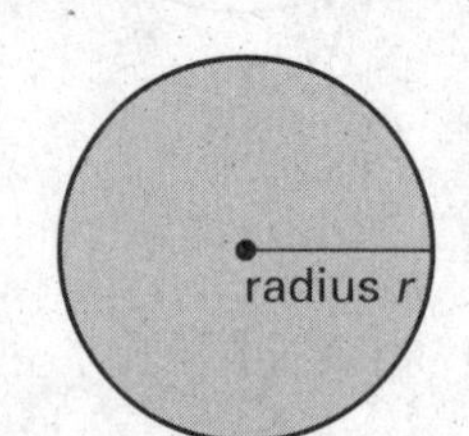

EXAMPLE 1 **Finding the Area of a Circle**

Find the area of the circle to the right. Use 3.14 for π.

$A = \pi r^2$ Write formula for area of a circle.

$\approx \left(\boxed{} \right) \boxed{}$ Substitute $\boxed{}$ for π and $\boxed{}$ for r.

$= \boxed{}$ Simplify.

Answer: The area of the circle is about [   ].

EXAMPLE 2 **Finding the Area of a Circle**

Irrigation A farmer uses an irrigation system to water his crops. The diameter of the circle formed by the system is 54 feet. Find the area of the irrigated area.

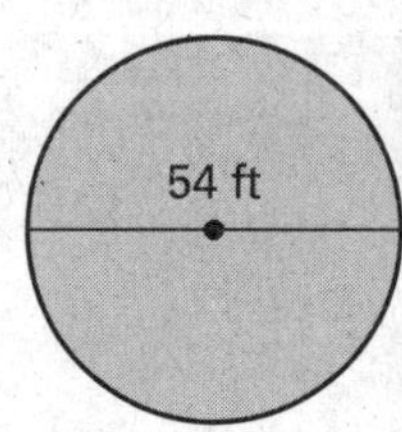

Solution

1. Find the radius.

$r = \boxed{} = \boxed{}$ ft

2. Find the area.

$A = \pi r^2$ Write formula for area of a circle.

$\approx \left(\boxed{} \right) \boxed{}$ Substitute 3.14 for π and $\boxed{}$ for r.

$\approx \boxed{}$ Simplify.

Answer: The area of the irrigated area is about 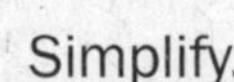 [   ].

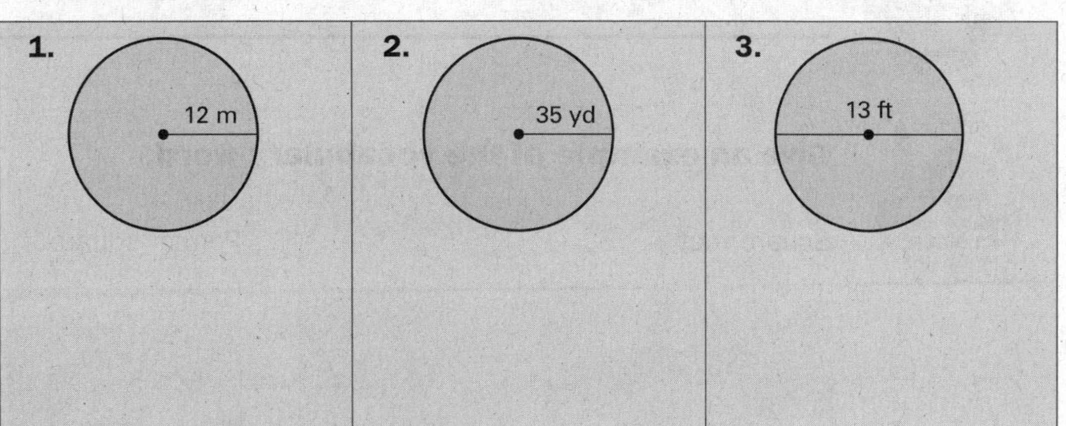

EXAMPLE 3   Finding the Radius of a Circle

Find the radius of a circle that has an area of 1384.74 square meters. Use 3.14 for π.

$A = \pi r^2$ Write formula for area of a circle.

[ ] $\approx$ ([ ])r^2 Substitute [ ] for π and [ ] for A.

[ ] $\approx$ [ ]   [ ] each side by [ ].

[ ] $=$ [ ]   Simplify.

[ ] $=$ [ ]   Take positive square root of each side.

[ ] $=$ [ ]   Evaluate square root.

Answer: The radius of the circle is about [ ].

Words to Review

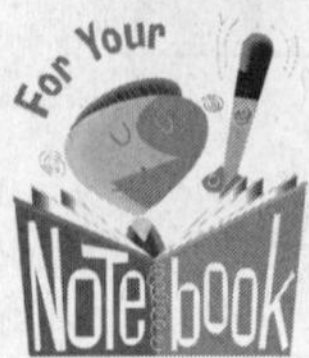

Give an example of the vocabulary word.

Square root

Perfect square

Radical expression

Irrational number

Real number

Hypotenuse

Leg

Pythagorean theorem

Base of a parallelogram

Height of a parallelogram

Base of a triangle

Height of a triangle

Bases of a trapezoid

Height of a trapezoid

Circle

Center

Radius

Diameter

Circumference

Review your notes and Chapter 11 by using the Chapter Review on pages 574–575 of your textbook.

Classifying Solids

Goal: Classify solids and identify their parts.

Vocabulary

Solid:

Prism:

Pyramid:

Cylinder:

Cone:

Sphere:

Face:

Edge:

Vertex:

Classify the solid as a *prism*, *pyramid*, *cylinder*, *cone*, or *sphere*.

a.    b. 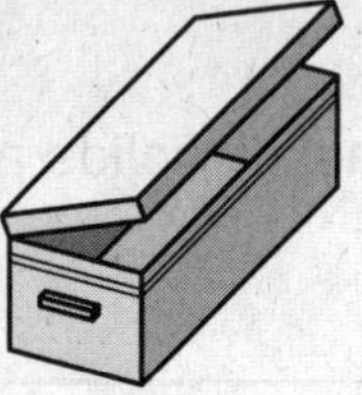   c. 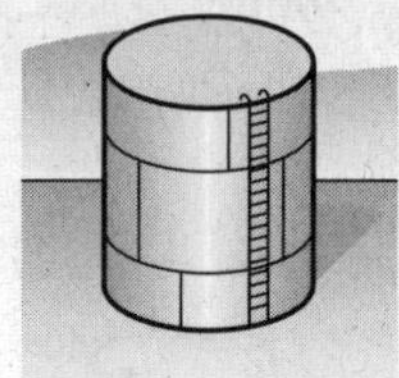

Solution

a. The baseball is a .

b. The trunk is a .

c. The water tower is a .

EXAMPLE 2 **Types of Prisms and Pyramids**

Classify the solid. Be as specific as possible.

a. 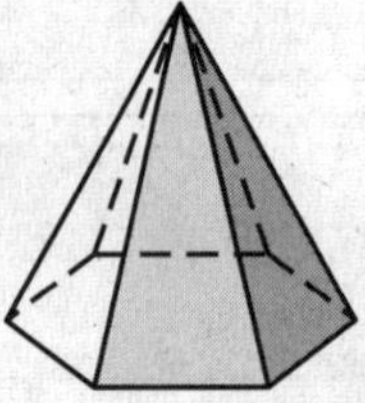   b. 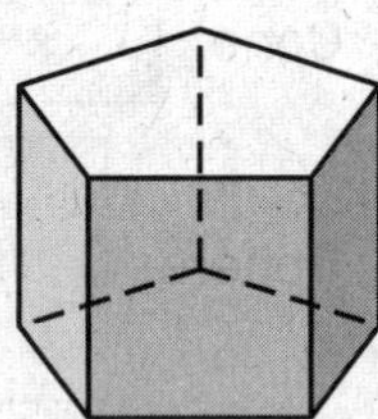

Solution

a. The base is a , so the solid is a .

b. The bases are , so the solid is a .

EXAMPLE 3 **Counting Faces, Edges and Vertices**

Count the number of faces, edges, and vertices in the triangular pyramid.

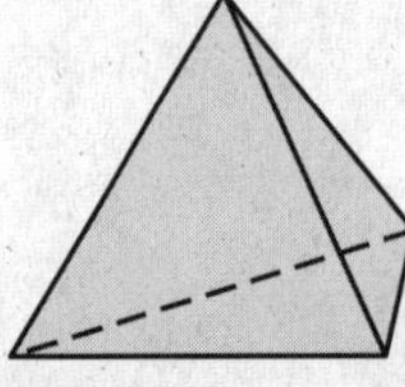   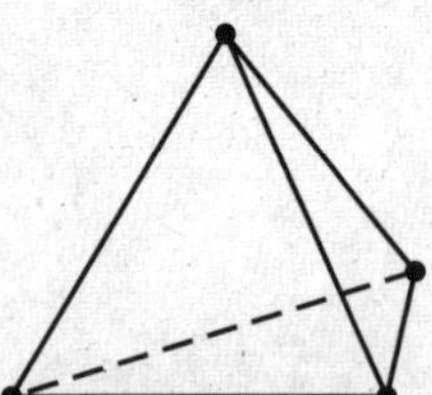

Dashed lines are used to show hidden edges of a solid.

Answer: The pyramid has  faces, 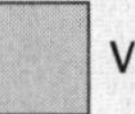 edges, and vertices.

1.
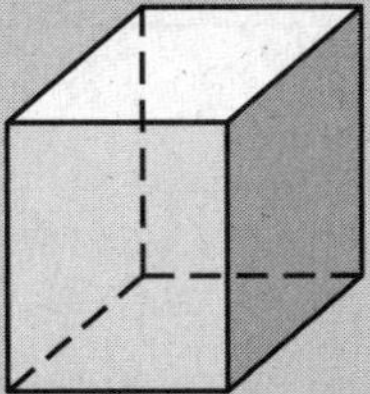

2.
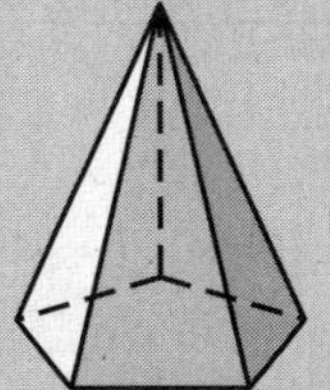

3.
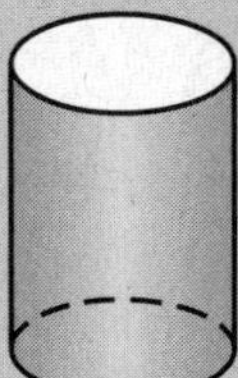

4. Count the number of faces, edges, and vertices in the solid in Exercise 1.

Sketching Solids

Goal: Sketch solids.

EXAMPLE 1 **Sketching a Prism**

Sketch a hexagonal prism.

1. Sketch two congruent hexagons.

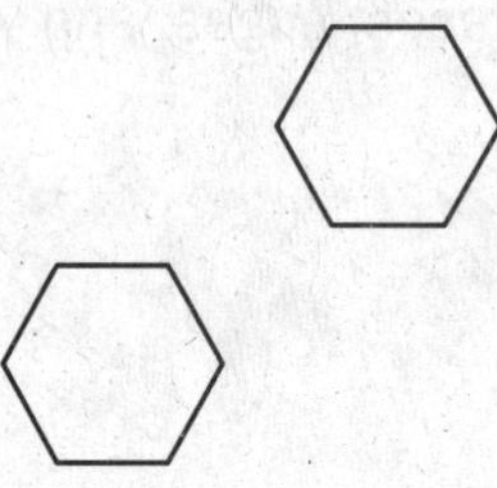

2. Connect the corresponding vertices using line segments.

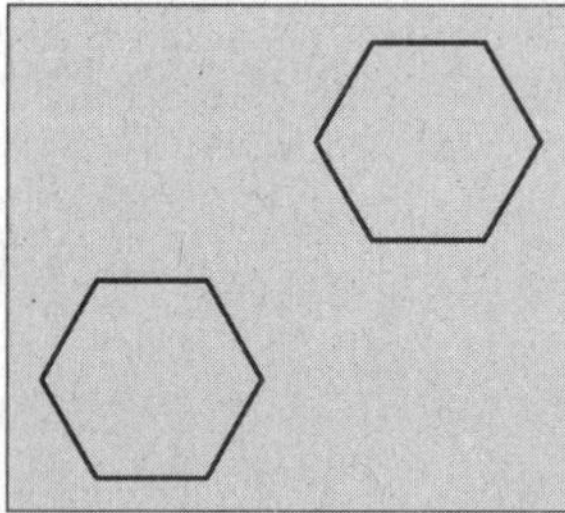

3. Make any "hidden" lines dashed.

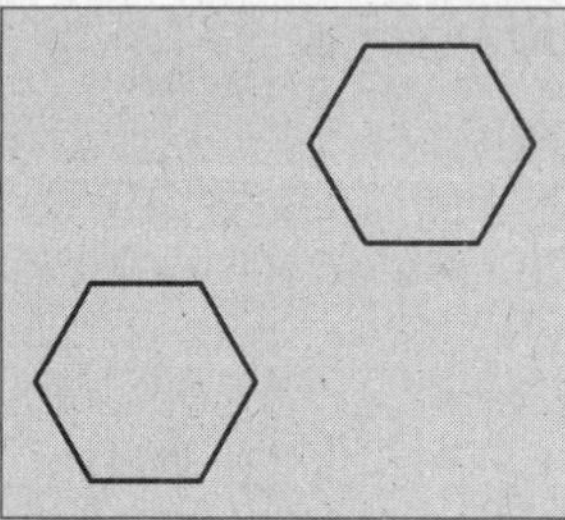

Your turn now **Sketch the solid.**

1. Rectangular prism	**2.** Pentagonal prism

 Sketching a Pyramid

Sketch a triangular pyramid.

1. Sketch a triangle for the base and draw a dot directly above the triangle.

2. Connect the vertices of the triangle to the dot.

3. Make any "hidden" lines dashed.

  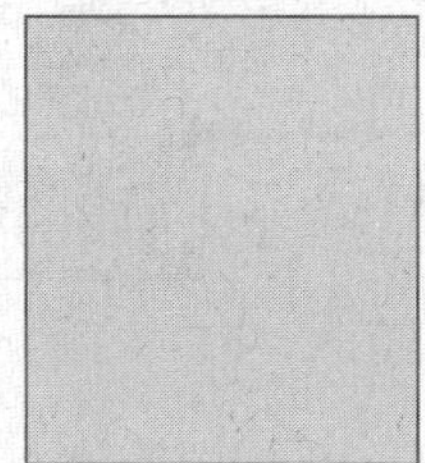

 Sketching Three Views of a Solid

Sketch the top, side, and front views of the cylinder.

Solution

The top view of a cylinder is a ☐.

The side view of a cylinder is a ☐.

The front view of a cylinder is a ☐.

Your turn now **Complete the following exercises.**

3. Sketch a pentagonal pyramid.

4. Sketch the top, side, and front views of the pentagonal pyramid you sketched in Exercise 3.

Surface Area of Rectangular Prisms

Goal: Find the surface area of rectangular prisms.

Vocabulary

Surface Area:

Net:

EXAMPLE 1 **Finding Surface Area Using a Net**

Find the surface area of the rectangular prism.

1. Find the area of each face.

   Area of top or bottom: [ ] = [ ]

   Area of front or back: [ ] = [ ]

   Area of either side: [ ] = [ ]

8 in.   2 in.   3 in.

3 in.   8 in.   2 in.   8 in.   2 in.

2. Add the areas of all six faces.

   [ ] = [ ]

Answer: The surface area of the prism is [ ].

Surface Area of a Rectangular Prism

Words The surface area S of a rectangular prism is the [ ].

Algebra [ ] = [ ]

Find the surface area of the rectangular prism.

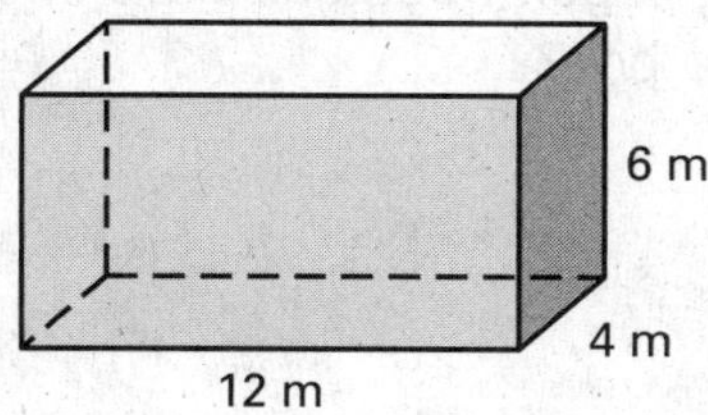

$S = 2\ell w + 2\ell h + 2wh$ Write formula for surface area.

$= 2\left(\boxed{}\right)\left(\boxed{}\right) + 2\left(\boxed{}\right)\left(\boxed{}\right)$ Substitute $\boxed{}$ for ℓ, $\boxed{}$ for

$+ 2\left(\boxed{}\right)\left(\boxed{}\right)$ w, and $\boxed{}$ for h.

$= \boxed{} + \boxed{} + \boxed{}$ Multiply.

$= \boxed{}$ Add.

Answer: The surface area of the prism is $\boxed{}$.

Your turn now Find the surface area of the rectangular prism. Check your answer by finding the area of the prism's net.

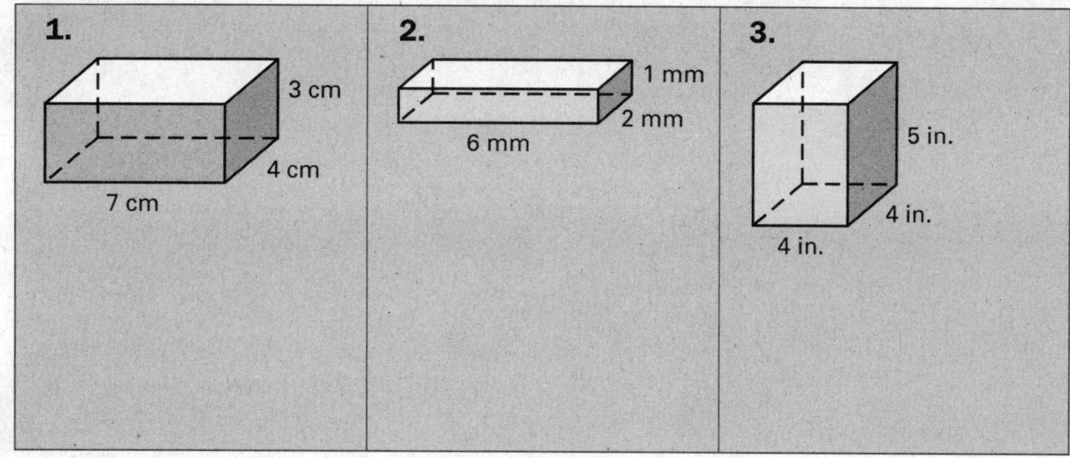

Gift Wrap Leann is wrapping a present for her father. She has 15 square feet of wrapping paper. Does she have enough wrapping paper to cover the box?

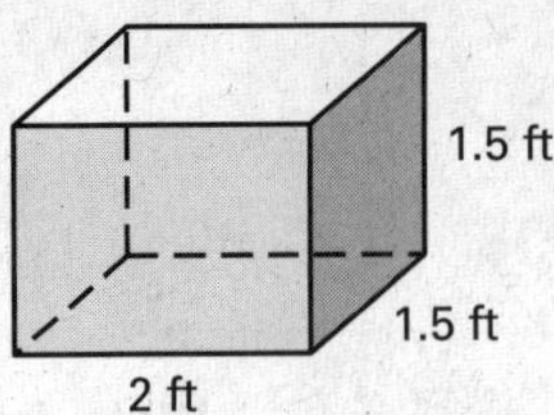

Solution

1. Find the surface area of the box.

$$S = 2\ell w + 2\ell h + 2wh$$ Write formula.

$$= 2()() + 2(\cdot)() + 2()()$$ Substitute values.

$$= $$ Simplify.

2. Compare the surface area to the amount of gift wrap Leann has.

Answer: Leann __________ have enough wrapping paper.

Surface Area of Cylinders

Goal: Find the surface area of cylinders.

Surface Area of a Cylinder

Words The surface area S of a cylinder is the [ ] of the area of the [ ] and the areas of the [ ].

Algebra [ ] = [ ]

EXAMPLE 1 **Finding the Surface Area of a Cylinder**

Find the surface area of the cylinder. Use 3.14 for π.

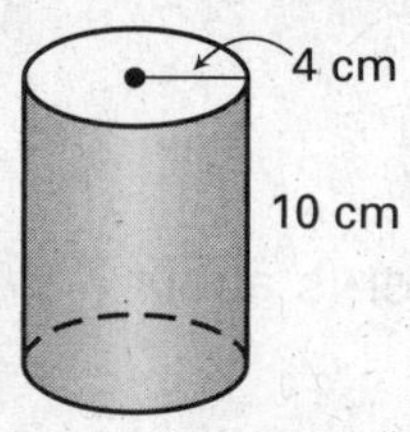

Solution

$$S = 2\pi rh + 2\pi r^2$$ Write formula.

$$\approx 2(\quad)(\quad)(\quad) + 2(\quad)\quad$$ Substitute values.

$$= \quad + \quad$$ Multiply.

$$\approx \quad$$ Add.

Answer: The surface area is about [ ].

Water Heater A company manufactures covers for cylindrical water heaters to help save energy and retain heat. The water heater has a radius of 1.5 feet. The cover uses 45 square feet of insulated fabric. Find the height of the cylinder. Use 3.14 for π.

Solution

$S = 2\pi rh + 2\pi r^2$ Write formula for surface area.

$\boxed{} \approx 2\left(\boxed{}\right)\left(\boxed{}\right)h + 2\left(\boxed{}\right)\boxed{}$ Substitute values.

$\boxed{} \approx \boxed{} + \boxed{}$ Multiply.

$\boxed{} - \boxed{} \approx \boxed{} + \boxed{} - \boxed{}$ Subtract $\boxed{}$ from each side.

$\boxed{} \approx \boxed{}$ Simplify.

$\dfrac{\boxed{}}{\boxed{}} \approx \dfrac{\boxed{}}{\boxed{}}$ Divide each side by $\boxed{}$.

$\boxed{} \approx h$ Simplify.

Answer: The height of the water heater is about $\boxed{}$.

  Find the surface area of the cylinder. Use 3.14 for π.

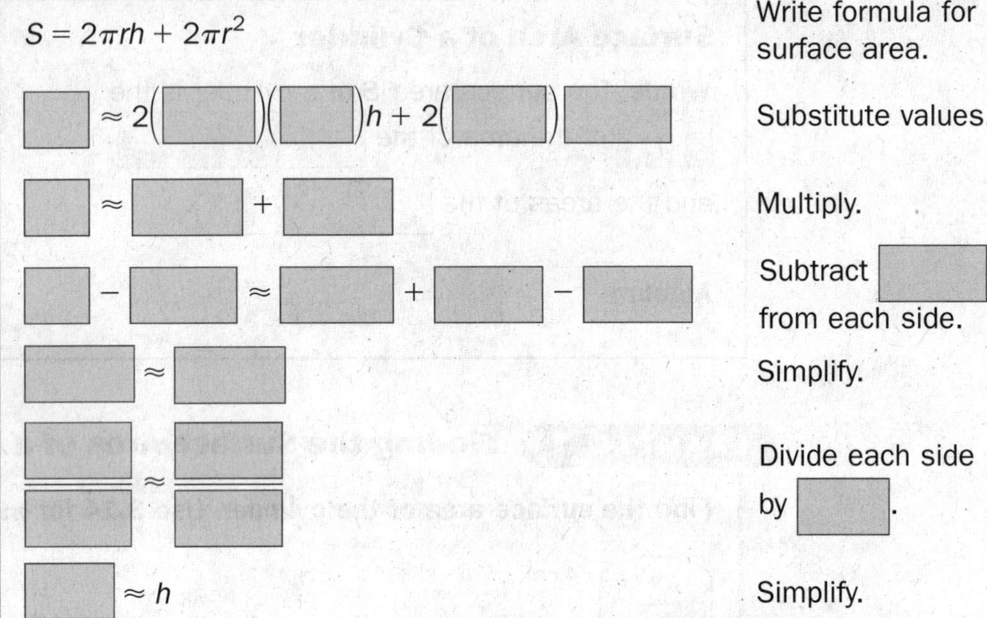

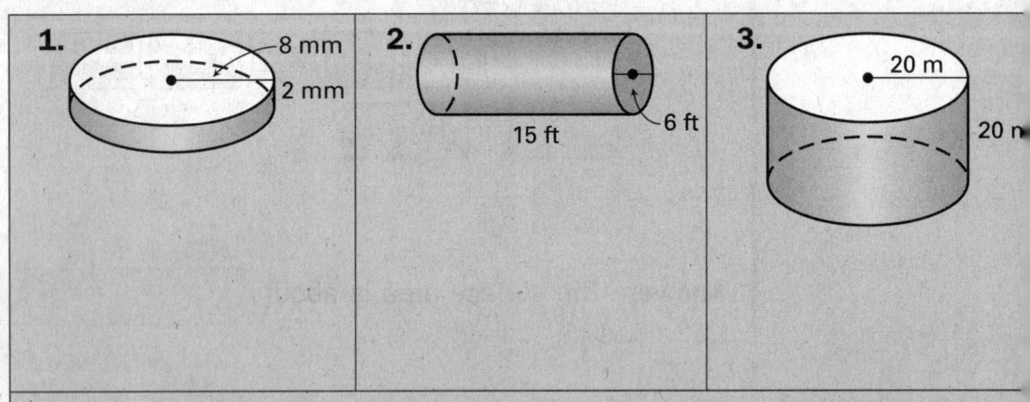

4. Find the height of a cylinder that has a radius of 9 meters and a surface area of 791 square meters. Use 3.14 for π. Round your answer to the nearest meter.

Volume of Rectangular Prisms

Goal: Find the volume of rectangular prisms.

Vocabulary

Volume:

Volume of a Rectangular Prism

Words The volume V of a rectangular prism is the

⬚ of the ⬚ , ⬚ , and ⬚ .

Algebra ⬚ = ⬚

EXAMPLE 1 Volume of a Rectangular Prism

Freezer The Gilbert family has a chest freezer that has a length of 48 inches, a width of 30 inches, and a height of 36 inches. What is the volume of the freezer?

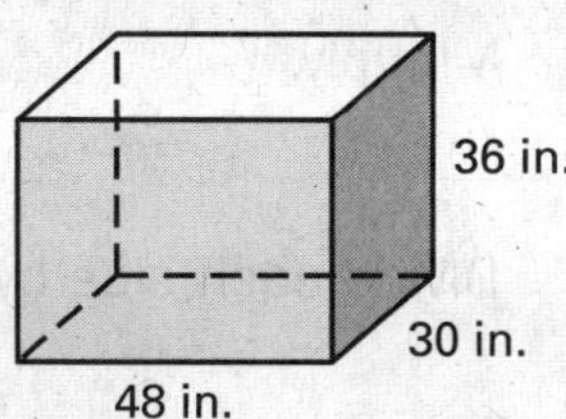

Solution

$V = \ell wh$

Write formula for volume of a rectangular prism.

$= (\quad)(\quad)(\quad)$

Substitute ⬚ for ℓ, ⬚ for w, and ⬚ for h.

$= \quad$

Multiply.

Answer: The freezer will hold ⬚ .

  Find the volume of the rectangular prism.

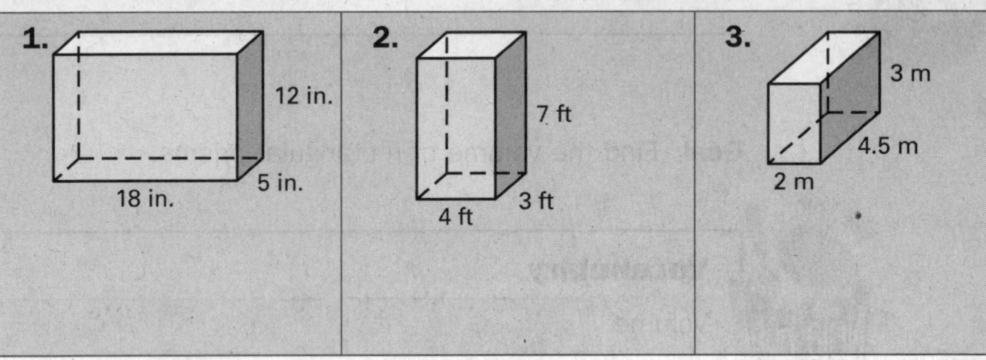

EXAMPLE 2 — Finding the Height of a Rectangular Prism

The rectangular prism shown has a volume of 2052 cubic millimeters. Find the prism's height.

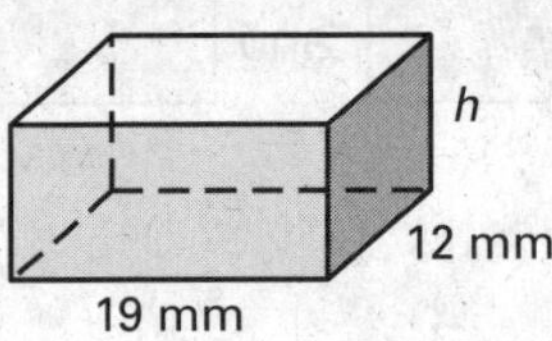

Solution

$$V = \ell wh$$

Write formula for volume of a rectangular prism.

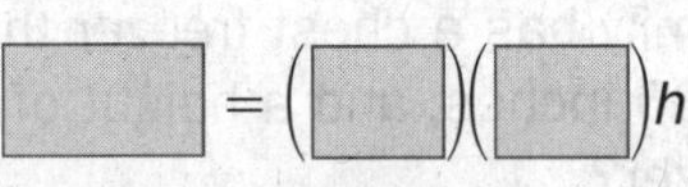

Substitute ☐ for V, ☐ for ℓ, and ☐ for w.

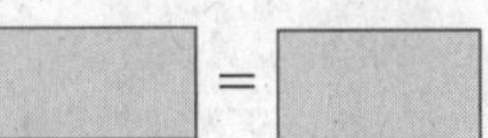

Multiply.

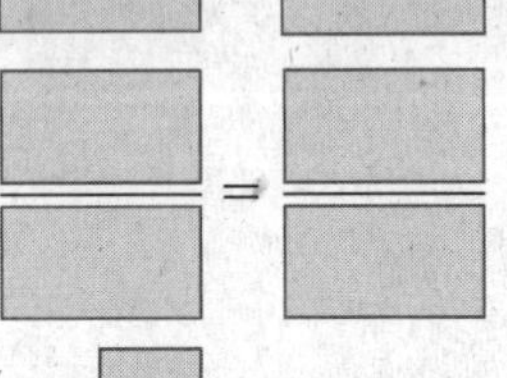

Divide each side by ☐.

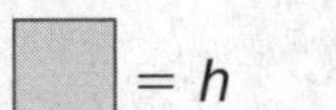$= h$

Simplify.

Answer: The height of the prism is ☐.

4. $V = 144 \text{ ft}^3$, $\ell = \underline{\ ?\ }$, $w = 3$ ft, $h = 6$ ft

5. $V = 308 \text{ cm}^3$, $\ell = 7$ cm, $w = \underline{\ ?\ }$, $h = 11$ cm

6. $V = 78 \text{ m}^3$, $\ell = 6.5$ m, $w = 4$ m, $h = \underline{\ ?\ }$

EXAMPLE 3 Using the Volume of a Rectangular Prism

Snack Mix A cereal box is 6 inches long, 10 inches tall, and 1.5 inches wide.
Marta is mixing a snack mix in a tin canister that holds 585 cubic inches.
How many boxes of cereal will Marta open in order to fill her container?

Solution

1. Find the volume of the cereal box.

$$V = \ell w h$$

$$= (\quad)(\quad)(\quad)$$

$$= \boxed{} \text{ in.}^3$$

2. To find the number of cereal boxes Marta will open, divide $\boxed{}$ cubic
inches by $\boxed{}$ cubic inches.

$$\boxed{} \text{ in.}^3 \div \boxed{} \text{ in.}^3 = \boxed{}$$

Answer: Because it doesn't make sense to open $\boxed{}$ boxes, Marta must
open $\boxed{}$ boxes of cereal to fill the container.

Volume of Cylinders

Goal: Find the volume of cylinders.

Volume of a Cylinder

Words The volume V of a cylinder is the ⬚ of the ⬚ of the base and the ⬚.

Algebra ⬚ = ⬚

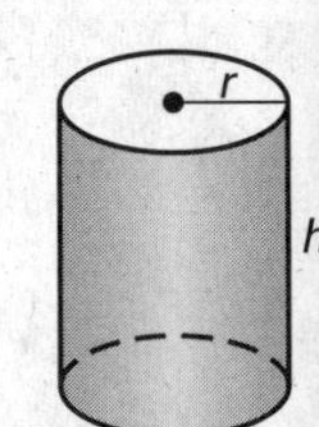

EXAMPLE 1 **Finding the Volume of a Cylinder**

Find the volume of the cylinder. Use 3.14 for π.

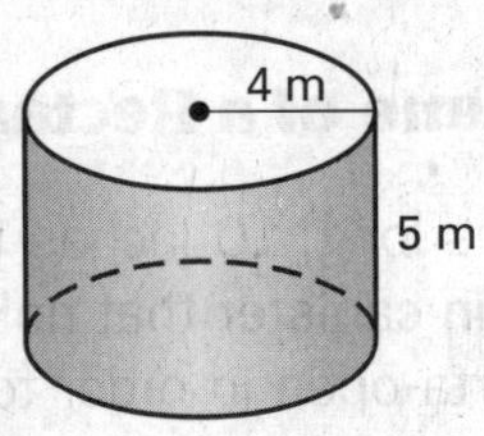

You have learned many properties and formulas related to solids. Writing a summary of what you have learned may help you prepare for the chapter test.

Solution

$V = \pi r^2 h$ Write formula for volume of a cylinder.

$\approx$ (⬚)(⬚)(⬚)   Substitute ⬚ for π, ⬚ for r, and ⬚ for h.

$=$ ⬚   Multiply.

Answer: The volume of the cylinder is about ⬚ .

EXAMPLE 2 **Comparing Volumes of Cylinders**

Tomato Sauce Carlos found two cans of tomato sauce in the pantry. One can has a diameter of 4 inches and a height of 5 inches. The second one has a diameter of 3 inches and a height of 6 inches. Which can has the greater volume?

Solution

1. Find the radius of each can, which is half of the diameter.

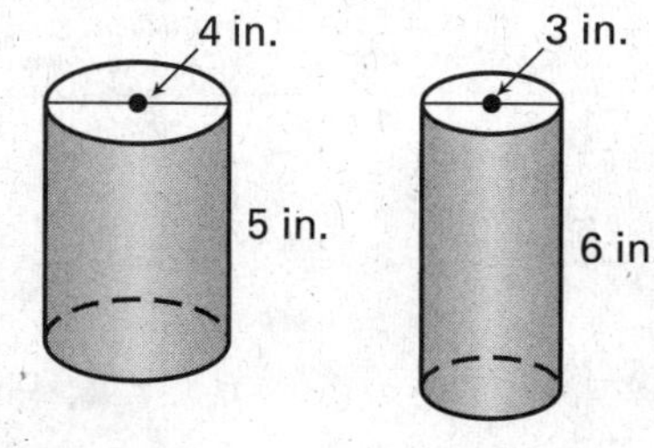

   Can 1: $r = \dfrac{\boxed{}}{} = \boxed{}$ in.

   Can 2: $r = \dfrac{\boxed{}}{} = \boxed{}$ in.

2. Find the volume of each can. Use 3.14 for π.

   Can 1:

   $V = \pi r^2 h$

   $\approx \left(\boxed{} \right)\left(\boxed{} \right)\left(\boxed{} \right)$

   $= \boxed{}$ in.^{3}

   Can 2:

   $V = \pi r^2 h$

   $\approx \left(\boxed{} \right)\left(\boxed{} \right)\left(\boxed{} \right)$

   $= \boxed{}$ in.^{3}

Answer: Can $\boxed{}$ has the greater volume.

EXAMPLE 3 **Finding the Radius of a Cylinder**

A cylinder has a height of 12 feet and a volume of 3768 cubic feet. Find the radius of the cylinder. Use 3.14 for π.

$V = \pi r^2 h$ Write formula for volume of a cylinder.

$\boxed{} \approx \left(\boxed{} \right)r^2\left(\boxed{} \right)$ Substitute $\boxed{}$ for V, $\boxed{}$ for π, and $\boxed{}$ for h.

$\boxed{} \approx \boxed{}$ Multiply.

$\boxed{} \approx \boxed{}$ Divide each side by $\boxed{}$.

$\boxed{} \approx \boxed{}$ Take positive square root of each side.

$\boxed{} \approx \boxed{}$ Evaluate square root.

Answer: The radius of the cylinder is about $\boxed{}$.

 Find the volume of the cylinder. Use 3.14 for π.

1. 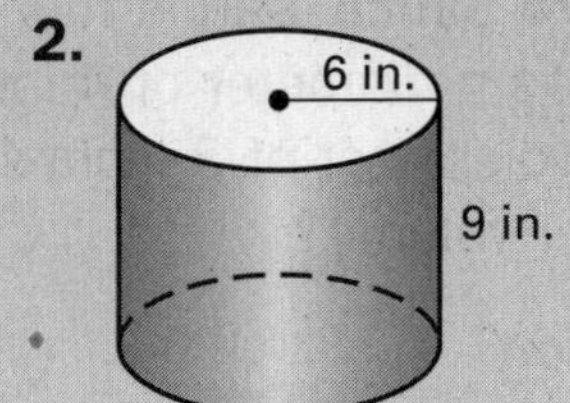

2.

3. 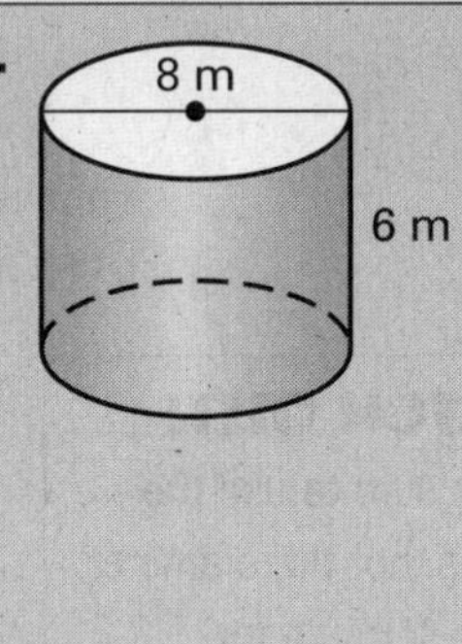

4. Find the radius of a cylinder that has a height of 7 inches and a volume of 351.68 cubic inches. Use 3.14 of π.

Words to Review

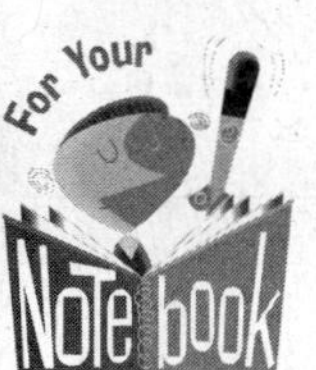

Give an example of the vocabulary word.

Solid

Prism

Pyramid

Cylinder

Cone

Sphere

Face

Edge

Vertex

Surface area

Net

Volume

Review your notes and Chapter 12 by using the Chapter Review on pages 618–619 of your textbook.

Introduction to Probability

Goal: Find probabilities.

Vocabulary

Outcomes:

Event:

Favorable outcomes:

Probability:

Theoretical probability:

Experimental probability:

EXAMPLE 1 Finding a Probability

Find the probability of randomly choosing a striped ball from the balls shown at the right.

Solution

$$P(\text{striped}) = \frac{\qquad}{\qquad}$$

⟵ There are ___ striped balls.

⟵ There are ___ balls in all.

You can write probabilities as fractions, decimals, or percents.

Answer: The probability of randomly choosing a striped ball is

___ , ___ , or ___ .

1. From the balls in Example 1, you randomly choose a spotted ball.

2. You get heads when you flip a coin.

3. You get a multiple of 3 when you roll a number cube.

EXAMPLE 2   **Finding an Experimental Probability**

Guests Robert tracked whether guests knocked on his door or rang his doorbell and wrote his results in the table at the right. Find the probability that the next guest will ring the doorbell.

Doorbell	15
Knock	10

1. Determine the number of successes and the number of trials.

Because a success is ▢, there are ▢ successes.

There are ▢ + ▢ = ▢ trials.

2. Find the probability.

$$P(\text{doorbell}) = \frac{}{}$$

← There are ▢ successes.

← There are ▢ trials.

$$= \frac{}{}$$

Answer: The probability that the next guest will ring the doorbell

is ▢ , ▢ , or ▢ .

4. In Example 2, what is the probability that the next guest will knock on the door?

5. At an auto dealership, of the last 150 vehicles purchased, 45 were sport utility vehicles. Find the probability that the next purchase will be a sport utility vehicle.

Tree Diagrams

Goal: Use a tree diagram to find all possible outcomes.

Vocabulary

Tree diagram:

EXAMPLE 1 **Making a Tree Diagram**

Sandwich Shop A sandwich shop has a daily special where customers can choose from ham, turkey, or roast beef. Customers can then choose between Swiss cheese and cheddar cheese. Make a tree diagram to find all the possibilities of sandwiches.

Solution

List the meats.   List the choices of cheese for each meat.   List the outcomes.

ham — Swiss
ham — cheddar

Answer: There are ☐ different choices of sandwiches.

1. At a children's photography studio, parents can choose from pink,
blue, black, or white for the background color and a rocking horse,
a truck, or a doll for the prop. How many choices of photographs do
parents have?

EXAMPLE 2   Making a Tree Diagram

Camp Scheduling You are scheduling your afternoon activities at camp. The
activities are at 1:00 P.M. and 3:00 P.M., and the choices are crafts, repelling,
weight lifting, horseback riding, and music. If you must choose two different
activities, how many afternoon activity schedules are possible?

Solution

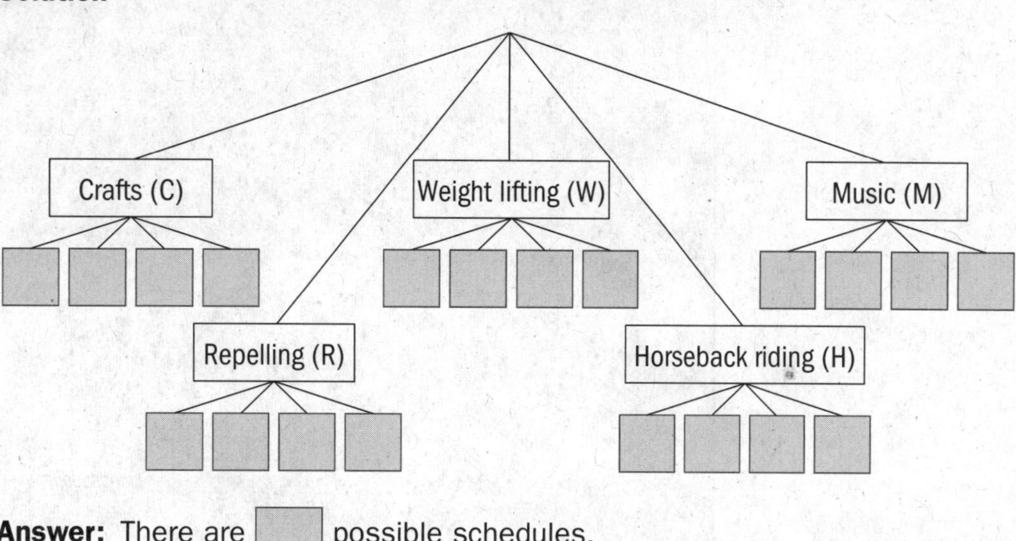

Answer: There are ☐ possible schedules.

 Using a Tree Diagram

A sack has three chips in it: a red chip, a blue chip, and a green chip. To find the probability of randomly drawing the same chip when drawing a chip from the sack, replacing it, and drawing again, make a tree diagram to find the outcomes.

Solution

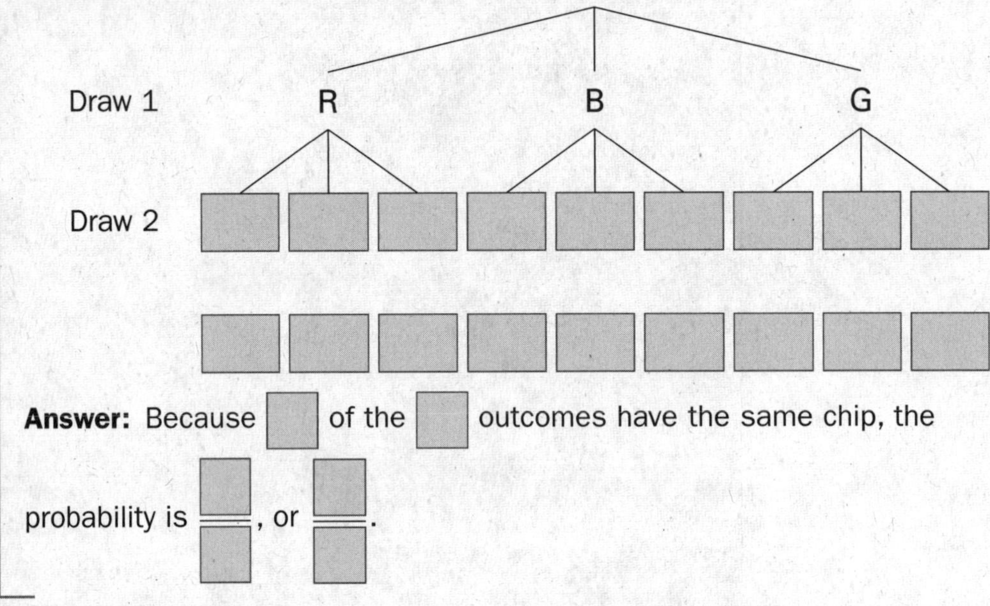

Answer: Because ☐ of the ☐ outcomes have the same chip, the probability is ☐/☐ , or ☐/☐ .

Your turn now **Use a tree diagram to find the probability.**

2. You roll a number cube and flip a coin. What is the probability that you roll a number greater than 4 and heads?

The Counting Principle

Goal: Use the counting principle to find outcomes.

The Counting Principle

If one event can occur in *m* ways, and for each of these a second event can occur is *n* ways, then the number of ways that the two events can occur together is ⬚ .

The counting principle can be extended to three or more events.

EXAMPLE 1 **Using the Counting Principle**

Dance Toward the end of a school dance, the disc jockey has three ballads, five pop songs, and two jazz songs to choose from. How many different choices does the disc jockey have if one ballad, one pop song, and one jazz song are to be played?

Number of ballads	×	Number of pop songs	×	Number of jazz songs	=	Number of choices
⬚	×	⬚	×	⬚	=	⬚

Answer: The disc jockey has ⬚ choices.

EXAMPLE 2 **Using the Counting Principle**

License Plates How many different 6 character license plates are possible, if each character can be a digit or a letter and can be repeated?

Solution

Use the counting principle to find the number of different license plates.

There are ⬚ + ⬚ = ⬚ choices for each character.

⬚ × ⬚ × ⬚ × ⬚ × ⬚ × ⬚ = ⬚

Answer: There are ⬚ possible license plates.

Student Identification Numbers Students at a small college are assigned student identification numbers. The IDs are made up of five digits. If the digits can be repeated, what is the probability that a randomly chosen student will be assigned the ID number 12345?

Solution

1. Find the number of different ID numbers.

$$\boxed{} \times \boxed{} \times \boxed{} \times \boxed{} \times \boxed{} = \boxed{}$$

Use the counting principle.

2. Find the probability that the ID number is 12345.

$$P(12345) = \boxed{}$$

Only $\boxed{}$ of the outcomes is 12345.

Answer: The probability that a randomly chosen student will be assigned the ID number 12345 is $\boxed{}$.

Your turn now Use the counting principle to solve the problem.

1. You have 36 baseball cards, 20 from American League teams and 16 from National League teams. How many outcomes are possible if you randomly choose 1 American League card and 1 National League card?

2. You spin a spinner with 6 different numbers (1 through 6) and another spinner with 8 different numbers (1 through 8). How many different outcomes are possible?

3. In Exercise 2, what is the probability that the first spinner lands on 3 and the second spinner lands on 7?

Permutations and Combinations

Goal: Use permutations and combinations.

Vocabulary

Permutation:

Combination:

EXAMPLE 1 Counting Permutations

Basketball Five players are introduced as the starting players of a basketball team. How many ways can the five players be introduced?

Solution

Use the counting principle.

Choices for first player	×	Choices for second player	×	Choices for third player	×	Choices for fourth player	×	Choices for fifth player	=	Ways to introduce players
☐	×	☐	×	☐	×	☐	×	☐	=	☐

Answer: There are ☐ different ways to introduce the players.

EXAMPLE 2 Counting Permutations

Spelling Bee There were 47 children entered in this year's city-wide spelling bee. In how many ways could the first, second, and third places be awarded?

Solution

Choices for first place	×	Choices for second place	×	Choices for third place	=	Ways to award first, second, and third place
☐	×	☐	×	☐	=	☐

Answer: There were ☐ ways to award first, second, and third place.

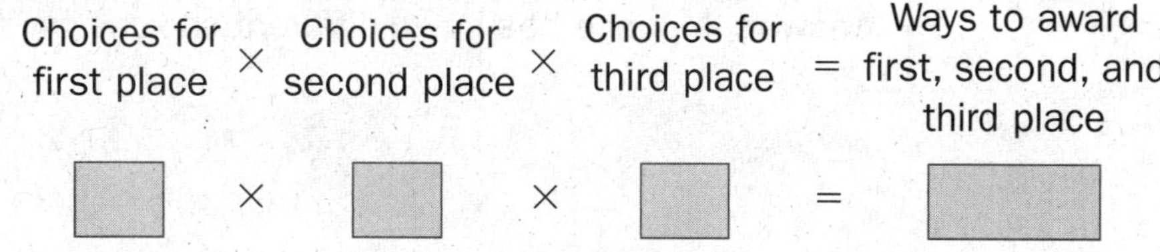

1. In how many ways can you arrange the letters in the word HOLIDAY?

2. There are 10 runners in a long distance race. In how many ways can the runners place first, second, and third?

EXAMPLE 3 Listing Combinations

Errands Maurice's mom asks him to choose two errands to run. He can pic from the grocery store (GS), the dry cleaners (DC), the car wash (CW), the post office (PO), and City Hall (CH). How many different choices does Mauric have if the order in which the errands are done does not matter?

Solution

Start by listing all of the permutations of 2 errands. Because the order in which Maurice chooses the errands does not matter, cross out one of any pair of permutations that lists the same two errands.

In Example 3, you can use a tree diagram to find the permutations of 2 errands. Then cross out one of any pair of permutations that lists the same two errands.

Answer: Maurice has ____ different choices for running two errands.

Vacation Allison is packing for a vacation. She owns 16 pairs of shoes, and plans on taking 3 pairs with her. How many choices does she have?

Solution

Because the order in which the pairs of shoes are chosen does not matter, you need to find the number of combinations.

1. Find the number of permutations when choosing 3 pairs from 16.

2. Find the number of permutations when arranging 3 objects.

3. Divide the number of permutations when choosing 3 pairs of shoes from 16 by the number of permutations when arranging 3 objects.

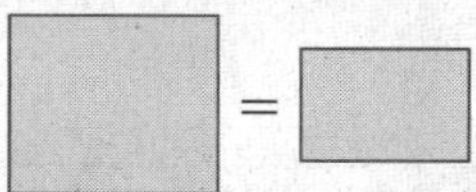

Answer: Allison has ☐ choices.

Your turn now   **Find the number of combinations.**

3. You want to see 6 different movies over spring break, but only have money to see 3. How many choices do you have if the order in which you see them is not important?

4. Your city is offering Museum Day, where you can visit any of the 12 museums for free. You have time to visit 4 museums. How many ways can you choose 4 museums if the order in which you visit them is not important?

Disjoint Events

Goal: Find the probability that either of two events occurs.

Vocabulary

Disjoint events:

Overlapping events:

Complementary events:

EXAMPLE 1   Disjoint and Overlapping Events

Tell whether the events involving the spinner are *disjoint* or *overlapping*.

Event P: Get a number greater than 4.

Event Q: Get an even number.

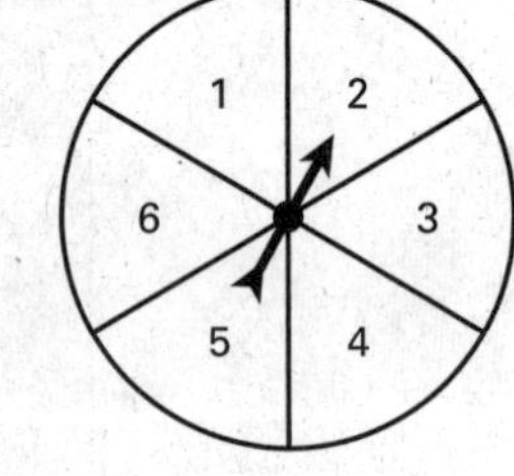

Solution

Make a list of the outcomes for each event. Then determine whether the events have any outcomes in common.

Event P: List the numbers greater than 4.

Event Q: List the even numbers.

Answer: There ______________ in common, so the events ______________.

> To help you understand the difference between disjoint and overlapping events, you can make a concept grid for each term.

1. Event J: Get a prime number.
Event K: Get a number greater than 5.

Probability of Disjoint Events

Words For two disjoint events, the probability that either of the events occurs is the [　　] of the probabilities of the events.

Algebra If A and B are disjoint events, then $P(A \text{ or } B) = $ [　　　　].

EXAMPLE 2   **Probability of Disjoint Events**

Television Viewing The table shows the types of television shows viewed by a family in a month. What is the probability that a randomly chosen show watched by the family that month is a sitcom or a news program?

Show type	Percent
Cartoon	31%
Sitcom	28%
Drama	17%
News	13%
Reality	11%

Solution

The events are disjoint because a news program is not a sitcom.

$$P(\text{sitcom}) + P(\text{news}) = \boxed{}\% + \boxed{}\%$$

$$= \boxed{}\%$$

Answer: The probability that the show is either a sitcom or a news program is [　]%.

2. What is the probability that a randomly chosen program is a reality program or a cartoon?

EXAMPLE 3   **Probability of Complementary Events**

Day Care Of the workers at Kids Kingdom Day Care Center, 78% of the employees have professional certifications. What is the probability that a randomly chosen employee at the center is *not* certified?

Solution

$P(\text{not certified}) = \boxed{} - P(\text{certified})$ Write verbal model.

$= \boxed{} - \boxed{}$ Substitute $\boxed{}$%, or $\boxed{}$, $P(\text{certified})$.

$= \boxed{}$ Subtract.

Answer: The probability that a randomly chosen employee is not certified is $\boxed{}$, or $\boxed{}$%.

Independent and Dependent Events

Goal: Find the probability of dependent events.

Vocabulary

Independent events:

Dependent events:

EXAMPLE 1 **Independent and Dependent Events**

A drawer contains 15 socks, 7 blue and 8 white. You close your eyes and pull out a blue sock first, then a white sock, without replacing the blue sock. Are these events independent or dependent?

Whether or not you choose a blue sock first [   ] affect the likelihood that you choose a white sock second. This is because the ratio of blue to white socks in the drawer [   ] after the first sock is pulled from the drawer and not put back.

Answer: The events are [   ].

Your turn now **A jar contains 8 red and 12 blue marbles.**

1. You randomly choose a marble, put it back, then randomly choose another marble. Are the events "choose a red marble first" and "choose a blue marble second" *independent* or *dependent*?

Probability of Independent Events

Words For two independent events, the probability that both events occur is the [______] of the probabilities of the events.

Algebra If A and B are independent events, the $P(A \text{ and } B) =$ [______]

Probability of Independent Events

Carnival Tara is playing a game at a carnival where she picks a rubber duck from a pond. There are 12 ducks in the pond for which there is no prize and 4 ducks that will award a prize. What is the probability that Tara picks a prize-winning duck, replaces the duck in the pond, then picks another prize-winning duck?

Solution

1. Find the probability of each event.

$$P(\text{win}) = \frac{}{} = []$$ There are [__] ducks in all.

$$P(\text{win}) = \frac{}{} = []$$ Because Tara replaces the first duck, there are [__] winning ducks for the second pick.

2. Because the events are independent, multiply the probabilities.

$$P(\text{win and win}) = []$$

$$= []$$

$$= []$$

Answer: The probability that Tara selects 2 winning ducks from the pond in a row is [______], or [____] %.

Probability of Dependent Events

Words For two dependent events, the probability that both events occur is the [______] of the probability of the first event and the probability of the second event [______].

Algebra If A and B are dependent events, then
$P(A \text{ and } B) =$ [______].

In common usage, being independent means being free from the control of others. This may help you remember the meaning of independent events.

Beverages Jeffrey's mother has 10 orange juice boxes, 7 grape juice boxes, and 3 lemonade juice boxes in the cooler for Jeffrey and his friends. Jeffrey randomly takes a juice box from the cooler, then randomly chooses another juice box without replacing the first. Find the probability that both juice boxes are grape.

Solution

Find the probability of the first event and the probability of the second event given the first. Then multiply the probabilities.

1. $P(\text{grape}) = \boxed{}$ Out of $\boxed{}$ juice boxes, $\boxed{}$ are grape.

2. $P(\text{grape given grape}) = \boxed{}$ Of the remaining $\boxed{}$ juice boxes, $\boxed{}$ are grape.

3. $P(\text{grape and grape}) = \boxed{}$ Multiply probabilities.

$= \boxed{}$ Divide out common factor.

$= \boxed{}$ Multiply.

Answer: The probability that both juice boxes are grape is $\boxed{}$.

  Refer to Example 3.

2. Find the probability that both juice boxes are lemonade when the first juice box chosen is not replaced.

Words to Review

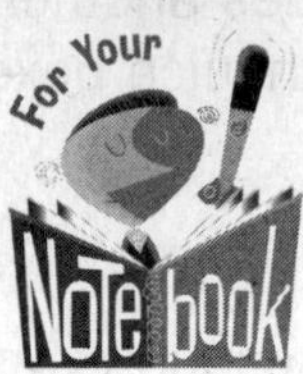

Give an example of the vocabulary word.

Outcomes

Event

Favorable outcomes

Probability

Theoretical probability

Experimental probability

Tree diagram

Permutation

Combination

Disjoint events

Overlapping events

Complementary events

Independent events

Dependent events

Review your notes and Chapter 13 by using the Chapter Review on page 672–673 of your textbook.